"A sure-fire way

"A daring challenge to be made over—from the inside out."

The Honorable Kay Coles James,
president, The Gloucester Institute

"This book is a life-changing must-read for those in a passionate pursuit of exploring God's heart."

Patsy Clairmont,
bestselling author,
Women of Faith speaker to more than
three million women worldwide

"My heart and passion for God's Word has changed my character. This book captures the process to see that same change in your own life."

Dr. Gary Smalley,
author of *Change Your Heart,
Change Your Life*

"This character-refining book reminds us to be clay in the Potter's hands—every day of our lives!"

Catherine Hart Weber, PhD,
therapist, author, speaker;
adjunct professor, Fuller Theological Seminary

"*Character Makeover* is an eight-week journey that will have profound implications for your life. Your soul will be flooded with the realization and exhilaration that God Almighty is intimately involved in this life-changing adventure."

Rev. Jeff Jernigan, pastoral counselor,
author of *The Power of a Loving Man*
and *Leadership with Panache*

Also by Katie Brazelton

Pathway to Purpose for Women

Conversations on Purpose for Women

Praying for Purpose for Women

Pathway to Purpose Personal Journal for Women

Pathway to Purpose Abridged Audio CD

Katie Brazelton and Shelley Leith

Character
Makeover

40 DAYS WITH
A LIFE COACH
TO CREATE
THE BEST YOU

ZONDERVAN®

ZONDERVAN.com/
AUTHORTRACKER
follow your favorite authors

Character Makeover
Copyright © 2008 by Katherine F. Brazelton

Requests for information should be addressed to:
Zondervan, *Grand Rapids, Michigan* 49530

Library of Congress Cataloging-in-Publication Data

Brazelton, Katie.
    Character makeover : 40 days with a life coach to create the best you / Katie Brazelton and Shelley Leith.
    p. cm.
    ISBN-13: 978-0-310-25653-3
    ISBN-10: 0-310-25653-4
    1. Character—Religious aspects—Christianity. 2. Christian life. 3. Self-actualization (Psychology)—Religious aspects—Christianity. 4. Personal coaching. I. Leith, Shelley. II. Title.
    BV4599.5.C45B73 2007
    248.8'43—dc22   2007029330

Interior design by Beth Shagene

Printed in the United States of America

07 08 09 10 11 12 13 14 • 25 24 23 22 21 20 19 18 17 16 15 14 13 12 11 10 9 8 7 6 5 4 3 2 1

To our families,
who give us confidence yet keep us humble,
who are generous with their love
and patient when we're unlovable,
and who have persevered with us on our journey
of perpetual character development

Contents

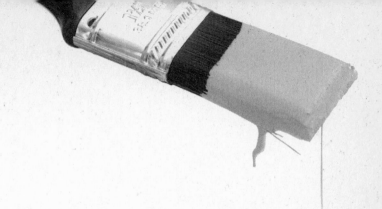

Remaking Your Character through Grace-Filled Coaching

Spiritual transformation is essential, not optional for Christ-followers.
Spiritual transformation is a process, not an event.
Spiritual transformation is God's work, but requires my participation.
John Ortberg, pastor, author

YOUR PERSONAL, VIRTUAL COACH

Have you ever wished that there was such a thing as a "life makeover," similar to when a salon fusses over your hair or a personal shopper over your wardrobe, and you come away transformed? I wish getting a life makeover were as painless as those times when I've dabbled in the surface-level, cosmetic approach to changing my outward appearance. Whether it was for a milestone birthday or for a family portrait, I must admit that I have found makeovers to be a lot of fun. In fact, I wish every woman could be treated at least once in her life to such a day of pampering!

I've also experienced a minor house remodel during which a fresh coat of paint and some new carpet profoundly changed the look of my home; the improvement was fairly quick and obvious. But there are also deeper renovations, the kind where families are displaced for months as a construction crew repairs a house foundation, removes walls, rewires electricity, or updates the plumbing. These types of changes are much more painstaking, messy, and costly—often emotionally and physically stressful—and they typically require the help of more than one expert.

Shelley Leith (my coauthor) and I have both delved deeply into the concept of remodeling character, or doing a character makeover. For Shelley and her husband, Greg, the approach they have used in raising their five children has been something she would call character-based parenting. They established the character traits they felt their kids needed in order to live as fruitful Christians, then set out to build those traits into them throughout their years at home. From another angle, Shelley and Greg are speakers for marriage conferences, and they have seen time and time again that the *lack* of strong character traits such as humility, contentment, self-control, patience, or perseverance can drive couples to the brink of divorce.

For me, this matter of character development has become my passion for different reasons. For years I have been a Life Purpose Coach®, helping women discover—to borrow Billy Crystal's phrase from the movie *City Slickers*—their "one big thing." I have been interested not only in helping them discover their unique purpose in life, but in creating a life plan to ensure that they leave a legacy. I even wrote a series of books (*Pathway to Purpose, Praying for Purpose, Conversations on Purpose*, and *Pathway to Purpose Personal Journal*) to help women find their specific, second-half-of-life mission.

Yet, it became evident to me after analyzing my own life patterns and those of my life plan clients for more than a decade, that some of us experience a gap between understanding our God-designed legacy and actually realizing that magnificent purpose. We self-sabotage, succumbing to well-worn patterns of defeat, woundedness, insecurity, unworthiness, or self-centeredness that keep us from carrying out God's best intentions for our lives.

You can know everything there is to know about yourself, your potential, and your goals, but if you are hesitant about developing some of the essential character qualities it takes to fulfill your godly dreams (such as humility, generosity, and confidence), you'll get derailed from your life's calling at every turn. I began to see that my coaching had to go further. Thus, *Character Makeover* was born. In this book, I become your personal, virtual coach—taking you on a forty-day adventure of deepening your character as you collaborate with God, role models, and myself ... preparing you to fulfill your legacy.

Pat Summitt of the University of Tennessee is the all-time winningest college basketball coach. Her 900-plus victories make her the only coach, male or female, to surpass the previous record of 900 wins. A college coach likely dreams about many things: coaching a national championship team, coaching an Olympic team, coaching players who become All-Americans and pros, being elected to the Hall of Fame. Summitt has achieved all of these pinnacles—in some cases, multiple times! In her book *Reach for the Summit* (Broadway Books, 1998), she has this to say about the role of coaching:

> Our players understand that all I'm trying to do is help them. They want to win a national championship. Well, I'm going to do everything I can to see to it.... Their long-term, repetitive success is a matter of building

a principled system and sticking to it. Principles are anchors; without them you will drift.

That sums up the essence of this book. Are you reaching for a personal dream—your "national championship," if you will? *Character Makeover* will coach you to realize your dreams by "building a principled system and sticking to it." Without character, as Summitt says, "you will drift," and drifters don't reach their goals!

Frankly, I'll be a good Character Coach for you, because I have been terribly hard on myself until the last six or seven years, and I distinctly remember what it was like to suffer from the "I'm not good enough" syndrome. You can trust that I now fully realize what a privilege it is to walk alongside you on this *grace-filled* (imagine that word underlined three times!) journey toward truth in your own life. This must be an exercise into newness and joy, not one that causes you to feel defeated. The latter would break my heart to hear. Life has enough struggles without me coming along and increasing your stress and guilt about living a holier life!

What you *do* need from me is to walk beside you and show you how character development will be the very thing that will carry you on angel's wings during the toughest seasons of your life. My commitment to you is that, with the remembrance of the grace and mercy of God shining brightly on my own muddled life choices, I will gently coach you, not judge you or push you beyond what you are able to bear.

Here are some important things we know up front: God cares more about the character we bring to our life mission than he does about our ministry's strategic plan. He cares more about our Christlike integrity than our kingdom-building productivity. He wants our honesty in all areas of our lives more than our accomplishments for him. In his Holy Book, learning to be holy is the bottom line (1 Peter 1:15–16). We who dream of doing something outrageously tremendous for the Lord are held to a higher standard by God Almighty himself. We, who have a heart for changed lives, cannot intentionally lead misguided lives. We must do all we can to become the leaders God is asking us to be in our homes, communities, churches, schools, ministries, and vocations.

CHARACTER VS. STRONGHOLDS

With literally dozens of character qualities to choose from, you may wonder why I selected the eight qualities you'll find in this book: *humility, confidence, courage, self-control, patience, contentment, generosity,* and *perseverance*. My choice has to do with the flipside of these very qualities, what the New Testament (2 Corinthians 10:4) refers to as strongholds.

What Are Strongholds?

The term *strongholds* refers to areas where our enemy, Satan, has set up camp and dug in, creating for himself a fortress from which he launches attacks and tries to destroy us. These are the places where we repeatedly experience discouragement, distress, defeat, and damage. These are the monsters that keep us from our God-given dreams.

The eight character qualities I've chosen address the most prevalent strongholds I see in women today. As you read through the following annotated list of character traits and strongholds, ask yourself, "Do I have any of these good qualities or opposite rough edges in my life? Am I 'soaring on wings like eagles' (Isaiah 40:31), or am I living an unfulfilled, wounded life, being held back by one of these forces?" I firmly believe when you and I are deliberate about strengthening these particular character qualities in our lives, the related, destructive strongholds are transformed into areas of victory.

You'll note that half of these character qualities are exhibited inwardly, and half are expressed more outwardly. And they also involve five different relationships which definitively and repeatedly affect the outcome of our life purpose:

Relationship to God

1. **Humility** drives at the *inner* strongholds of pride, self-centeredness, judgmentalism, and—believe it or not—worthlessness. (By the way, humility is foundational; if we don't start with humility, any work we do in other areas of character could make us prideful!)

Relationship to Ourselves

2. **Confidence** is an *inner* quality that speaks to strongholds of insecurity, poor self-esteem, and perfectionism.
3. **Courage** is an *outward* quality desperately needed by women who struggle with fear, anxiety, or untruthfulness.

Relationship to Others

4. **Self-control** is what women need to exhibit *inwardly* if they are impulsive, addictive, undisciplined, overemotional, or stress-prone.
5. **Patience** is a great *outward* character quality for women who are intolerant or demanding.

Relationship to Things

6. **Contentment** is an important *inner* characteristic for women who battle strongholds of envy, dissatisfaction, or perpetual restlessness.
7. **Generosity** is an *outward* expression that comes against greed and an entitlement mentality.

Relationship to the Future

8. **Perseverance** is an *outward* character quality that's needed when women feel like quitting, hesitating, avoiding a decision, or not following through.

Customize Your Reading Sequence

You might want to do something different and try reading this book out of sequence. Look at the character qualities in the preceding list, and invite the Holy Spirit to speak to you about each one. Do you recognize any of these strongholds as your personal battleground? Are you experiencing unusual trials, or do you feel a sense of brokenness in one of the areas? That may be the starting place God has in mind for you. Try going through this book in a sequence directed by the Lord, addressing the character qualities in which you feel the weakest first; then progressing from there.

THREE WAYS TO COLLABORATE

Building character is a collaborative effort, mainly between God and you. It is ignited with your salvation and continues until you have become like Christ, a process which isn't completed until the moment you see him face-to-face (1 John 3:2). God speeds up this process by giving you character-building opportunities—circumstances that are orchestrated to develop the character you need to honor him more with your daily efforts. For instance, if you find yourself in a slew of irritating situations, ask yourself if God is trying to teach you *patience*. If your circumstances are making you fearful, it might be *courage* that God is working into your life. Do you keep encountering people whose lives you envy? Anybody want to talk about *contentment*?

Every time you forget that character
is one of God's purposes for your life,
you will become frustrated
by your circumstances.

Rick Warren, pastor, author

Has God been giving you some frustrating circumstances? Don't forget that God uses such circumstances to build your character. When you start viewing your circumstances as God's character-deepening tools, then you're ready for your part in the character-building collaboration. In this book, I will coach you to develop your character using three age-old, proven methods of collaborating with God: preparation, prayer, and practice.

1. Preparation

One way we collaborate with God to build character is through preparation. This simply means that through this book, we will learn all we can about what God wants of us, which helps us get his principles ingrained into our thinking and attitudes.

2. Prayer

Another essential way we join God's work of making us more Christlike is by praying—which, as you know, is simply a conversation with God. Through the written prayers in this book, we will invite God to transform us and then rely on the Holy Spirit's power to build into us the principles of character we are addressing.

3. Practice

Character Makeover helps you be proactive and take steps to develop and deepen eight key character qualities that greatly impact God's plan for your life and your readiness to serve him however he commands. You may have never thought that your character was something you could decide to work on, but through the Action Plan you will set up for yourself, you will partner with the Holy Spirit to do just that.

How to Get the Most Out of This Book

For each of the eight character qualities in *Character Makeover*, there are five days of readings, assessments, directed journaling, and prayers. My strong recommendation is that you do not blaze through all five days in one sitting. Come to a full stop at the end of each day's reading. Dwell on the concepts and meditate on the verses. Dig deep and be honest; don't settle for shallow answers that enable you to tread water in your spiritual life. Pray the prayer aloud or write out a prayer of your own.

To keep us organized in this endeavor, each day's reading transports you to a special coach-client setting, so you can focus intently on a specific topic:

Day 1: Welcome Back to My Place! Each week, I want you to imagine you are meeting with me at my home. We may choose to sit in my living room or dining room; relax on my front porch bench or on the swing chair in my backyard; or take a stroll around my block. The mental picture I will paint for you will be of my real-time, real-life surroundings, with no phony airs or pretense. When you visit with me in my own home environment, you will begin to see how similar we are in many respects. As your personal Character Coach (or Spiritual Growth Partner or Dream Collaborator!), I want to actually invite you into my life and into my heart, so you will more readily feel the encouragement I have to share with you.

Day 1 starts with strength training where we build the foundation for the week's targeted character quality. We begin by learning about the character trait and how it can be exhibited best in our lives. More importantly, we learn about a complementary quality of God's ways—such as his mercy, compassion, power, or love. Our firm foothold and belief in each of God's attributes will help us deepen the characteristic in our own lives and break free from the strongholds that are blocking our holiness and productivity for God.

Day 2: A Virtual Message. Each week, you will receive a Virtual Message from me. You can either go to my website to actually download it, so you can hear my voice—or you can simply read the text right from this book. Day 2 examines the strongholds that are addressed by the week's character quality. This 360-degree bird's-eye view will give you a broader knowledge base, much more truth to prayerfully consider, and a deeper conviction to ensure your next steps.

On either Day 2 or Day 3, I will introduce you to a precious friend of mine who is a real, everyday woman just like us, a woman who is trying to deepen specific character qualities in her own life. I can't wait for you to meet these imperfect, but oh, so lovable, friends—each a Life Purpose Coach® herself. These woman are passionate about obediently completing the work God gave them to do!

Day 3: You've Got Mail. Each week, you will receive an Email Message from me. I want you to imagine that you have given me your email address and that my words of encouragement have landed in your inbox. You can even blog a response to me at www.LifePurposeCoaching-Centers.com/CM if you'd like. Day 3 drills deeper into the character quality—because by now you will have seen both sides of it, the good and the ugly, and you will be wanting further information about how to live it more diligently in your own life. Enjoy the cyberspace coaching!

Day 4: Perspective-Changing Outing. Each week, I have a field trip treat planned for us! We will "meet" away from my home, somewhere conducive to helping us change our perspective and get out of the ho-hum, doldrums box of how we do life. On this special day, plan to "get out of town," to let your hair down, and to return home refreshed and invigorated to begin anew. Day 4 is a critical juncture in this process. It is when I gracefully help you evaluate yourself, asking you to honestly respond to questions about how you are doing in each given area. The progress on this day will pole-vault you further into fulfilling the tasks God assigned to you before you were born.

Day 5: Sitting Quietly with Your Maker. Day 5 is a time for reflection and solitude in the privacy of your own quiet-time space with God. This day's exercise will allow you to adopt practices that will deepen the week's character quality in your life. Your final decisions are between God and you. (A good coach or collaborator will never try to push you into doing something you are not ready to do; that just never works out for anyone!) There are prayer strategies, Scripture studies, research ideas, and challenge goals you can use to formulate your action steps.

MASTER ACTION PLAN

You will be prompted to select one key step from your Action Plan each week—one thing you will commit to doing first—to help build a Master Action Plan. If you can take one solid step toward deepening a specific character quality in your life, you will find the rest of the steps will follow more naturally. (See appendix A on page 322 if you'd like a sneak preview.)

Three Ways to Deepen Your Experience

1. **Character Journal:** Try starting a character journal in which you record your thoughts, write out your own prayers, and journal even more questions and answers as you make your way through *Character Makeover*.
2. **Forty Days:** As previously noted, take at least forty days (five days per week for eight weeks) to work through this book. Or, if you prefer, you may extend it to fifty-six days (seven days per week for eight full weeks) by reading for five days, then spending two days meditating on the Scripture prayer in appendix B before moving on to the next week's character topic.
3. **Accountability Partner:** Enlist a reading and prayer partner who knows you well enough to give you feedback and hold you accountable as you work your way through the book.

A COACH'S PRAYER FOR YOU

Before we turn our attention to our first topic, I want to ask you the all-important renovation question: Are you really sure you want to do this? (That's what every good hairstylist would ask before cutting off your two-foot-long locks, right? Or what a savvy construction foreman would ask before starting an overhaul on your house.) I will assume, if you're still reading, that your answer is: "Yes, I want to be the best me I can be for God!"

Above all, remember to give yourself some grace as you learn more about Christlike character in this book. Even the apostle Paul said, "For I do not do the good I want to do, but the evil I do not want to do—this I keep on doing" (Romans 7:19). I love Paul's honesty when he admits that he is merely human. Know that God is pleased when he sees the effort you are making. He will be applauding you for your improvements, not waiting in the wings to berate you for your shortcomings. As I already said, if this book is not filled with love and hope, what good is it to you? The last thing you need is more pressure. So, breathe deeply and get ready to enjoy becoming the best godly woman you can be!

When the going gets tough on this dream-collaborating character makeover —and let's be clear that it will get tough!—I want you to commit to keeping your eyes on the prize of Christlike character that will better position you to live out the dream God has always had in mind for you. Now as we begin, I'm going to do something vital to every coaching session, and that is to pray.

Precious Lord,

My sister in Christ is embarking upon holy work to be the best she can be for you. She has picked up this book about making over her character because, at her deepest core, she wants to please you. You, Lord, are the architect of her life, and you have been building something beautiful in her since before she was born. She wants to join you in your work in her life. She wants to prepare her heart, pray for change, and practice the disciplines of a woman of character.

She has a dream of doing something for you, but she is being held back by strongholds that the enemy is using to discourage and defeat her. Lord, show her who you really are and who she is through the truth of your Word and the power of your Holy Spirit, so she may overcome those persistent strongholds.

I pray for your protection to surround her as she starts on this challenging renovation. Bring her encouragement along the way at just the moment when obstacles or self-condemnation threaten to derail her efforts. Show her which character quality you want her to start with, transform her prayer life, and help her persist to the end. I claim your blessings upon her collaboration with you to become that humble, confident, courageous, self-controlled, patient, content, generous, persevering woman you created her to be. May the time and energy she devotes to developing her character cause you to use her all the more powerfully for your kingdom-building purposes, which will reap eternal rewards for her and those you want her to serve.

In the mighty name of Jesus, I pray, amen.

The Making of a Right Relationship to God

Chapter 1

Humility

Do nothing out of selfish ambition or vain conceit.
Rather, in humility value others above yourselves.

Philippians 2:3

Seeing God

We'd all like to be humble.
But what if nobody notices?
John Ortberg, pastor, author

WELCOME TO MY HOME!

Welcome to my home! Won't you join me in my living room, so we can begin to talk about the modernizing makeover you've chosen to undergo? I'm definitely excited for you. I've got a comfy, oversized chair you may like—I think it's called a *chair-and-a-half.* Kick off your shoes and curl up with the fuzzy throw. Rearrange the marshmallow-soft pillows as needed. I've turned on the small, tabletop waterfall to create some soft background sounds for you, and I'll get our snacks out of the fridge momentarily—but first, let's begin this forty-day adventure together in prayer:

Dear Sweet Lord,

No makeover is ever easy, whether it's our appearance, home interior, curbside appeal, or our character. As we begin today, we don't need a curling iron or a paint roller or a garden hoe as a tool; we only need you and the wisdom of your Word. We know that this character remodel won't happen while we stand by idle and passive; it will only happen if we willingly engage in the process. Lead us boldly as we explore humility. Impress your humility on our hearts today. Help us to see how this characteristic is foundational to developing all the other character traits and to completing the incredible plan you intend for our lives. Sit with us now as we begin this transformation of our souls, this character makeover.

Amen.

Shall we dive into the life-changing concept of humility, which will truly help us to see with the eyes of God?

KATIE: HAVING BEEN DULY HUMBLED

I remember my cocky attitude many years ago when I was a director of public relations for a very profitable, publicly held company. It was my heyday of wearing expensive clothes and costly jewelry, and being treated well by my employer—financially and emotionally. I was in the inner circle of those few who got invited to the owner's home for Christmas parties. I had arrived! I think what I loved most about that job was that my opinion counted; I had a voice. The problem was that I wasn't embarrassed to brag about my good fortune. Then, in the blink of an eye, a corporate reorganization occurred as the company was being positioned for sale, and I was "on the streets" looking for a job with many other coworkers.

It was about that time that someone called me *vapor-ware*. It was one person's unique way of saying that I only had vapor inside the personal Tupperware® of my life, that I had nothing to offer. Zip. Zilch. Nada. My heart sank. I was humiliated! I knew that statement was not true, but it hurt me deeply to realize that someone thought that poorly of me. What I learned that day was that cruel humiliation is not God's way, only man's way. What I decided to do about the unkind remark was life-changing. I went on a personal quest to "get real" and fill my plastic life with Christlike substance. I'd say that God used the layoff from a pride-producing job, as well as the humiliating comment, to get my attention and cause me to want to work on building more of him, more humility into my life. For that, I will be eternally grateful.

CLASSIC CASES OF HUMILITY

Humility is a compelling, attractive quality in a person. Truly humble people are likeable, even irresistible. When I think about some of the well-known stories I grew up with, I realize that the thing that makes them so captivating is that they feature humble, others-centered people. In *Willie Wonka and the Chocolate Factory*, we root for poor little Charlie Bucket, the only kind child on the chocolate factory tour. Cinderella is a criticized yet servant-hearted girl who wins our hearts on her way to winning the prince. *To Kill a Mockingbird* draws us to a white attorney in the deep South named Atticus Finch, a truly humble man, who greatly respects the black man he's defending. George Bailey is so humble it takes an angel to get him to believe that he is significant to people in *It's a Wonderful Life*. And *Chariots of Fire* is the true story of Eric Liddell, a missionary-turned-Olympic athlete who earns our respect by honoring God above his potential medals. It's these unlikely heroes, the humble, unself-conscious people, who endear themselves to us, both in fiction and in life.

HUMILITY IS THE RIGHT PERSPECTIVE

So, how does one go about becoming humble? Does it require coming from humble circumstances, like Charlie Bucket? Or being mortified, like Cinderella? Should we endure slander for helping the accused, like Atticus Finch? Or be self-deprecating, like George Bailey? Does it mean to sacrifice our own glory, as did Eric Liddell? In actuality, none of these approaches guarantees humility. They could just as easily produce anger, self-righteousness, vengeance, pride, and/or depression.

The only sure path to humility is through gaining the right perspective. Humility is a natural result of having an accurate view of who God is and having the right perspective of who you are in relation to him. Truly humble people compare themselves not with other people, but only with Christ. They realize their sinfulness and understand their limitations.

On the other hand, they also recognize their gifts and strengths and are willing to use them as Christ directs. A truly humble person will serve God in any capacity, even if she doesn't feel particularly gifted in that area. What about the person who dutifully shows up every week to sharpen the pew pencils? Is that person truly gifted in pencil sharpening? No, she knows that the job needs to be done and doesn't feel that she is above that task or think she should conserve her energy for something more attuned to her talents. How often, when a church ministry is seeking volunteers, do we hear, "That's not my area of giftedness"? Can that be just another way of saying, "I can get more kudos doing something I'm really good at"?

We may be thinking that humility is something that it's not. We may assume that humility is discovering our inner doormat, but as my personal example illustrates, humility is not the same as humiliation. Humiliation is self-mortification that evokes the sense of being debased, unworthy, shamed. It screams at us that we have done something wrong and are therefore worthless! Frankly, I want to be clear that God loves us too much to ever want us to feel that way; his desire is not to shame us or humiliate us. That is the demeaning work of the Devil. The Bible tells us that God honors us; he chooses us; he pursues us; he sacrifices for us; he woos us; he protects us; and he provides for us; but never once does it say that he humiliates us. Granted, he does discipline us to get our eyes off ourselves and onto him, but discipline is not the same as humiliation.

Humility can coexist with self-worth, esteem, and personal value. Right thinking about yourself in relationship to God is realistic thinking—a full-orbed picture of your strengths and weaknesses, your actual appearance, genuine talents, negative habits, and real worth. Thinking that you're more wonderful than you really are is pride, and thinking that you're more wretched than you really are is false humility, which is another form of pride because it's still self-focused.

Make no mistake about it: We are God's chosen ones, his prized possessions. Isaiah 62:4 (MSG) tells us:

> *No more will anyone call you Rejected,*
> *and your country will no more be called Ruined.*
> *You'll be called Hephzibah (My Delight).*

Bottom line, we need to get this false humility versus godly humility versus pride thing straight in our minds by understanding that our value rests in God, not in ourselves. To picture this on a continuum, think of humility as being at the middle of a scale:

False humility is at the extreme left side of the scale—thinking everyone else is better than you. At the extreme right end of the scale is boastful, prideful thinking. Humility is balanced in the middle, with a right view of who you are and who you're not, and who God is and that you just ain't him! When your eyes are on yourself and how great thou art, that equals pride. When your eyes are on God, you can't help but be humble.

HUMILITY IS THE FOUNDATION

Of all the character qualities we're going to work on together, humility is not only the most endearing quality, it is also the foundational character quality to all the others. You can't build genuine character qualities without having humility as a component of all of them. Let me put it this way. It would be natural for me, with my coaching bent, to use the "Ten Easy Steps to Character," or "Twenty Ways to Be Your Best," or "Eight Character Qualities of Winners" approach to character development, and thus reduce the process to a shallow formula. The problem with shallow formulas is that once you follow the blueprint, you could end up thinking you had *achieved* character, when in actuality you would have just gone through an exercise in pridefulness. It's the potentially dangerous "power of positive thinking" mentality that says, "If I believe, then I can achieve." This rules out dependence upon God and steals any glory from him in the process.

A humble woman gets her strength for the journey from God, then gives the credit to him when something good happens. Humility must be our starting place for the narrow passage to deeper character. Without it, we'll all turn into highly principled overachievers who are no closer to true Christlikeness than when we started. And that's surely not where we want to end up!

HUMILITY IS SELF-CONFIDENCE

Speaking of Christlikeness, it's fascinating to discover how Jesus described his own character. There is only one recorded instance of him talking about himself in this way, and in that discussion he used only two words to describe himself. The two words may surprise you. They're not "strong and mighty," or "all-knowing and wise," or "perfect and God-man." His self-description is: *I am gentle and humble in heart* (Matthew 11:29b). It was later, at the end of his life, that Jesus gave his disciples a graphic illustration of his gentle and humble character when he washed their feet.

> *Jesus knew that the Father had put all things under his power, and that he had come from God and was returning to God; ⁴so he got up from the meal, took off his outer clothing, and wrapped a towel around his waist. ⁵After that, he poured water into a basin and began to wash his disciples' feet, drying them with the towel that was wrapped around him.*
>
> John 13:3–5

This story starts not with what Jesus did, but with what he knew. Jesus knew his strengths, yet he did not use them to dominate or manipulate; his strength was under God's control—which is the biblical definition of gentleness. And he was humble. But notice that humility doesn't mean downplaying who you are by saying things like, "Oh, I'm really not that talented," or "I just threw something together—it's nothing at all." Jesus fully knew and honestly acknowledged his true nature, his strengths, his full identity, and his brilliant future. Yet, see what happens next? Unannounced, he interrupted his meal, quietly made his preparations, and commenced humbly serving others. Out of his strong self-image, he humbly served.

Have you ever assumed that strong self-image and humility are contradictory concepts? Jesus does not. His humble act of service was born out of a sure sense of all that was good and true about himself. The lesson here is that it takes a strong self-image to perform truly humble acts of service. G. K. Chesterton, an influential English writer of the early twentieth century, said, "It is always the secure who are humble."

SHOULD YOU PRAY FOR HUMILITY?

Asking God for humility is a scary thing. All I can say is this: Be careful what you ask for! You may wonder: Will God answer my prayers for humility by embarrassing me? Debasing me? Well, I certainly thought the answer was yes, many years ago, when I was a house cleaner for wealthy families. One day, after I had cleaned a palatial master bathroom for an hour, I found myself on my hands and knees downstairs, scrubbing a marble floor that seemed to stretch for miles from the front door through the formal living room and family room on into the kitchen and out to the back slider door. All of a sudden, I looked up to heaven, shook my fist at God, and cried out in anger, "This is how you answer my heartfelt and constant prayer for humility? How dare you treat me this way!" I was furious at God. I had been praying that he would break me of all pride, but scrubbing toilets and floors week after week was too much! Notice that even my enraged reaction to God was evidence of a heart not humbled. (By the way, this happened in 1989, immediately prior to getting the cushy public relations job—and we've already exposed my pride there!)

Now, the big question: Had God caused me to be a housecleaner, so he could answer my prayer for humility? No, being an overspending, single mom in graduate school had caused me to be a housecleaner. I had orchestrated part of my circumstances myself. But, even when I *looked up* at him in anger, he knew the desire to be humble was on my heart. I didn't have to clean toilets to get humble—I had to focus on God's power and humility would follow. I must admit that my process was a long, convoluted one (as you may already suspect), but I am grateful that he was patient with me. Final warning: Be careful what you pray for!

Journal

If humility is having the right perspective about who God is and who I am in relation to him, let's start by getting that perspective firm in our minds. This concept is powerfully described in Psalm 103. Read each portion of the psalm, then summarize your answers to the three questions:

Psalm 103:1–5

Who is God? _He is the Giver (of forgiveness, benefits, etc)_

Who am I in relation to him? _I am the Recipient_

How can this understanding help me become humble? _____

_____

_____

Psalm 103:6–10

Who is God? _____

Who am I in relation to him? _____

How can this understanding help me become humble? _____

_____

_____

Psalm 103:11–14

Who is God? _____

Who am I in relation to him? _____

How can this understanding help me become humble? _____

_____

_____

Psalm 103:15–18

Who is God?_____

Who am I in relation to him? _____

How can this understanding help me become humble? _____

_____

_____

Psalm 103:19–22

Who is God? *Sovereign Ruler over all*

Who am I in relation to him? *Subject- servant*

How can this understanding help me become humble? *I am God's servant, He is not mine. God has the right to call the shots in my life*

PRAYER

Precious Lord,

  Thank you that you don't cause our humiliation, but that you redeem it for good in our lives. That's a relief. I want to be humble, but it's daunting to pray for humility, imagining what circumstance you might use so that I'll learn it! But I trust you, Lord, and I submit myself to you to teach me humility however you choose. Reassure me about my identity in you so that I can be secure enough to be humble. Get my eyes firmly locked on you so that I start to lose my self-focus. Show me the needs of those around me; then help me to do something about what you show me. And as I stop thinking about myself and start focusing on you and others, I look forward to being seen by you as one of your humble servants.

  Amen!

                              In the name of Jesus, amen.

Pride: Exposing Your Inner Buzz Lightyear

Pride is the root of every sin and evil.

Andrew Murray, 1828–1917, Dutch Reformed minister and author

A VIRTUAL MESSAGE

NOTE: *It's Day 2, so you have the option of listening to today's message by downloading it from my website, www.LifePurposeCoachingCenters.com/CM, or reading the message text below. Enjoy the virtual coaching and don't forget to open in prayer!*

THE FLIP SIDE OF PRIDE

The 1995 animated movie *Toy Story* tells the tale of the rivalry between Woody, the honest-Abe cowboy toy, and Buzz Lightyear, the prideful, fancy spaceman toy. The problem with Buzz is that he is convinced he is a real space ranger who must single-handedly save the galaxy from destruction. He is so self-absorbed he doesn't realize he is a mere toy. Woody feels compelled to point out Buzz's blind spot at every opportunity. For example, when Buzz sets his laser from stun to kill, Woody retorts, "Oh, great. If anyone attacks, we can blink 'em to death." When Buzz deploys his terillium-carbonic alloy wings, Woody sneers, "That wasn't flying! That was falling with style!"

Buzz was obsessed with himself—his powers, his weapons, his important mission, his pivotal role in saving the world. Because of his pride, he lost touch with the reality that his powers came from batteries; his abilities came from kids who moved his arms or threw him in the air; and his mission was all in his head. That's what pride does. It makes us delusional. We get so focused on our own inflated capabilities, our possessions, our appearance, our importance, and our indispensability that we become oblivious to the reality that everything we are is from God and that we can do nothing without him.

In *Toy Story*, Buzz has an accident while arguing about his ability to fly, necessitating his rescue by Woody. It goes to prove that well-known verse, "Pride precedes a disaster, and an arrogant attitude precedes a fall" (Proverbs 16:18 GWT).

THE MANY FACES OF PRIDE

Pride at its essence is a problem of being me-centered. There is a whole range of pride-driven sins, which are most commonly seen in the ways we *mis-value* ourselves and others—by exalting ourselves, belittling ourselves, attacking others, or ignoring others. Pride sets us up against God and attempts to seize his lordship for ourselves.

Exalting myself: "It's all about me."

Exalting pride occurs when we *overvalue* ourselves by trying to build ourselves up. Let's consider some of the behaviors women might use to exalt themselves:

- Constantly showing off the accomplishments of their children.
- Exaggerating, because the simple truth doesn't get enough reaction.
- Serving to be noticed. (This was a particular problem of mine for a season. Once when I was on a missions trip to Africa, my pride reared its ugly head. As we washed the street children, I was having a really bad hair day, so ... I simply decided to avoid the photographer who was snapping candid shots of all the activities. Prideful? Yes, but here's where the more devious side of pride kicked in: All of a sudden, I felt really angry that I wouldn't be in any of the photos that would circulate back home!)
- Feeling entitled to star treatment, especially during times of sacrificial work.
- Maneuvering for a preferred position in their extended family, community, or workplace.

"You're hopeless, you Pharisees! Frauds! You love sitting at the head table at church dinners, love preening yourselves in the radiance of public flattery."

Luke 11:43 MSG

Ouch. Jesus sure knows how to say it like it is! When we exalt ourselves, we aren't exalting God. In fact, exalting ourselves amounts to seizing the credit that belongs to God ... claiming it as if we achieved our position through our own merit.

Belittling myself: "Woe is me."

Worthlessness is the most deceptive form of pride. This type of pride masquerades as humility, but it's really a reverse method of attracting attention. Women who belittle themselves are masters at *undervaluing* their worth. Think of some methods you have seen women use to tear themselves down, in hopes that someone will notice and build them back up. How about these?

- Women who overwork and let others take advantage of them.
- Women who have a difficult time accepting help, gifts, or compliments because they don't feel worthy, or who feel like it's shameful or awkward to need help.
- Perfectionists who secretly try to prove they are worthy by absolutely controlling some area of their lives.
- Women who are down on themselves and constantly pointing out their shortcomings, failures, or areas where someone else is better.

"And when you fast, don't make it obvious, as the hypocrites do, who try to look pale and disheveled so people will admire them for their fasting. I assure you, that is the only reward they will ever get."

Matthew 6:16 NLT

Attacking others: "You're not as good as me."

Pride that attacks others is a judgmental spirit, one which *devalues* others by tearing them down. You'll notice this in women who are critical, irritable, intolerant, argumentative, and self-righteous. Read this unusual adaptation of the well-known passage about the speck in your neighbor's eye and the log in your own for a fresh perspective on this type of pride:

"Don't pick on people, jump on their failures, criticize their faults—unless, of course, you want the same treatment. ²That critical spirit has a way of boomeranging. ³It's easy to see a smudge on your neighbor's face and be oblivious to the ugly sneer on your own. ⁴Do you have the nerve to say, "Let me wash your face for you," when your own face is distorted by contempt? ⁵It's this whole traveling road-show mentality all over again, playing a holier-

than-thou part instead of just living your part. Wipe that ugly sneer off your own face, and you might be fit to offer a washcloth to your neighbor."

Matthew 7:1–5 MSG

Attacking others and trying to change them actually amounts to commandeering the place of the Holy Spirit in people's lives.

Ignoring others: "You're not the boss of me."

When my daughter was young, she constantly told her older brother: "You can't make me. You're not the boss of me!" This type of ignoring others obviously *undervalues* their input. Women who are too proud to receive input deal with some of these issues:

- Not being teachable. The attitude of "I already have my act together" closes women to the efforts of others to speak into their lives.
- Remaining stuck in bad patterns. Some women see their past and their personality as a trap in which they're stuck, instead of realizing they can choose either to stay the same or change their behavior. For some, the statement "You need to accept me the way I am" is a smoke screen they use to avoid changing bad habits.
- Never admitting fault. This is the "hard of hearing" woman, who doesn't seem to perceive or internalize any words of correction, advice, rebuke, instruction, or warning.

Israel's pride will cause their defeat; they will not turn back to the LORD their God or look to him for help in all this.

Hosea 7:10 NCV

Ignoring others is a refusal to be influenced by those the Holy Spirit is trying to use to speak into your life. It is saying to God: I'm fine just the way I am.

BETTE'S STORY OF BROKENNESS

You may have heard that brokenness is a stepping-stone to humility. But . . . it might first lead to a step in the opposite direction! My friend Bette's brokenness caused years of compensating for her shame, which actually turned into pride. As a very young child, Bette's friendships were marred by several instances of sexual abuse that she kept secret. One instance, in particular, was manipulated by a female babysitter, a teen, who convincingly made the violation a "condition of true and lasting friendship" — and friendship was what Bette craved. By age nine she was eating to gain weight to make herself ugly in order to keep any more predators away. In her teens, she compensated for her shame and poor self-esteem by becoming an overachiever. Yet when she was eighteen, she overheard a coworker say that she would never amount to anything, a cutting remark that Bette spent the next thirty years trying to prove wrong.

Bette sought self-worth by taking charge. She worked her way up in the escrow industry, angling for better titles and bigger salaries by hiding her inadequacies behind exaggeration and self-promotion. She covered her relational insecurity by buying friends gifts for every occasion—from the most prestigious stores—with money she didn't have. She hid her fear that she wouldn't measure up by trying to be the perfect mom, the perfect friend, the perfect church member.

A turning point came in 2001. In Bette's words, "One day, alone at home, while listening to a song, I discovered that I was burdened with shame. I heard the word 'shame' and suddenly the tears were gushing. No longer did I want to live ashamed of the person God created me to be!"

In 2003, in obedience to the unmistakable leading of God, Bette and her family left California and moved to their family homestead in Texas. She started letting go of her compensation methods, one after the other, and in the process she discovered a life of simplicity and honesty without those prideful, shameful masks. Bette no longer had the prestige of a job as vice president and general manager. She couldn't afford a gift-buying frenzy at Christmas, but after the initial embarrassment of not meeting people's perceived expectations, she felt a freeing sense of a return to true friendship based on love, not gifts.

When her new pastor learned about her past experience as head of women's ministries, he invited her to fill that role in their church. But because she couldn't get confirmation from God, she chose not to grab for the approval and acceptance of that "easy fix." Instead, she remained in the background, doing temporary projects when asked and waiting for the ministry the Lord wanted her to have. With her freed-up time, she took seriously the exhortation of her aunt who told her, "You're the spiritual influence in your extended family," and she made her family the focus of her ministry energy.

Bette says, "I have discovered that 'doing church' isn't always just walking through a set of doors on Sunday. It is often simply walking through a set of doors to give a hug to family members or helping them meet a deadline for a project they may be working on at the time. I now have a fresh perspective on my life."

Pride Test — But Only for the Strong of Heart!

This test is a rigorous self-examination to detect pride in your life. Circle the number corresponding to how frequently you think you have exhibited each type of prideful attitude within the last several weeks. Warning: Take only if you are having a good day!

Never Rarely Sometimes Frequently

Exalting Myself

1 2 3 (4) Asserting my rights: I am concerned about getting what I deserve.

1 (2) 3 4 Bragging: I boast about successes (mine or my kids') without crediting God.

1 2 3 (4) Entitlement: I deserve special treatment because of my condition or position. *25*

1 (2) 3 4 Exaggerating: I embellish the truth to get attention.

1 (2) 3 4 Name dropping: Knowing important people makes me feel important.

1 2 3 (4) Self-centeredness: I am blind to the needs of others. "It's all about me."

1 2 (3) 4 Showing off: I call attention to my possessions, abilities, or sacrifices.

1 2 3 (4) Vain: I am obsessed with the areas where I am better than others.

Belittling Myself

1 2 (3) 4 False humility: I point out my shortcomings, looking for reassurance. *27*

1 2 (3) 4 Overly independent: I can't receive help or gifts. That would be awkward or shameful!

1 (2) 3 4 Overworking: I work to exhaustion; it makes me feel worthy.

1 2 (3) 4 Overserving: I serve beyond the call of duty, looking for affirmation.

1 2 3 (4) Perfectionism: I try to be perfect; it makes me feel acceptable.

1 2 3 (4) Woe is me: I often have a catastrophe to lament, looking for pity.

1 2 3 (4) Works: I have to do more to deserve God's approval.

1 2 3 (4) Worthlessness: I rely on the reassurance of others to bolster my self-esteem.

(cont.)

Never Rarely Sometimes Frequently

Attacking Others

(1) 2 3 4 **Argumentative:** I choose to find what I disagree with and engage in a quarrel.

1 2 (3) 4 **Controlling:** I manage the actions of others to make sure they do things my way.

1 2 (3) 4 **Critical spirit:** I look for ways others don't meet my standards and point them out.

1 (2) 3 4 **Intolerance:** I won't accommodate opinions different than my own.

1 2 3 (4) **Irritability:** I get annoyed easily and lash out at those who bother me.

1 2 (3) 4 **Judgmentalism:** I assume the worst or exhibit a condemnatory attitude.

(1) 2 3 4 **Put-downs:** I intentionally belittle others with cutting or snubbing remarks.

(1) 2 3 4 **Self-righteousness:** I justify poor treatment of others by my holiness.

Ignoring Others

1 (2) 3 4 **Pouting:** If I don't get my way, I clam up.

1 2 3 4 **Ignoring correction:** I'm never wrong (plus I'm hard of hearing!).

1 2 (3) 4 **Isolated:** I reject help from others, preferring to go it alone.

1 2 (3) 4 **Refusal to change:** This is just who I am, so accept me.

1 2 (3) 4 **Rigidity:** I can't be flexible or adjust my plans.

1 2 (3) 4 **Stubborn:** I am obstinate.

1 (2) 3 4 **Unsubmissive:** I won't receive leadership. "You're not the boss of me."

1 2 3 (4) **Unteachability:** I am closed to input or guidance. I have my act together.

Section Score:

Exalting Myself Total: 25

Belittling Myself Total: 27

Attacking Others Total: 18

Ignoring Others Total: 20

TOTAL SCORE: 90

Scoring:

1–33   You are a model of genuine humility.

34–64   You are learning to be more and more humble. Way to go!

65–96   Thank you for your honesty. That's the first step to humility!

97–128 Hmm! You have some work to do. Keep reading!

CURE FOR PRIDE

First, congratulate yourself for being brave enough to take that test. Scanning through it, you probably realized that the questions would be hard, soul-searching, and even a little embarrassing. It's not easy to examine the very ugliest part of yourself, write it down, and then analyze it. Yikes! That's true courage right there. Since pride is wrong thinking about who you are in relation to God, then it makes sense that the cure for any pride you noted on the Pride Test would be to start thinking rightly about who you are in relation to God. Look back at the test and see where you scored the highest —which is not good in this case! Now, take a look at the following solutions to your type of pride.

- **Do you exalt yourself?** You can decide to die to self and stop attempting to steal God's glory. This is a conscious choice; it is a daily decision.
- **Do you belittle yourself?** You can learn who you are in Christ as his precious daughter and stop lying to yourself about your lack of value.
- **Do you attack others?** You can declare that God is God and stop trying to be president of the world. (This was a hard one for me. It took me years to resign!)
- **Do you ignore others?** You can start seeing people as God's instruments and stop resisting their input.

In case you don't know the end of our Disney story, Buzz Lightyear does end up learning humility when he acknowledges his shortcomings and accepts who he really is. After saving the day by "flying" with rockets taped to his back, he deflects a compliment by echoing Woody's earlier jab: "Aw, that wasn't flying. That was falling with style!"

Journal

When Satan tempted Jesus in the wilderness, he tried three different appeals to Jesus' pride. The first temptation was *to be self-sufficient* and self-reliant by making a stone turn into bread to eat (Luke 4:3). In what areas do you resist depending upon God and the people he has sent into your life? Refer to your answers in the "Ignoring Others" part of the self-test and write down your observations about how you see this type of pride in your life.

Mostly by being closed to what I can learn from those around me. I do not have a "teachable spirit"

The second temptation Jesus resisted was the temptation *to be powerful* by being in charge of the whole world (Luke 4:6). In what areas do you act like you're the "president of the world"? Refer to your answers in the "Attacking Others" part of the self-test and write down your observations about how you see this type of pride in your life.

Critical spirit & irritability

The third temptation Jesus resisted was the temptation *to be spectacular* by throwing himself off the temple into the hands of angels (Luke 4:9). In what areas do you suffer from the celebrity mentality? Refer to your answers in the "Exalting Myself" and "Belittling Myself" portions of the self-test and write down your observations about how you use either positive or negative attention-seeking methods to bolster your self-esteem.

Self-centered & perfectionistic - constantly in need of reassurance & obsessed w/ my own recognition/approval

PRAYER

Precious Lord,

I confess to you that I've been claiming to fly, when all I can really do is "fall with style." I've been taking credit for things that I can only do because of your power and your gifts, and I've been attempting to steal your glory. I'm sorry. At other times I have been belittling myself, criticizing your creation (me), and making myself out to be a loser. I'm harder on myself than you are on me, demanding more of myself than you ever have. I'm sorry. Sometimes, I turn against other people. I take out my insecurities on them, judging them harshly and demanding more of them than you ever have. I'm sorry. And I close myself off to people. I'm rigid and stubborn toward the very ones you have put into my life to help me be more like you. I'm sorry. Help me to stop ignoring the presence of these issues in my life and to call them what they are: *pride.*

In the name of Jesus, amen.

How God Redeems
Brokenness

It is possible to be too big for God to use you,
but never too small for God to use you.

Encyclopedia of 15,000 Illustrations

YOU'VE GOT MAIL

To:	"The Best You" Woman	Sent:	Day 3
From:	Katie Brazelton		
Subject:	Humility		

It's Day 3, so here is your first Email Message. Feel free to blog me a response at my website, www.LifePurposeCoachingCenters.com/CM, if you'd like. Enjoy the email-coaching and don't forget to open in prayer!

WHAT WE CAN LEARN
FROM CHUCK COLSON ABOUT HUMILITY

One day, as Chuck Colson, imprisoned for his central role in the Watergate coverup, waited on a platform to speak to a group of inmates, he had an epiphany. He realized that God was using his biggest failure—the fact that he was an ex-convict—to achieve his greatest victory, the creation of the Prison Fellowship® ministry. Up to the time of his imprisonment, Colson had much to be proud of—scholarships and honors earned, legal cases argued and won, great decisions made from lofty government offices, and a prestigious position next to the most powerful leader in the world. But his life of success was not what riveted the attention of those inmates that day—it was his failure and resulting humility. As Colson recounted in his book *Loving God* (Zondervan, 1983), God chose the one experience in which Colson could not glory for *his* glory.

What part of your life do you think is most useful to God? Do you think there is great potential for your musical talent, your organizational skills, or your leadership abilities? Is your greatest contribution in the area of teaching or training, cooking or counseling, design or discipleship, missions or medicine, writing or witnessing? Those areas where you shine are probably quite influential, but think about something here: where is your point of pain? What was your hardest hour of being humbled? When did you experience brokenness? Did you know that your greatest suffering will never go unnoticed by God? He wants to use the pain he has allowed you to feel, and it can become your greatest honor. God is a master at helping us use our negative experiences to minister to others.

HUMILITY: THE ESSENTIAL INGREDIENT

Humility is an essential ingredient in the Christian life. Just like the human body needs oxygen, flowers need water, and bread needs yeast, humility is vital for a growing Christian. The following eight core practices of Christian living are all powerless unless they partner with humility.

1. Worship

It takes humility to truly worship God. A prideful spirit, which in essence is worship of self, cannot coexist with the worship of God. True worship attributes worth to God, and in so doing, it magnifies the contrast between God and us. God is powerful; we are weak. God is holy, which just points out our comparative sinfulness. God is Creator and Savior; we are the created and the saved. Worship is the ultimate act of declaring that God is God and we are not.

2. Self-Esteem

A humble person has healthy self-esteem. Does that seem contradictory? Bette's story in Day 2 showed us that shame, fear, and the insecurity of poor self-esteem were camouflaged in prideful behaviors such as bragging, criticizing, and being a perfectionist. But a humble person is someone who has let go of everything she thought made her great, and in doing so, she discovers the true self God created her to be. God doesn't want our success, achievements, or perfection. He wants *us*. When we know we're wanted by God—that builds our self-esteem on an unshakable foundation.

3. Honesty

It takes humility to be truly honest. Pride tells lies, exaggerates, hides, pretends, and misrepresents, with the purpose of covering up our shortcomings, failures, and sins. A lie is like a signal flag that identifies the presence of another sin. Whether you lie to yourself, to God, or to another person, a lie is never independent—it is always born of a need to hide another sin related to pride. Humility, on the other hand, acknowledges the truth about what we have done and who we are. It is humbling to truthfully reveal something we have done that we'd rather not make known.

4. Obedience

It takes humility to obey. Obedience requires giving up my way, my rights, my entitlements. We justify our lack of obedience in different ways: "God would want me to be happy" or "I don't want to jeopardize my relationship" or "I'm sacrificing in this other area, so a little compromise is okay" or "I have worked so hard I deserve a break" or "I don't want to hurt another person." But God is more interested in our holiness than our happiness. He doesn't demand our sacrifices; he wants our obedience. Our job is to obey; his job is to take care of the consequences of our obedience.

5. Teachability

It takes humility to be teachable. In order to be a learner, we need to set aside our expertise or life experiences or age, and be receptive to another's influence. Knowing a lot doesn't automatically qualify us as the authority, the spokesperson, or the teacher. Humble people are lifelong learners who do not disregard the input of others, even in areas where they feel knowledgeable. They count the suggestions of others as valuable information.

6. Servanthood

It takes humility to serve. Servanthood requires us to set aside our prestige, position, and rights in order to serve others. Having great gifts and talents doesn't mean they all have to be in use all the time. The humble path sometimes means setting aside our capabilities and simply serving where there is a need. Humility can narrow our field of service. For example, God may call

This is a big one for me :)

us in this season to humbly serve only within our own family—and that may be the toughest assignment for us ever!

7. Waiting

It takes humility to wait. Waiting involves letting God give us our role, instead of self-promoting and assuming we should serve wherever we please. Waiting means allowing God to direct us instead of pushing our agenda. Waiting can also be as simple as closing our mouth until God clearly gives us release to speak.

8. Brokenness

A humble person is a broken person. Have you noticed this? The person who exudes genuine humility is invariably someone who has had an experience that has broken her pride, such as Bette's loss of job, friends, and ministry, or Chuck Colson's imprisonment. Failure or loss has a way of stripping away our false values and selfish obsessions. Then, God steps in and uses the very thing in which we can't glory for his glory. At the point we feel most useless, that's when God can choose to transform us into the highest usefulness.

See www.LifePurposeCoachingCenters.com/CM for a self-test on how well you have woven humility into these ingredients of Christian living.

Journal

Read 2 Corinthians 12:9–10:

> *But he said to me, "My grace is sufficient for you, for my power is made perfect in weakness." Therefore I will boast all the more gladly about my weaknesses, so that Christ's power may rest on me. [10] That is why, for Christ's sake, I delight in weaknesses, in insults, in hardships, in persecutions, in difficulties. For when I am weak, then I am strong.*

Paul names five types of problems in which he delights, because his weaknesses serve to illuminate God's power. List several examples from your own life in each of the following categories. Additional synonyms from various Bible translations have been provided to help trigger ideas.

Weaknesses, infirmities, limitations

driving phobia; shy/timid - fear weenie-hood of spirit (anxiety) struggle w/ depression

Insults, reproaches, abuse, suffering, mistreatment

feeling 2nd class @ work - boss's favoritism of Mary Ann

Hardships, needs, accidents, constraints, hard times, catastrophes

House fire;

Persecutions, opposition, perplexities

Difficulties, distresses, bad breaks, calamities, troubles, pressures

Joe's lack of work - joe's alcoholism overwhelmed @ my job - current trouble w/ memory/forgetting

Rewrite 2 Corinthians 12:9–10 in your own words, inserting your name, and listing some of the specific weaknesses, insults, hardships, persecutions, and difficulties you are experiencing.

> **Example:** *But my heavenly dad said to me, "I have plenty of grace for you, Katie, for my power is all the more powerful when you're collapsing." Therefore I can get excited when I feel like I can't go on, because I know that's when Christ's power kicks in. That is why, in the power of Christ, I can rejoice when I get a panic attack, when I am criticized by my friend, when I get bronchitis, when I receive a mean email, when I miss a flight. It's when I'm at my weakest that I give up and let Christ take over, and his power in me makes me strong.*

My grace is all you need, Tonja – because it's in your weaknesses that My strength is clearly seen. So when you are fearful & anxious, when you are ignored or treated as 2nd best, when times are difficult @ home – that's when you can joyfully experience My power in you!

PRAYER

Precious Lord,

I worship you. With all my heart I mean that. You are God and I am not. Help me let go of the masks I wear to bolster my self-esteem. Help me to stop covering my sins with various types of lies. Strip away all my excuses for not obeying you. I want to have the beauty of a lifelong learner. Show me where I should serve, and I'll do what you say. Tell me when I should speak, and until you do, I'll wait. Take all my broken places and transform them into humility so that I can be most useful to you.

In the name of Jesus, amen.

Your Humility Coach

May the love of Jesus fill me, as the waters fill the sea;
Him exalting, self abasing, this is victory.

**Kate Wilkinson, 1859–1928,
writer of "May the Mind of Christ, My Savior"**

PERSPECTIVE-CHANGING OUTING

In my town there is a manmade lake with a lovely walking path encircling it. There are park benches, weeping willows, paddleboats, a sloping beach, and gentle inlets. When I come here with a friend for a chat, we usually first stop in at the coffee shop for a latte to sip while we walk. Then along our route, we sometimes pause to feed the ducks, or just sit on a grassy knoll and gaze at the glimmering water gently lapping at our feet. It's a peaceful setting for a heart-to-heart conversation such as the one you and I are about to have. So let's get our favorite beverages, take a stroll around the lake as we pray silently, and then talk together about how you're doing in the area of humility.

As we get started, let me ask you this: Do you know who Jesus named as the greatest person ever born? Well, it wasn't Moses of the Red Sea and Ten Commandments fame; it wasn't David, who was a "man after God's own heart"; it wasn't Abraham, the father of the nation of Israel; or Joseph, who braved grave injustices to rescue the Israelites from the grip of a famine. Rather, it was the scruffy, wild-eyed hermit, John the Baptist, of whom Jesus said, "Truly I tell you, among those born of women there has not risen anyone greater than John the Baptist" (Matthew 11:11). Now, why am I asking you about the greatest person ever born just before we talk about humility? Because humility was one of the primary characteristics that caused John the Baptist to be Jesus' top pick. And John had a formula for humility that we're going to use as our measure for today's discussion: "He must increase, but I must decrease" (John 3:30 KJV).

HE MUST INCREASE

"He must increase" doesn't refer to an increase of Jesus' divine abilities ... or authority ... or glory, but to our vision of his greatness.... The closer we come to him, the bigger he seems to get.

Charles Swindoll, pastor, author

The problem with working on humility is that it's impossible to achieve by working on it directly. The more you focus on humility, the more you are focusing on yourself, which is an entrée to pride. And the minute you say, "I have achieved humility," oops — that's prideful too! So, how on earth are you supposed to work on a quality that eludes you if you work on it? <u>Well, the prescription for humility starts not with working on humility, but work-ing on increasing your vision of God</u>. As you grow closer to him, spend more time concentrating on him, set your sights firmly on him, invest yourself in learning about him and talking with him, he will take up more and more of your field of vision. True, this does require practice, devotion, dedication, and concentration on your part. Becoming unself-conscious is really a matter of becoming other-conscious, isn't it?

How God-conscious are you? For each of the following passages, assess how you are doing at seeking God in the way described. Then write down ideas from each verse for making God a bigger and bigger part of your life.

And all of us have had that veil removed so that we can be mirrors that brightly reflect the glory of the Lord. And as the Spirit of the Lord works within us, we become more and more like him and reflect his glory even more.

2 Corinthians 3:18 NLT

But if from there you seek the LORD your God, you will find him if you seek him with all your heart and with all your soul.

Deuteronomy 4:29

_____

_____

_____

"You're blessed when you've worked up a good appetite for God. He's food and drink in the best meal you'll ever eat."

Matthew 5:6 MSG

_____

_____

_____

As the deer pants for streams of water, so my soul pants for you, my God.

Psalm 42:1

_____

_____

_____

I MUST DECREASE

It is well to remember that the entire population of the universe, with one trifling exception, is composed of others.

John Andrew Holmes, 1823–1872, physician and author

There is a natural phenomenon that occurs when God takes up more of your field of vision: your focus on yourself automatically gets smaller. But, if you try to decrease yourself in a vacuum, with no corresponding increase of God, it is just as ineffective as straining to become humble. Here's how Chuck Swindoll explains it:

Ironically, those who strain to become humble, who try to engineer their own decrease, only call attention to themselves. Socrates once pithily mocked a man for dressing with ostentatious poverty: "I can see your vanity, Antisthenes, through the holes in your cloak."

On the other hand, people who aspire to exalt Christ divert attention from themselves. Commentator Arthur W. Pink said, "The more I am occupied with Christ, the less shall I be occupied with myself...."

The question then is not "How can I humble myself?" but "How can I occupy myself with Christ?" (*John the Baptizer*, Insight for Living, 1991)

Using Philippians 2:3–8 (NCV) as a measuring stick, indicate with a check mark how you are doing in the following ways of decreasing yourself.

Verse 3: *When you do things, do not let selfishness or pride be your guide. Instead, be humble and give more honor to others than to yourselves.*
Imagine a simple scale for measuring your actions in the past week. If you were to put all your actions designed to gain honor for yourself on one side, and all your actions giving honor to others on the other side, which side would be heavier?

☐ Honor for myself   ☐ Honor for others

In what ways can you give more honor to others?

_____

_____

_____

Verse 4: *Do not be interested only in your own life, but be interested in the lives of others.*
Imagine another scale; this one is for this past week's conversations. If you were to put all your stories about yourself on one side, and all your questions of others and listening to their stories about themselves on the other side, which side would be heavier?

☐ My stories   ☐ Stories of others

What can you do to shift the balance and draw out more from others about themselves?

_____

_____

_____

Verse 6: *Christ himself was like God in everything. But he did not think that being equal with God was something to be used for his own benefit.*

The next scale weighs how you used your capabilities. On one side, put all the times you used your skills, abilities, or talents to benefit yourself in some way this week. On the other side put all the times you used your skills, abilities, or talents to benefit others. Which side is heavier?

☐ Benefit for myself   ☐ Benefit for others

How can you use your skills, abilities, or talents to bless others more often?

_____

_____

_____

Verse 7: *But he gave up his place with God and made himself nothing. He was born as a man and became like a servant.*

This scale measures this week's rights. Think of the times you insisted on your rights, demanded your way, or made use of your status or position. Those times go on one side. Next, think about the times you gave up your rights, let someone else have his/her way, or served others. Place those times on the other side. Which side is heavier?

☐ My rights   ☐ Serving others

In what situations can you let go of your rights and serve instead?

_____

_____

_____

Verse 8: *He humbled himself and was fully obedient to God, even when that caused his death—death on a cross.*

The last scale measures this past week's obedience when it hurt. If, on one side, you were to put all the times you excused yourself from obeying because it would hurt, and on the other side you were to put all the times you obeyed God, even when it hurt, which side would be heavier?

☐ Excusing when it hurt ☐ Obeying when it hurt

In what situation do you need to let go of your fears and obey?

My final question for you today is this: What encouraging thing did you notice about yourself in this exercise?

PRAYER

Precious Lord,

Examine me, Lord. If you were to set up a scale of humility, and place my prideful acts on one side and my evidence of humility on the other, how would I measure up? If you were to give me an eye exam and assess how much of my field of vision is filled with you and how much is focused on myself, how would I measure up? Look deep into my heart and my mind and reveal to me the truth about which one of us truly has precedence in my life—you or me. Lord, may you increase. I want to know you more today than yesterday, and less than tomorrow. I want to become more enamored with you. I want to engage with you more and more frequently throughout my day. Show me how to decrease. As you fill more of me, help me to let go of more of myself. Help me honor, listen to, benefit, and serve others. And help me obey you, even when it hurts.

In the name of Jesus, amen.

Steps to Humility

Being totally committed to Christ's increase ...
means letting our lives act as a frame that shows up the masterpiece—
Jesus Christ. And a worthy frame isn't tarnished or dull, plain or cheap;
yet neither is it so elaborate that it overpowers its picture.
Instead, with subtle loveliness, it draws the observer's eyes
to the beautiful work of art it displays.

Charles Swindoll, pastor, author

SITTING QUIETLY WITH YOUR MAKER

Today is a time of reflection and solitude for you in the privacy of your own quiet-time space. You will be putting all your decisions into a Humility Action Plan, with steps to follow and practices to adopt that will deepen this character quality in your life. You will take a look at developing humility from three perspectives: developing a right view of God, developing a right view of yourself, and developing a right view of others.

Ask yourself how deeply you are able to focus on increasing your humility during this season of your life. Then select the appropriate action steps on pages 53–55, whatever you feel you can realistically experiment with this week. It's your plan, your life, and your prayerful decision—nobody else's. If you feel God impressing on you to concentrate on your humility right now, go for these exercises with gusto—without further ado or delay! I am confident that whatever effort you are able to devote to improving your humility will be richly rewarded by him on earth and in heaven.

Humility Action Plan

PRAYER FOCUS: Worship God by praying about some of his characteristics (faithfulness, kindness) or his names (Protector, Provider, King, Holy One). Ask him to show you where you have overvalued yourself and where you have undervalued yourself. Get your eyes off yourself by praising him for a person in your life and pray for an opportunity to share that praise with someone today.

DEVOTIONAL FOCUS: Choose one of the following Scripture passages on the topic of humility: To focus on *developing more of a right view of God*, read Revelation 5:8–14 and marvel at who he is. To focus on *developing more of a right view of yourself*, read the story of Naaman's healing in 2 Kings 5:1–19 and meditate on areas of your life in which pride has made you overvalue yourself to the degree that you struggle with obeying God. To focus on *developing more of a right view of others*, read the passage about the log in your eye and the speck in someone else's eye from Matthew 7:1–5, possibly using a few different translations for a fresh perspective.

EXTRA PERSPECTIVE: Read books to help you better understand God's nature, such as *Knowing God*, the classic on this topic by J. I. Packer. Or get creative and and take the focus off yourself by giving extra attention to a friend who could use it right now.

Action Steps: Developing a Right View of God

Instructions: Prayerfully choose one or two action steps to experiment with this week.

Start Date

_____ ☐ **I will worship God.** I will turn more events of my day into a prayer so that he will increase and I will decrease. I will include God in my thoughts while I'm driving, walking, working, chatting with someone, or watching television. I will acknowledge his great power by talking to him about my worry, fear, anger, frustration, and anxiety, as well as my delight and cheer!

_____ ☐ **I will study God.** I will dive deep into exploring who God is. I will do this through studying his names, his character traits, and his love toward me in Scripture. (For a list of verses in these categories, go to www.LifePurposeCoachingCenters.com/CM.)

_____ ☐ **I will hunt for God.** I will go on a daily God Hunt, journaling where I see him show up in my day: the things I see in nature, the interruptions, the serendipities, the detours, the provisions, the difficulties, the connections with people, and/or the answers to prayer. I will share with at least one person something I saw on my daily God Hunt.

_____ ☐ **I will develop** a right view of God by *(add your idea here)*

_____

_____

Action Steps: Developing a Right View of Myself

Instructions: Prayerfully choose one or two action steps to experiment with this week.

Start Date

_____ ☐ **I will stop trying so hard to be perfect.** I will intentionally let some non-life-threatening thing go, and when someone notices, I will laugh about it instead of apologizing or fixing it.

_____ ☐ **I will not tear myself down.** I will see my attitude of worthlessness for what it is—pride. I will replace my negative self-talk with thanks to God for how he has made me.

_____ ☐ **I will not boast.** I will not maneuver conversations to create opportunities to brag. I will not exaggerate when I am telling a story. I will not show off.

_____ ☐ **I will try to learn** one new thing every day, even in my area of expertise. I will be open to correction, teaching, and the opinions of others.

_____ ☐ **I will check my motives.** I will carry a card in my wallet that says, "Check Your Motives," to remind myself to check for any prideful motives before I speak or act. I will regularly ask myself about my reasons for volunteering, name-dropping, emailing/calling, dropping hints, etc.

_____ ☐ **I will obey God in an area in which I have been holding back.** Instead of saying "That's just the way I am," I will work on areas—with the power of the Holy Spirit—in which I am offensive, irritating, hurtful, selfish, or out of control.

_____ ☐ **I will develop** a right view of myself by *(add your idea here)*

_____

_____

_____

Action Steps: Developing a Right View of Others

Instructions: Prayerfully choose one or two action steps to experiment with this week.

Start Date

_____ ☐ **I will be an encourager.** I will stop comparing myself to others, and instead turn my attention to others and freely give genuine compliments. I will not be judgmental. I will replace my tendency to be harsh, opinionated, and critical, with words and acts of kindness, affirmation, and understanding.

_____ ☐ **I will be a helper.** I will get my eyes off myself, especially if I am going through a difficult time. I will look for ways to turn my attention outward and be a help to someone else. I will shift the balance from being more of a taker to being more of a giver.

_____ ☐ **I will be a servant.** I will deliberately choose to serve somewhere I will not be noticed. I will not compete or be concerned about who gets credit.

_____ ☐ **I will be a receiver.** I will accept help, gifts, or compliments from others graciously, allowing others the dignity of exercising their gifts of helps, generosity, or encouragement.

_____ ☐ **I will be a mentor.** Rather than doing everything myself, I will develop others and help them discover their areas of giftedness, being their cheerleader when they succeed.

_____ ☐ **I will develop** a right view of others by *(add your idea here)*

_____

_____

_____

MASTER ACTION PLAN

Now, select only one major action step from this Day 5 exercise and record it on your Master Action Plan in appendix A on page 322. When you have finished reading this book, continue to refer to that one major action step on your Master Action Plan (as well as this Humility Action Plan, of course, as your season of life permits!). Remember, in order to become more like Christ in your character, you need to collaborate with God in three ways: preparation, prayer, and practice. You have done the work of preparation by learning God's truth about humility. Now, internalize it by praying for the Holy Spirit's help and practicing your action steps, one by one.

HUMILITY PRAYER

Precious Lord,

I wish I did not struggle in this area, because it makes me so sad to think about the terrible ripple effects my pride has on others. Worse, though, I am deeply sorry for my pride which attempts to make me the president of the universe and steal glory from you. Today, I just want to go on record as saying: I love you. I am sorry for my prideful ways. Thank you for loving me in spite of myself, and most of all, thank you for your extreme kindness and willingness to take me from where I am today. That is truly remarkable to me. It may very well be the first thing I thank you for when I get to see you in heaven.

In the name of Jesus, amen.

PART 2

The Making of a Right Relationship to Myself

Chapter 2

Confidence

The Fear-of-GOD builds up confidence,
and makes a world safe for your children.

Proverbs 14:26 MSG

Faith in God

Confidence gives you courage and extends your reach.
It lets you take greater risks and achieve far more
than you ever thought possible.
Jack Welch, chairman and CEO of General Electric

WELCOME BACK TO MY PLACE— *CHARACTER MAKEOVER STUDIO*!

Hi there. I'm glad you mentioned last week how much you love the outdoors, because it dawned on me that you might just enjoy a beautiful rustic path around the corner from my house. We'll be surrounded by trees with chirping birds and have a view of a canyon with a stream running through it. What do you say? How about a leisurely stroll as we chat? There are even a few benches we can use along the way, as needed. Good! I think the prayer that is on my heart before we head out is this, but feel free to add to it ... if you'd like:

Heavenly Father,
    You are the Ruler of all creation. Thanks that we will have a chance today to breathe in some of the fresh air you've given us and hear the rustling of the trees you made. Thank you for walking with us for this coaching session. We give you absolute authority over the path of life you would like us to follow.
Amen.

Now, off we go to discuss today's topic: confidence.

CONFESSIONS OF A NONCONFIDENT COACH

It's true confession time. I hate to admit this, but people used to call me "helmet head." You see, for years I felt ugly and self-conscious about my looks, so I compensated for that by spraying on so much hairspray that I cemented every hair in its perfect place. I'm telling you—a hug with a head-bump from me could have knocked you out! I may have felt embarrassed about my general appearance, but I was confident about my hairstyle!

Confidence is an important quality for women of character. Confidence gives us that inner self-assurance that helps us interact effectively with others. It equips us with the belief that we can live out our purpose in life. Without confidence, we shrivel up and hide, and we don't believe in ourselves or in God's power working through us. Certain self-help gurus suggest that confidence is built upon little tricks, such as good posture, dressing for success, a strong handshake, powerful deodorant, or having an image consultant. (And ... yes, I've tried all of those too, in addition to the hairspray!) Confidence, they say, is a matter of looking right and acting like you believe in yourself. The problem is this: What happens if you don't think you look right? What happens when you let yourself down?

SELF-CONFIDENCE VS. GOD-CONFIDENCE

Self-confidence comes *not* from believing in yourself but from having faith in God. Pervasive self-confidence is not self-confidence at all, but God-confidence. That's another one of those spiritual paradoxes, like losing your life to find it, or the last shall be first. Confidence is only as good as the one in whom you place your confidence. If you try really hard to work up your confidence by doing your hair right or putting on a dazzling smile, your confidence will last only as long as your hairspray or your tooth whitener, and it could be destroyed by a rainy day or bad breath.

So, if confidence is only as good as the one in whom you place your confidence, who better to trust than God himself? A radical shift from self-confidence to God-confidence makes all the difference. Sociologists tell us that our self-esteem is based on what we believe the most important person in our life thinks about us. If you are picking up your self-esteem cues from a parent or a best friend or a mate or your own self-talk, your confidence suffers when you get a negative message. But, if you are looking to God for your self-esteem cues, how much more solid and unshakeable could your confidence possibly be? You will know, despite what anyone else says—and despite what you might tell yourself—that you are worthwhile; you are lovable; you are acceptable; you are desirable; you are forgivable.

DEBORAH: A PICTURE OF CONFIDENCE

The Bible is full of stories about confident people, those who found strength and unexpected leadership abilities as a result of placing their trust in God. One of the most alluring stories of confidence is about the judge-prophetess named Deborah, a woman who was a national leader in a culture that largely ignored women. There are a few, very powerful women in Scripture—such as Queen Esther, the Queen of Sheba, and Queen Jezebel—but Deborah is the only woman who rose to her prominent position of authority by popular demand. Among a slew of judges over a span of a few hundred years who demonstrated increasingly blatant character flaws, Deborah is the only one of her time who consistently exhibited integrity, character, wisdom, and a confidence in God that drew people to follow her bold leadership.

One day, as people were waiting their turn for Deborah to settle their disputes and dispense justice, she received a prophetic message from God for Barak, the military commander: assemble an army and attack the Canaanites. Now let's just stop a minute here to realize how audacious this idea was. The Canaanites boasted an invincible army with iron chariots (Judges 1:19). Earlier generations of Israelites had been so terrified of them that they surrendered before they even prayed. Well, the Canaanites still had their chariots, but Israel now had a secret weapon—Deborah's abiding faith in God. Barak was willing to face those chariots only if Deborah would come along. He said: "If you go with me, I will go; but if you don't go with me, I won't go" (Judges 4:8).

So off went Deborah and Barak, and due to her inspirational leadership, ten thousand tribesmen gathered with them to place their lives on the line for an impossible cause. Deborah's complete faith in God became the strength of the army as she raised the battle cry, "Go! This is the day the LORD has given Sisera into your hands. Has not the LORD gone ahead of you?" (4:14). The charge of the brave Israelite army coincided with a great thunderstorm, and the invincible Canaanite chariots were mired in a sea of mud, resulting in the utter destruction of the Canaanite army.

Deborah displayed absolute confidence in God, unshakable faith, extreme devotion to her nation, passion for her people, and confident leadership despite leading in a male-dominated culture. Yet, we don't see an ounce of pride in her as she gives all the credit and glory to God for their military victory (see Deborah's song in Judges 5).

LESSONS IN CONFIDENCE

Deborah exhibited several important qualities of a confident person:

- **Problem-solver.** Deborah saw a situation that demanded action, and she organized a solution. She did not let her gender or her lack of experience stymie her.
- **Risk-taker.** By faith in God, Deborah rallied an army and inspired the men to go to battle. This was not the behavior of a fearful, unsure woman, but that of a woman with a solid faith in a powerful God.
- **Realistic about strengths.** Deborah attracted followers by virtue of her devotion to God, but the people's attention didn't make her self-conscious. She didn't put herself down by saying, "Oh, I'm just a woman. You shouldn't be listening to me. Go talk to Barak."
- **Competent.** Deborah's sense of competence did not come because she dispensed her own wisdom or controlled people. She felt competent because she listened to God, spoke his words, and pointed people to him. She didn't claim credit for her success—she acknowledged God as the giver of victory.
- **Knowing purpose.** Deborah understood her strengths and exerted her influence. When faced with a great obstacle, she rose to the challenge knowing that this was the moment and purpose for which God had placed her in that position. She was decisive, not a people-pleaser or a conformist.
- **Awareness of *not* being qualified.** We see nothing in this story that explains why Deborah was used by God in this dramatic way. She did not come from a long line of leaders. She had not distinguished herself in battle before this. From what we can tell, God used her simply because she was usable, obedient, and faithful. It seems that he must have said, "Wow! A woman sold out to me? That's all I ask!"

It's time to check in with you to see how confident you are. Try the self-assessment on the next page in order to take your *confidence pulse*:

Confidence Self-Test

For each pair of thirteen statements, check the one that more frequently describes you, then total your score to determine whether you lean more toward confidence or insecurity.

Confidence	Insecurity
I find the positive side ☐ of negative events.	☐ I see a negative event as a reason to quit.
I look for solutions to problems. ☐	☐ I feel stuck when problems arise.
I see mistakes as learning ☐ opportunities.	☐ I see mistakes as embarrassing; I hide them.
I accept myself, even when I fail. ☐	☐ Failure is proof that I'm unworthy.
I take risks and try new things. ☐	☐ I fear failure and avoid risk.
When I'm new in a group, ☐ I focus on others.	☐ When I'm new in a group, I'm self-conscious.
I realistically acknowledge ☐ my strengths.	☐ I put myself down.
I am able to receive ☐ compliments graciously.	☐ I discount compliments as undeserved.
I do the right thing, ☐ even when criticized.	☐ I'm driven by what I think will make others happy.
I have a strong sense of who I am. ☐	☐ I conform in order to be accepted.
I generally feel competent. ☐	☐ I feel out of control, incapable, inadequate.
I know what my life purpose is. ☐	☐ My life is meaningless; I'm confused.
My self-esteem is based ☐ on what God says.	☐ My self-esteem is based on approval of others.
TOTAL CONFIDENCE SCORE ___	___ TOTAL INSECURITY SCORE

Reflecting on the results of this self-test may help you answer the following journal questions more realistically.

Journal

Read Deborah's battle cry again: "Go! This is the day the LORD has given Sisera into your hands. Has not the LORD gone ahead of you?" (Judges 4:14).

1. What "day" is this for you—what battle is taking place in your sphere of influence? In what area are you finding your confidence the most shaken or susceptible right now?

_____

_____

_____

2. What is God saying to you about this area? If God is telling you to "go!" or charge or move ahead, what would that obedience look like?

_____

_____

_____

3. Picture God going ahead of you into your battle. How would placing your faith in him instead of yourself (or your appearance, or your past successes, or what your friends say about you, or whatever you typically rely on for your self-confidence) affect your confidence?

_____

_____

_____

PRAYER

Precious Lord,

Thank you that I don't have to rely on how I feel about myself for my confidence. Lord, help me have faith in you when I lack confidence. You have proven over and over again that you use people even when there is something in their lives that could erode their self-confidence. You raised up Deborah to be a national leader, even though she was a woman. You made Sarah the mother of a nation, even though she was too old. You used Rahab to protect Hebrew spies, even though she was a prostitute. Ruth is in the genealogy of Jesus, even though she was an outsider — a Moabitess. You made Esther a queen who saved her people, even though she was an orphan. You let Martha serve you, even though she was a worrier and a complainer. You inspired the Samaritan woman to evangelize her village, even though she was a five-time divorcée. And you taught a lesson in generosity through the widow who gave two pennies, even though she was destitute. Please go before me and win the battle in the area about which I feel most vulnerable. I want to make the shift from self-confidence to God-confidence.

In the name of Jesus, amen.

Insecurity: Exposing Your Inner Charlie Brown

Another belief of mine: everyone else my age is an adult,
whereas I am merely in disguise.

Margaret Atwood, novelist

A VIRTUAL MESSAGE

 NOTE: It's Day 2, so you have the option of listening to today's message by downloading it from my website, www.LifePurposeCoachingCenters.com/ CM, or reading the message text below. Enjoy the virtual coaching and don't forget to open in prayer!

THE FLIP SIDE OF CONFIDENCE

"I got a 'C' in everything. I'm a straight 'blah' student!" This is a typical self-assessment from Charlie Brown, that hapless star of the *Peanuts* comic strip, who is constantly battling his anxieties and shortcomings. He is resigned to his loser status: "I'm not a poor loser; I'm a good loser. I'm so good at it I lose all the time!" And he lets Lucy dominate him: "You, Charlie Brown, are a foul ball in the line drive of life. You are a miscue. You are three putts on the eighteenth green. You are a seven-ten split in the tenth frame. You are a dropped rod and reel in the lake of life."

Poor Charlie Brown. I wonder if his parents were as critical and demanding as Lucy! Were they overprotective and controlling? If so, they probably greatly contributed to Charlie Brown's feelings of inadequacy and inferiority. After all, everything *else* gets blamed on parents! If only they had made Charlie Brown feel accepted, even when he made mistakes, he probably wouldn't have been so hard on himself when he missed the football or got his kite stuck in a tree. Remember that Charlie Brown didn't necessarily lack ability; he just focused too much on other people's expectations and let others shape his self-concept.

CONFIDENCE ROBBERS

We all have areas about which we are insecure. Simple things like gaining ten pounds, getting criticized, or feeling left out can shake our confidence. But there are deeper threats that can cause a more deep-seated insecurity: the confidence robbers of false identity, lack of purpose, and self-sabotage. Fortunately, you can prevent your confidence from being stolen by: (1) knowing who you are; (2) knowing why you are here; and (3) knowing what you are worth!

You need to know who you are.

If you don't have a strong sense of who you are, then your identity may depend on what other people tell you about yourself. If you have friends like Charlie Brown's, this could be rather discouraging! When people around you are habitually critical, or if they label you or insult you, your confidence can erode and you can be left feeling like a *nobody* and a failure. We all know the importance of choosing our friends wisely and limiting our exposure to those who put us down, degrade us, or treat us like we're worthless.

With their mouths the godless destroy their neighbors.

Proverbs 11:9

The words of the reckless pierce like swords.

Proverbs 12:18

Another factor that can sway your confidence is if you compare yourself to others. Comparison can lead to pride if you feel superior to others, or it can lead to insecurity if you think others are better than you. If you are someone who tends to gauge your status by measuring yourself against other people, then you'll be on an identity seesaw, depending upon whom you're comparing yourself to that day.

We do not dare to classify or compare ourselves with some who commend themselves. When they measure themselves by one another, and compare themselves with one another, they do not show good sense.

2 Corinthians 10:12 NRSV

You need to know why you're here.

Nothing helps you overcome confidence-barriers more than a sense of purpose. When you know why you're here on earth and what you were made to do, it gives you a tremendous sense of meaning in life. You may notice that when you're operating in your gift area, whether that's singing or teaching or painting or managing or phone calling, you have boundless energy. You feel you could just keep going and going as if you have an endless tank of gas. You also may find that you keep bouncing back after a failure, trying again and again at something you believe in and know you're supposed to do, undeterred by detours or setbacks. But if you are confused about your direction or unsure of your purpose, you are far more susceptible to fatigue and failure.

This is exactly what happened to Peter. Jesus' arrest was Peter's unhinging. All along he thought he knew what his purpose was—to be at Jesus' side when he was crowned king of the Jews. But when that glittering destiny was ripped away at the hands of an angry mob, Peter lost his confidence, which set the stage for him to succumb to fatigue and failure. He stumbled into a courtyard, upset that all his dreams and plans had been dashed, worn out from his all-nighter in Gethsemane. With his reserves depleted, he couldn't withstand the taunts of strangers and ended up retorting three times that he didn't even know Jesus (see Luke 22:54–62).

You need to know what you're worth.

A person with low self-worth can self-sabotage by being perfectionistic, controlling, or depressive. This makes her harder to be around, which only reinforces feelings of low self-esteem and isolation. Look closely at each category, paying special attention to ways you can stop the self-sabotage:

Perfectionism: A particularly insidious method of self-sabotage is perfectionism. It's the syndrome that says, "If I could just be perfect, everybody would like me," which mistakenly assumes that we can control what other people think of us. It can sound like this: "I have to have so-and-so's approval or I'll die." Or, "If it's not perfect, I've failed; and if I fail, I'll die." If that's the case, perfectionists are doomed! Being perfect is the unattainable goal of a woman who is trying to prove her worth. But worth is not something we earn or achieve. Worth is something we learn to perceive. We come to realize that we have worth because God created us, redeemed us, and loves us.

Long before he laid down earth's foundations, he had us in mind, had
settled on us as the focus of his love, to be made whole and holy by his love.

Ephesians 1:4 MSG

Control: Some insecure people have a high need for control. A perfectionist tries to make *herself* perfect, while a controller tries to make *her world* perfect. It can feel threatening to be out of control, such as when a coworker has a different opinion than you, your house is a mess, your children are misbehaving, you're jobless, or your husband is late getting home. If your self-image relies on being right, looking right, parenting right, or doing right, then you might become a controller. Usually, forcing the people and things in your world to line up with your perception of "right" only succeeds in alienating those you are trying to control.

Depression: Another common method of self-sabotage for insecure people is depression. In depression, you are attacking yourself. Many things can cause depression. For me, it was a thyroid condition that exacerbated the post-partum blues after my daughter was born. But, once I was in a state of depression, my chronic insecurities converged to prolong it. Even after I trudged back to the land of the living, I moved into hyperactive mode in order to avoid feeling pain and plunging into another pit. Looking back on it now, I believe that if I had been more secure in my identity in Christ, known my purpose in life (which I was almost frantic to discover at the time), and had not been so perfectionistic and controlling, I would have recovered more quickly and the aftermath would have been less turbulent.

I encourage you to use this next self-assessment to get a better idea of how confidence robbers may be intruding on your life.

Confidence Robbers Checklist

Check any of the following confidence robbers you have experienced, as illustrated by the sample statements for each. For everything you check, pray about what you discover and what God might be inviting you to change.

☐ **Perfectionism:** "It has to be perfect, or I have failed."

☐ **Control:** "I need to make my family look 'right'—they're a reflection on me."

☐ **Mistaking feelings for fact:** "I *feel* stupid, so I'm sure I *am* stupid."

☐ **Projecting:** "I know they're laughing at me," or, "She probably thinks I'm boring."

☐ **Deflecting compliments:** "You liked the meal? I'm sorry it wasn't gourmet."

☐ **Downplaying:** "My success wasn't my doing—it was good luck/chance/ because of someone else."

☐ **Comparison:** "I'm not as pretty/talented/thin/successful/capable/ well-dressed/outgoing/holy as she is."

☐ **Entrenchment:** "I was raised in a dysfunctional home, so I'll always be dysfunctional."

☐ **Futuring:** "Since I got laid off, that means I'm never going to make it in this industry."

For an additional confidence assessment, go to www.LifePurposeCoaching Centers.com/CM.

Beware Extreme Thinking

We tend to think in extremes. Be careful about doing that because confidence robbers feed off extreme thinking. Look through the following pairs of statements for classic examples of such behavior:

Unrealistic assessment...	... as opposed to realistic assessment
"I'm a terrible mother."	"I have to work late sometimes."
"If my children aren't well behaved, they're completely bad."	"Everybody has good days and bad days."
"If my dishes are not done, my house is entirely messy."	"I haven't gotten the dishes done yet."
"I'm useless."	"I've got a lot to learn."
"I'm lazy."	"I'm feeling tired today."

CONFIDENCE RESTORERS

Let's return to the scene where Jesus washed his disciples' feet that we talked about in relation to humility. There are lessons here that will also help restore the confidence stolen by the three confidence thieves. To set the stage again, let's look in on the upper room:

> *Jesus knew that the Father had put all things under his power, and that he had come from God and was returning to God;* ⁴*so he got up from the meal* ... ⁵*and began to wash his disciples' feet.*
>
> John 13:3–5

This passage tells us that Jesus knew three things about himself:

1. **He knew who he was.** *He had come from God.* Jesus knew that his identity was sourced in God.
2. **He knew where he fit.** *The Father had put all things under his power.* His position was one of authority, and he knew that his authority was given to him by his Father.
3. **He knew his destiny.** *He was returning to God.* Jesus knew his purpose was to redeem humankind, and he was so confident that he would accomplish his purpose that he knew he would return to the presence of his Father in heaven.

Notice one very important thing about Jesus' self-image: It was entirely based on God. There is no mention of Jesus thinking: "I wonder what they'll think of me," or "I need to do this to be noticed," or "It makes me feel so good just to serve." Jesus' self-image was not reliant on the approval of others, on achievement, or on being the best. His self-image was based on who God made him to be (he had come from God), what God gave him (all power), and God's destiny for his life (completing his purpose and returning to God).

Journal

True and lasting confidence comes by basing our self-esteem in what God says about us. For each of the following verses, summarize what the Bible says about you and how this affects your self-esteem.

My identity (who I am)

Psalm 139:14–18 _____

_____

Ephesians 1:4–5 _____

_____

My position (where I fit)

Romans 12:4–5_____

_____

Ephesians 2:6_____

_____

My purpose (why I'm here)

Matthew 5:16 _____

_____

John 15:16_____

_____

2 Corinthians 5:20 _____

_____

PRAYER

Precious Lord,

I have felt like a Charlie Brown–type loser at times. I have been guilty of giving more credence to what the Lucys in my life say about me than what you say about me. I have compared myself to others and come up short. I have felt like I don't fit in—like I'm alone and rejected. I have become confused about my purpose, and I find myself more tired, more discouraged. And the more insecure I feel, the more I try to fix myself through perfectionism, or fix my world through control, or retreat to a place of depression where I'm numb. Lord, I don't want to be like that anymore. Help me to believe you when you tell me you made me just the way I am, and that you chose me. Help me to remember that I am part of something larger, to know where I fit in your family. And give me a vision for your purpose for my life. I want to be the best me I can be. I want to be the person you see when you look at me through your eyes of love. Thank you that you love me for being me.

In the name of Jesus, amen.

How to Be Nice to Yourself

A realization of the universal lack of self-confidence
tends to strengthen one's own.
Anonymous

YOU'VE GOT MAIL

To:	"The Best You" Woman	Sent: **Day 3**
From:	Katie Brazelton	
Subject:	Confidence	

It's Day 3, so here is your weekly Email Message. Feel free to blog me a response at my website, www.LifePurposeCoachingCenters.com/CM, if you'd like. Enjoy the email-coaching and don't forget to open in prayer!

WHAT WE CAN LEARN FROM RICK WARREN ABOUT CONFIDENCE

A number of years ago my pastor, Rick Warren, said something in a sermon that really struck me. He said that *we consider our problems unique, but not our potential.* About our *problems* we might say, "You don't know how hard it is for me ... you don't know my kids ... you don't know the man I have to live with ... you don't know how lonely I am." But when we talk about our *potential*, we think we're not unique at all. We'll say, "Anybody can speak ... lots of people can organize ... there's nothing special about cooking."

God's Word tells us just the opposite of this. It says that our *problems* are not unique — they're universal:

No temptation has overtaken you except what is common to us all.

1 Corinthians 10:13

Scripture also points out that our *potential* is not typical — it's unique:

But in fact God has placed the parts in the body, every one of them, just as he wanted them to be. [19]*If they were all one part, where would the body be?*

1 Corinthians 12:18–19

And here's the kicker, according to Pastor Rick: God only made one you, so he's never going to say, "Why weren't you more like so-and-so?" But he might have to say, "Why weren't you more like you?"

KATHRYN'S STORY ABOUT BEING AVERAGE

"Kathryn is average, and she'll never be anything but average." With that disparaging comment from her fourth grade teacher, my colleague Kathryn launched on a lifelong quest to prove her teacher wrong. No one up to that point would have characterized young Kathryn as average. She was an only child in a loving Christian family, made to feel special and unique. But the negative attitude of a teacher marked a turning point in her life.

For the next three decades, Kathryn worked at accomplishing more than everyone else. By seventh grade, for example, she was back on the honor roll and stayed there all through high school, college, graduate school, and her doctorate. Her papers were the longest, her notebooks the biggest, and her doctoral dissertation was six times as long as necessary. She became a teacher, and her students benefited from extra programs she started — a newscast, a school store, the chess club, and competitive academic teams such as Knowledge Masters and Stock Market. She eventually became the chair of the elementary education department at North Greenville University.

Her spiritual dedication was just as intentional, starting at age twelve when she publicly surrendered her life to God to do whatever he asked of her, and continuing into adulthood with mission trips to Africa, China, India, Thailand, Brazil, and several eastern European countries. She started an adoption agency and a ministry to women called Go Fish! All the while, no matter what she accomplished, she never believed it was enough. Her perfectionism drove her to work longer and harder than everyone else, and sometimes kept her from trying those things that she feared she wouldn't be able to do perfectly. Her self-talk included statements such as: "There's nothing special about me." "I have to be better than everyone else." "I'm not good enough." "I can't write because I'm a horrible speller." "I have to be perfect." "I'm average."

This all changed in 2005 when a friend challenged Kathryn, as she was relating the story about her teacher's comment. These words changed her life: "Isn't it time you surrendered that comment and let it stop controlling your life?" Her answer? Yes! Kathryn became aware of her negative self-talk and started replacing negative statements with positive ones. Now, instead of telling herself she's depressed, Kathryn thinks, "I choose to be happy." She tells herself that she's worthy, since God made her. She dwells on God's blessings instead of her problems. And in regard to her writing, instead of believing she would never write, she started saying things like, "Computers have spell checkers now!" and "At least I'm a good editor" and "I have something God wants me to say." She has now published several articles and is working on a book. She has changed her inner voice recording to say, "I am special and God has an awesome plan for my life that is more exceedingly abundant than I can even imagine." Her advice to women struggling with confidence? "Spend time daily with God, developing a love relationship with him. Then surrender your negative self-talk. You can't trash yourself without slamming the one who created you."

SUREFIRE CONFIDENCE BUILDERS

Kathryn's story points out an important principle: In order to surrender your negative thoughts and statements, you have to replace them with positive ones. Kathryn actually asked friends to catch her when she said something negative about herself; then she would write down the negative statement and ask God to give her a new, replacement statement that would honor him.

The Bible affirms this commonsense strategy:

> *Finally, brothers and sisters, whatever is true, whatever is noble, whatever is right, whatever is pure, whatever is lovely, whatever is admirable — if anything is excellent or praiseworthy — think about such things.*

> Philippians 4:8

Let's examine this verse phrase by phrase and find some surefire confidence builders that you can memorize and use when you uncover something negative that you've been telling yourself. It's as simple as remembering what

God says about you, believing it, and then saying those things to yourself that a loving Father would tell you.

Whatever is true

Are you making sweeping, unsupportable statements about yourself, such as, "I can't do anything right"? Do you need to let go of something someone said a long time ago about you that just isn't true? Are you going to believe what a *person* said about you or what *God* says about you?

> *"Then you will know the truth, and the truth will set you free."*
>
> John 8:32

Whatever is noble

Do you tell yourself you are dishonorable, crushed, embarrassed, humiliated? No matter how unworthy you may feel, God's love can't be shaken.

> *"Though the mountains be shaken and the hills be removed, yet my unfailing love for you will not be shaken nor my covenant of peace be removed," says the LORD, who has compassion on you.*
>
> Isaiah 54:10

Whatever is right

Has a great wrong been done to you? Are you telling yourself that your life isn't fair? God promises to take care of us if we're wronged.

> *Though my father and mother forsake me, the LORD will receive me.*
>
> Psalm 27:10

Whatever is pure

Are you saying that what you have done cannot be forgiven? Do you feel impure, dirty, unclean, or unacceptable? There is nothing you have done that is beyond the reach of God's cleansing power.

> *Through what Christ would do for us ... he [God] decided then to make us holy in his eyes, without a single fault—we who stand before him covered with his love.*
>
> Ephesians 1:4 LB

Whatever is lovely

Do you feel ugly? Have you been telling yourself that you're unlikable, that you don't measure up, that you're flawed? God wants to replace your injured, broken, and destroyed places with beauty.

> *[He will] bestow on them a crown of beauty instead of ashes.*
>
> Isaiah 61:3

Whatever is admirable

Do you tell yourself that your character is less than commendable, that there is nothing you do that anyone else would admire? Do you feel like you can't lead, that you're afraid to speak from your heart, or that you need to shrink into the background?

> *I have strength for all things in Christ Who empowers me — I am ready for anything and equal to anything through Him Who infuses inner strength into me; I am self-sufficient in Christ's sufficiency.*
>
> Philippians 4:13 AB

If anything is excellent

Do you feel like you're unworthy or worthless? Do you tell yourself that you're just average? God's care for you proves your level of excellence in his eyes.

> *"God feeds [the birds] … and you are far more valuable to him than any birds!"*
>
> Luke 12:24 LB

Or praiseworthy

When someone compliments you, do you rebuff them? Do you feel you don't deserve kindness, praise, affirmation, or positive attention? God made us acceptable, which results in praise to him.

> *To the praise of the glory of His grace, by which He made us accepted in the Beloved.*
>
> Ephesians 1:6 NKJV

Self-Talk Checklist

Mark the three types of positive self-talk you need the most:

☐ **Whatever is true:** I need to let go of a lie someone said about me and believe God.

☐ **Whatever is noble:** I need to affirm that God loves me even when I feel dishonorable, crushed, embarrassed, or humiliated.

☐ **Whatever is right:** I need to remember God will take care of the wrong done to me.

☐ **Whatever is pure:** I need to declare that God says I am forgivable.

☐ **Whatever is lovely:** I need to see the beauty God has given me for my "ashes."

☐ **Whatever is admirable:** I need to claim God's sufficiency when I feel inadequate.

☐ **If anything is excellent:** I need to state that I'm valuable when I feel average.

☐ **Or praiseworthy:** I need to thank God that I'm acceptable when I feel undeserving.

Journal

Following Kathryn's recommendations, the first step to replacing negative self-talk is to write down your negative statements. Referring to the items you checked on the Self-Talk Checklist on page 80, write out your three most typical negative statements.

1. _____

_____

2. _____

_____

3. _____

_____

Now, replace those statements with positive, true statements, drawing your ideas from the surefire, confidence-building verses found on pages 78–79.

1. _____

_____

2. _____

_____

3. _____

_____

Proverbs 18:21 (GWT) says that "the tongue has the power of life and death," so speak these positive, true statements *out loud* at least once a day—during your quiet time with God, or while driving, or whenever you catch yourself putting yourself down.

PRAYER

Precious Lord,

Sometimes I get it mixed up; I think my problems are unique, but my potential is not. Lord, you are my confidence-booster. If I speak negatively about myself, I'm trashing your creation — me! Forgive me for being down on myself. Help me to replace my negative self-talk with statements about myself that are true, that affirm what is noble about me. Remind me to thank you for justice to come, to embrace how you have made me pure, to rejoice in the loveliness you have given me, to claim your strength to be admirable, to affirm my excellence, and to receive praise graciously. My confidence comes from what you think of me, Lord, and I promise to dwell on your surefire confidence builders instead of on the lies of the confidence robbers I have listened to in the past.

In the name of Jesus, amen.

Your Confidence Coach

God expects of us the one thing that glorifies Him —
and that is to remain absolutely confident in Him, remembering what
He has said beforehand, and sure that His purposes will be fulfilled.

Oswald Chambers, 1874–1917, Scottish Protestant minister

PERSPECTIVE-CHANGING OUTING

Today you and I are meeting at a delightful tearoom you discovered. It's in a restored Victorian house, and the walls are covered with old photos, intricate needlework, and hats with sweeping plumes and elaborate ribbons. We say a prayer of thanksgiving and then select from a vast variety of teas—I pick Chrysanthemum, you pick Lavender Dream—and as we steep our tea leaves, we study the old photos. They make us think of history and destiny, and we wonder who those people were and what they did with their lives.

Let's turn our attention to your life. Our conversation today is about confidence. How are you doing at having confidence in God, and knowing who you are, where you fit, and why you're on earth? Throughout our discussion, we're going to look at the confidence of Jesus and use the lessons of his life as the trigger for our evaluation. Let's get started.

HOW GOD-CONFIDENT ARE YOU?

Jesus showed great confidence in God every time he did a miracle, but raising Lazarus from the dead is perhaps the most revealing.

*Jesus, once more deeply moved, came to the tomb.... [39]"Take away the stone,"
he said. "But, Lord," said Martha ... "by this time there is a bad odor, for he
has been there four days." [40]Then Jesus said, "Did I not tell you that if you
believe, you will see the glory of God?" [41]... Then Jesus looked up and said,*

"Father, I thank you that you have heard me. [42] I know that you always hear me, but I said this for the benefit of the people standing here, that they may believe that you sent me." [43] ... Jesus called in a loud voice, "Lazarus, come out!" [44] The dead man came out, his hands and feet wrapped with strips of linen, and a cloth around his face. Jesus said to them, "Take off the grave clothes and let him go."

John 11:38–44

Consider Jesus' words. He prays aloud so the people nearby can hear. But notice that he starts off by saying that God has already heard him. He must have been praying before he ever got there, which is how he received his marching orders from the Father. Then, with full confidence in God, he speaks the impossible, and the impossible happens — Lazarus walks out of the grave.

Jesus had a habit of prayer that prepared him for this moment. If you were to find yourself in a daunting situation right now, how well would your current patterns of connecting with God equip you to be confident?

Jesus pointed people to God by reminding Martha about a truth and by praying aloud. In what ways do you point people's attention away from yourself and toward God (i.e., I give praise reports about the "impossible" things God has done in my life. In times of public prayer, I often unabashedly thank God for his mercy on me.)?

Jesus had confidence in God when it seemed impossible. Think about an impossible situation in your own life. How would you describe your level of belief in God's power in that impossible situation?

HOW WELL DO YOU KNOW WHO YOU ARE?

Jesus had a true, unshakeable knowledge of who he was. He would describe himself, using varying terms that fit the occasion. For instance, he told the woman at the well, "I am the living water"; to the blind man he said, "I am the light of the world"; after feeding the five thousand he declared, "I am the bread of life"; and before raising Lazarus, he assured Martha, "I am the resurrection and the life." Jesus knew without a doubt who he was, and he knew which aspect of himself was most needed by the person to whom he was speaking.

List four words about yourself that describe who you really are to the people around you. (Try to avoid names that depict roles, such as "I am Tyler's mother." Instead, use character qualities, such as: nurturer, encourager, helpmate, confidante, prayer warrior, mentor.)

Jesus knew Scriptures that described who he was. Write out your favorite phrases from Scripture that describe your true identity in Christ. (You may want to refer to verses in the journal exercise from Day 2, page 73, or look up the following passages for additional ideas: John 1:12; John 15:15; Ephesians 2:10.)

Looking back at the phrases you selected, what conclusions can you draw about what God thinks of you? How does that line up with what you think of yourself?

How Well Do You Know Where You Fit?

If you recall, before Jesus washed his disciples' feet, he already knew that the Father had put all things under his power. Jesus knew the extent of God's power, and he knew where he fit into God's plan in any given circumstance. In the midst of a storm, for example, he knew that his role was a position of authority over the weather.

> *That day when evening came, he said to his disciples, "Let us go over to the other side."... ³⁷A furious squall came up, and the waves broke over the boat, so that it was nearly swamped. ³⁸Jesus was in the stern, sleeping on a cushion. The disciples woke him and said to him, "Teacher, don't you care if we drown?"*
>
> *³⁹He got up, rebuked the wind and said to the waves, "Quiet! Be still!" Then the wind died down and it was completely calm.*
>
> *⁴⁰He said to his disciples, "Why are you so afraid? Do you still have no faith?"*
>
> *⁴¹They were terrified and asked each other, "Who is this? Even the wind and the waves obey him!"*
>
> Mark 4:35, 37–41

Knowing where he fit in God's plan on a daily basis gave Jesus utter confidence in a humanly terrifying circumstance. His confidence was so complete that he was even able to rest while a storm raged.

What event or concern is shaking your confidence today? What understanding do you need to develop in order to be more unshakable in your daily roles? Is it learning more about God's power, or about how you're gifted, or about where your problems and solutions fit in God's plan? How can you develop this understanding?

_____

_____

_____

Jesus was so confident in God and in his role that he was able to rest. How have you responded during a crisis? What did you do to find rest and peace when things were in turmoil?

_____

_____

_____

How Well Do You Know Why You're Here?

Jesus knew his purpose on earth, and just before he was arrested, he looked toward heaven and told his Father that he had completed the work he had given him to do.

"Father, the hour has come. Glorify your Son, that your Son may glorify you. ²For you granted him authority over all people that he might give eternal life to all those you have given him.... ⁴I have brought you glory on earth by finishing the work you gave me to do. ⁵And now, Father, glorify me in your presence with the glory I had with you before the world began."

John 17:1–2, 4–5

What was the work the Father gave Jesus to do? Jesus described it in various ways, but without wavering:

"For the Son of Man came to seek and to save what was lost."

Luke 19:10

"I have come that they may have life and that they may have it more abundantly."

John 10:10 NKJV

"I have come down from heaven not to do my will but the will of him who sent me."

John 6:38

"As the Father knows Me, even so I know the Father; and I lay down My life for the sheep."

John 10:15 NKJV

Describe the purpose of your life. Even if you don't have a succinct purpose statement, try to summarize how you think God might want to use you in the world (i.e., to give women hope that God has a plan for their lives; to listen to the lonely and hurting, offering biblical counsel).

_____

_____

_____

Jesus said that he brought glory to God by completing the work God gave him to do. In what ways do you give God glory by the way you are living your life?

_____

_____

_____

PRAYER

Precious Lord,

My strongest confidence comes from consistent prayer that connects me with you. Help me to rely more on prayer and less on my capabilities, especially when I'm feeling insecure. My strongest identity comes from what you say about me. Help me to embrace your words about me and live like I believe them. My strongest role is that of being a daughter of you, the King. Help me to draw upon that when my foundation is shaken. My strongest purpose is to bring glory to you. Help me to be the best me I can be, since you made me the way I am to fulfill a unique part in your grand plan. That is stunning to realize, Lord. Thank you. Thank you.

In the name of Jesus, amen.

Steps to Confidence

We probably wouldn't worry about what people think
of us if we could know how seldom they do.
Charlie "Tremendous" Jones, motivational speaker

Whether you think you can, or think you can't,
you're probably right.
Henry Ford, founder, Ford Motor Company

SITTING QUIETLY WITH YOUR MAKER

Today is a time of reflection and solitude for you in the privacy of your own quiet-time space. You will be putting together a Confidence Action Plan. Considering everything we talked about this week, you are going to look at developing confidence by liking yourself and forgiving yourself. I'm confident that you will put together a great plan!

Ask yourself how deeply you are able to focus on increasing your confidence during this season of your life. Then select the appropriate action steps on pages 90–92, whatever you feel you can realistically experiment with this week. It's your plan, your life, and your prayerful decision—nobody else's. If you feel God impressing on you to concentrate on your confidence right now, go for these exercises with gusto—without further ado or delay! I know that whatever effort you are able to devote to improving your confidence will be richly rewarded by him on earth and in heaven.

Confidence Action Plan

PRAYER FOCUS: Thank God for the way he made you—your appearance, abilities, talents, and strengths. Release to God the things you wish were different about you. Pray for God's help to make changes where you should, and accept his sovereignty for the things he chooses not to change. Thank God that Jesus died for you. Pray that God will reveal to you when you are not forgiving yourself. Receive his forgiveness and payment for your sins.

DEVOTIONAL FOCUS: Choose one of the following Scripture passages on the topic of confidence: To focus on *liking yourself more*, read the story of David preparing to face Goliath in 1 Samuel 17:12–50, noticing the ways David stayed true to who he was. Or, to focus on *forgiving yourself more*, read the story of the Prodigal Son in Luke 15:11–32 to remind yourself how much God values you.

EXTRA PERSPECTIVE: Read *Grace Awakening* by Chuck Swindoll. Or get creative and plan an outing with a woman who affirms and encourages you!

Action Steps: Liking Myself

Instructions: Prayerfully choose one or two action steps to experiment with this week.

Start Date

_____ ☐ **I will use my own measuring stick.** I will evaluate myself based on what God says, how I feel about my efforts, and how I did compared to last time. If I don't feel great about myself, I will examine why. It may be that I am feeling fearful about what someone else will think, which is letting myself be manipulated and controlled by others. Or I may be comparing myself to someone else, which is irrelevant because everyone is unique.

_____ ☐ **I will lighten up.** I will laugh at myself when I do something dumb; I will cheer for myself when I do a little thing right ("Yes, indeed—I got the laundry started before 3 p.m.!"). Also, I will find one new thing every day that I like about myself and write it down ("I like my smile—it reminds me of all the things I've had to smile about").

_____ ☐ **I will replace my self-consciousness.** When I'm unsure of myself in a social situation, I'll get my mind off myself by looking for what I can do to help. I'll make others feel valued by asking them a question, such as "What do you love to do?"

_____ ☐ **I will tune in to my body language.** When I'm nervous, my body screams out to people, "Keep away." I will change my body language so that I don't appear to be unapproachable. I will smile more, or at least relax my facial muscles. I will look around the room instead of keeping my eyes down. I will uncross my arms.

_____ ☐ **I will work** on liking myself by *(add your idea here)*

_____

_____

_____

Action Steps: Forgiving Myself

Instructions: Prayerfully choose one or two action steps to experiment with this week.

Start Date

_____ ☐ **I will let go of my guilt.** My unresolved guilt is destroying my confidence. I will accept God's forgiveness and stop living like God is mad at me. There is nothing I can do to myself or add to my punishment that will make me any more acceptable to God. *Area of unresolved guilt I will release:*

_____

_____

_____ ☐ **I will not view my past as a permanent mold.** I am not stuck in the mold of my childhood. Early influences do not have control over me now. I will separate myself from false messages about who I am and choose to believe the truth.

_____ ☐ **I will give myself grace.** God gave me grace, but I need to give myself undeserved favor more often. I will give myself credit for trying, not just for achieving. I will distance myself from people who don't know how to give grace and are more likely to be judgmental, negative, or discouraging.

_____ ☐ **I will let go of my perfectionism.** I will watch for sentences that start with "I should … I must … I ought to … I have to …." When I set an unattainable standard of perfection, I'll let myself off the hook. I will remind myself that God and others don't expect perfection and that I won't be letting anyone down by relaxing into a sane standard. I will pleasantly surprise someone today by letting my flaws show!

_____ ☐ **I will work** on forgiving myself by *(add your idea here)*

_____

_____

_____

MASTER ACTION PLAN

Now, select only one major action step from this Day 5 exercise and record it on your Master Action Plan in appendix A on page 322. When you have finished reading this book, continue to refer to that one major action step on your Master Action Plan (as well as this Confidence Action Plan, of course, as your season of life permits!). Remember, in order to become more like Christ in your character, you need to collaborate with God in three ways: preparation, prayer, and practice. You have done the work of preparation by learning God's truth about confidence. Now, internalize it by praying for the Holy Spirit's help and practicing your action steps, one by one.

CONFIDENCE PRAYER

Precious Lord,

What a great friend you have been to me! Thank you so much. You are the type of friend who breathes confidence into me, because you are an encourager. I can tell how much you want me to succeed. I can hear your whispers of "You can do it" and "I believe in you." My biggest prayer now is that I will believe you. Fill my lifetime with the knowledge of who you are and who I am in you. That will be a gloriously full life.

In the name of Jesus, amen.

Chapter 3

Courage

Be strong and courageous.
Do not be afraid; do not be discouraged,
for the LORD your God will be with you wherever you go.

Joshua 1:9

Indwelled by God

Courage is not the absence of fear;
it is the mastery of it.
Encyclopedia of 15,000 Illustrations

WELCOME BACK TO MY PLACE!

Welcome back to my place—for more exciting character remodeling! The week just flew by, didn't it? I thought that today we could sit in my backyard; I fondly call it my Prayer Garden. I have a huge, blue-cushioned swing chair that's got a nice, wide-brimmed covering on it. And … I think I know what your favorite beverage and nibbles are, so let me get those out of the kitchen. I'll meet you outside. By the way, I turned on the garden fountain to spiff up the ambience out there a little bit. Hope you like it.

Let's pray together as we begin:

Dear God,

As you already know, this week's tough topic is courage. We have much to learn in this area, so we want to lean not on our own understanding, but rather, rely completely on your wisdom. Grant that favor to us, we pray expectantly.

Amen.

YOUR SCAREDY-CAT COACH

Public speaking used to scare me silly. There was a time years ago when the prospect of giving a speech made me physically ill. I spent more time in the bathroom being sick than I did giving the talk! As it became obvious that I was going to have to do more and more speaking, I went to my accountability group in despair and whined: "I can't do this! I'm not good enough. My presentation is scattered; my mouth gets so dry I can't enunciate; and my knees shake so bad I'm sure everyone can see them. Plus, I'm not smart enough, holy enough, or attractive enough!'"

You know what my group told me? They said, "Katie! Stop worrying and just be yourself!"

"You're crazy!" I retorted. "I'm a bumbling idiot when I'm up in front! I can't string two sentences together." But you know something? Despite all my own internal perfectionistic voices screaming at me that just being myself wasn't enough, I tried it anyway, and something happened. I realized two things: First, this was not about me; this was about the audience — those women out there whom God loved and to whom he wanted to speak. Second, this was not about *my* talk; it was about *his* vision, *his* message. I was just the messenger. So, if God wanted to use me as a human voice, then he was going to have to communicate to the audiences in spite of my shaky delivery. It was tremendously freeing to stop worrying about my image as the speaker and let the Holy Spirit give me his message. Miraculously, he has taken away my fear of public speaking, and for that I will be eternally grateful.

WHAT IS COURAGE?

Courage is an outward display of the inward character quality of confidence. Courage is the strength to take risks, face danger, endure difficulty, or withstand fear. Notice, I didn't say courage is an *absence of* fear. Rather, it *withstands* fear — you have to experience fear in order to be courageous! For instance, speaking in front of a group was a courageous act for me, because it scared the living daylights out of me, but for Shelley, my writing partner, speaking is fun (go figure!) — she never even gets butterflies. So, giving a speech is not an act of courage for Shelley. You need the fear in order to call it courage.

ESTHER'S COURAGE

One of the greatest chronicles of courage in the Bible is the dramatic story of Esther. When my kids were young, this is the story they constantly asked me to tell them — probably because of all the drama and plot-thickening suspense. The central cast of characters includes: Esther, the orphan who hides her Jewish heritage and wins a beauty contest to become queen; Haman, the wicked henchman who plots to annihilate all Jews because of one Jewish man who would not bow to him; and Mordecai, the Jew who didn't bow, whose stirring words of exhortation challenged his niece, Esther, to face her fears and appeal to the king to save the Jews from disaster.

What was Esther afraid of? *She was afraid to risk dying*, which was the penalty for approaching the king uninvited (Esther 4:11).

What did Mordecai say to that? You're going to die anyway. If you think your fear is protecting you, a Jewish woman, think again. You're *possibly* doomed if you risk the king's wrath, but you're *for sure* doomed if you do nothing. Here are Mordecai's actual words:

> *Do not think that because you are in the king's house you alone of all the Jews will escape. ¹⁴For if you remain silent at this time, relief and deliverance for the Jews will arise from another place, but you and your father's family will perish. And who knows but that you have come to royal position for such a time as this?*
>
> Esther 4:13–14

How did Esther show courage? Basically, she said: *Okay, if I die, I die!* Esther made up her mind to risk violating the rules of the king's court. She called for a three-day fast and prayer service for all the Jews in the city, after which she planned to approach the king. The story ends with Esther being able to dramatically reveal Haman's plot, causing Haman to be hanged on the very gallows he built for Mordecai.

COURAGE COMES FROM BEING INDWELLED BY GOD

Esther found courage in three ways, and there are three lessons for us in her story: (1) she used her fear to find her faith; (2) she prepared herself; and (3) she shifted the focus of concern from herself to others.

Esther used her fear and found her faith.

If Esther had heard about the royal decree to kill the Jews and said, "No problem! I'll just pop on into the throne room and set my husband, King Xerxes, straight," we wouldn't have called her courageous—we would have called her foolhardy, reckless, and rash. Instead, Esther's fear caused her to put on the brakes and approach with caution. She spent time focusing on God and asking him for the strength and courage to proceed. The lesson for us is this: *A courageous person is one who is indwelled by faith in God, in spite of feeling fearful.*

Be strong and courageous. Do not be afraid or terrified because of them, for the LORD your God goes with you; he will never leave you nor forsake you.

Deuteronomy 31:6

The contrast in Scripture between our own strength and what we can do in God's strength is always striking. Courage seems to follow when you take God at his word, believe he'll do what he says, remember his protection in the past, and place yourself in his care. The more faith you have in God's power, the more courageous you'll be.

When you are afraid, what is your first response? Do you hide? Or do you let your fear direct you to seek God, shift your faith to him, and ask for his power and courage to indwell you?

Esther prepared herself.

Esther put everything on pause for three days. She used that time to think through and pray about her plan. Before Esther took those brave steps to the throne room, she had an established plan that gave her assurance. At the point of her greatest fear, she relied on her plan that was formulated out of her deepest convictions about justice, obedience, and God's sovereignty. The next lesson for us is this: *A courageous person is one who is indwelled by God's convictions, in spite of outside pressure.*

I have taken an oath and confirmed it, that I will follow your righteous laws.

Psalm 119:106 NIV

When my kids were teenagers, I talked to them about all types of peer pressure situations that would most probably come up. I encouraged them to settle in advance what their convictions were so that they wouldn't be swayed in the moment and cave in to their fear of losing their friends. Similarly, we adults need to have our moral, ethical, and relational choices determined in advance. Although we can't always anticipate all the crises that might come our way, our predetermined convictions can better equip us to face what does happen. Then, when we find ourselves in a dilemma (expected or not), we can act with courage by putting into practice what we have already decided.

When you are hesitant, what do you do? Do you cave in and do what others are demanding, or have you thought through your decisions in advance so that you can be more confident in the moment of fear?

Esther shifted from self-preservation to concern for her people.

Once Esther got her eyes off herself and thought about the greater issue—the preservation of her people—she found a reservoir of courage for making the right decision and carrying it out. When she was worried about her personal safety, she was hesitant, fearful. But once her perspective changed, she rose to the occasion and found the courage to put her own safety on the line. The third lesson for us is: *A courageous person is one who is indwelled by God's caring nature, in spite of the personal cost.*

We see this type of courage in the apostle Paul, who time after time put his own safety aside for the sake of reaching one more city for Jesus:

> *We had previously suffered and been treated outrageously in Philippi, as you know, but with the help of our God we dared to tell you his gospel in the face of strong opposition.*

1 Thessalonians 2:2

We've all seen news stories that feature brave heroes who rescued people in danger. Sometimes, when asked how they found the courage to jump in the icy river or run into a burning building or lift a crushed car, they shrug it off as something anyone would do. To those newly minted heroes, their acts of bravery feel not so courageous as perhaps kind, caring, or logical. Bravery was ignited when they saw someone in need and lost all thought of themselves.

When you feel fearful, what is at its source? Are you focused on yourself? That was my problem when I was afraid of public speaking. I was so self-conscious, all I could think about was what people were probably thinking of me. But when my concern grew for the women who needed to hear our God's loving message, I found courage I didn't know I had.

Courage Self-Assessment

Courage is just plain hard, because it only gets called into play when you're up against a barrier. Based on the three ways Esther found courage, mark one to two types of courage you exhibit most often with a ♥ , and mark one to two types of courage you need to develop with a ➜.

Courage to do something scary

____ Take a risk; try something new; stretch myself

____ Be myself; tell the truth; admit when I'm wrong

____ Face daily challenges—such as illness, disability, or distress

Courage to stand by my convictions

____ Defend my beliefs and do what's right, even if everyone else doesn't

____ Fight against evil or injustice with my actions, not just my words

____ Do what I prefer, even if no one else wants to join me

Courage to help someone

____ Be friendly; talk to someone I don't know

____ Reach out and assist someone who needs help

____ Put myself on the line for the sake of someone who is being wronged

Journal

When Psalm 34 Gave Shelley Courage

My coauthor, Shelley, and I were discussing the fact that she rarely has trouble with courage, as I mentioned earlier in connection with her love of public speaking. But Shelley did recall a time in her life when the Lord met her and helped her through a terrifying experience:

"When I was sixteen, my parents got divorced, and I had to appear in court for a hearing to determine which of my parents would get custody. As I waited all by myself in the big echoey hall outside the courtroom, I was terrified. I envisioned an austere, forbidding judge blaming me for what had happened. Deciding between my two parents was going to be excruciating. The judge turned out to be a very kind man who sympathetically asked many questions, seemed to understand I would be equally happy with either parent, and ultimately awarded custody to my mother, which was customary in those days. I had brought my Bible along, and as I looked through Psalms, the Lord gave me this passage that I have returned to again and again whenever I feel a need for rescuing."

> *I sought the LORD, and he answered me; he delivered me from all my fears.*
> *⁵Those who look to him are radiant; their faces are never covered with shame.*
> *⁶This poor man called, and the LORD heard him; he saved him out of all his troubles. ⁷The angel of the LORD encamps around those who fear him, and he delivers them.*
>
> Psalm 34:4–7

Using the text of Psalm 34:4–7, which meant so much to Shelley during her time of insecurity and fear, complete the following chart:

What I am supposed to do	What God does in response
Example: v. 4 *I seek the Lord*	*Example:* *He answers me and delivers me from all my fears*
v. 5	

v. 6	
v. 7	

Of the four actions on the chart, which one do you need to do more of and why? What will be the result?

_____

_____

_____

_____

_____

PRAYER

Precious Lord,

I need courage. Thank you, that when I am most fearful, my faith in you will infuse me with courage. Thank you, that when I am most hesitant, you will help me forge my convictions so I can stand against what is wrong. Thank you, that when I get my eyes off myself, I can find the inspiration to help someone else.

Help me to seek you instead of seeking escape. Help me to keep my eyes on you instead of on keeping myself from embarrassment. Help me to call out to you instead of copying what my friends are doing. Help me to reverence you more than I do the opinions of others. Help me to remember that you are my greatest source of courage.

In the name of Jesus, amen.

Fear: Exposing Your Inner Pinocchio

The only way we can create a place secure from
fear is to do nothing and go nowhere.
If you find yourself living in a tiny,
fear-enclosed box about what God
is asking you to do with your life today,
here's an idea — pray for claustrophobia!
At least that way your instinct will be to break out!

Katie Brazelton, *Pathway to Purpose for Women*

A VIRTUAL MESSAGE

 NOTE: It's Day 2, so you have the option of listening to today's message by downloading it from my website, www.LifePurposeCoachingCenters.com/ CM, or reading the message text below. Enjoy the virtual coaching and don't forget to open in prayer!

THE FLIP SIDE OF COURAGE

Pinocchio had fear issues. The Blue Fairy had told him, "Prove yourself brave, truthful, and unselfish, and someday you will be a real boy." But Pinocchio's fears kept him from being any of those things. His fear of not being accepted kept him from being brave and resisting peer pressure, so he skipped school at the insistence of the fox and the alley cat. His fear of not getting the Blue Fairy's approval kept him from being truthful about the real reason he didn't go to school. His fear of not being *real*, like the other boys, drove him to Pleasure Island with them to fulfill his every selfish desire. Pinocchio ignored his conscience and compromised until, as the story is told, he had grown donkey's ears and a tail. It wasn't until he got his focus off himself, in order to rescue Gepetto from the great fish, that Pinocchio exhibited bravery, truthfulness, and unselfishness — and then became a real boy.

Our fears can act as a prison, keeping us trapped and powerless. I'd like to introduce you to my friend Geri, and let her tell you her story of fear.

GERI'S STORY OF FEAR

"I have experienced a fear that has held me down in many different ways for all of my adult life. I suffered sexual abuse by my mentally ill brother starting when I was thirteen until I escaped and went to college. Since then, when I am alone, I can't sleep. My brain tells me 'sleeping alone equals not being safe.' If my husband is away on a business trip, I begin to feel tight in my stomach as bedtime approaches, and throughout the night my body snaps into this physiological response pattern at the slightest noise. Having chronic anxiety is like being in a room where the walls are steadily moving in on you, closing you in until you cannot even breathe. When dealing with sleep issues, anxiety is all-powerful, because you must be relaxed to fall asleep. But the thought of not being able to sleep brings on anxiety that prevents you from doing exactly what you need to do — relax. And so the vicious cycle goes.

"After seeking help through counseling and doctors and lots of prayer, I still felt no relief, so I came to terms with this as something I would just have to order my life around — like a physical handicap, so to speak. I avoided ministry or social or career opportunities if they meant being alone at night. Despite experiencing a deep process of healing from the memories and pain — which included forgiving my brother — the effects of the abuse still held power over me.

"My approach to my fear was radically altered by Katie Brazelton's discussion of courage in her book, *Pathway to Purpose for Women*. I had always felt that I must conquer fear before I could move forward. It revolutionized my life to realize that courage is not the absence of fear, but moving forward in spite of fear! The icing on the cake was reading the simple but profoundly freeing truth that God can and will use us, even when we have fear. She said: 'God does not need our courage to proceed with his plans.' When I began to apply my newfound insights on courage and fear, this thorn in my flesh lost its power over me."

COMPANIONS OF FEAR

Once fear has you trapped in its wicked grasp, it blocks creativity, productivity, and relationships. It can lead to health issues such as fatigue, high blood pressure, ulcers, and premature aging. It can cause psychological problems such as phobias or paranoia or hypochondria. But let's look more deeply at three of the most common companions of fear: worry, anxiety, and lying.

Worry

Worry happens when you rehearse your fear about a past or future event, causing mental distress, torment, disturbance, or agitation. The root from which we get the word *worry* comes from the term "to strangle." Worry goes around in maddening, futile circles, visiting the fear again and again with no resolution, gradually strangling you emotionally. For instance, if you worry about an event *in the past*, you might stew over mistakes you made; go over things you wish you had done differently; magnify every little mishap; and imagine negative things people must think of you. People who worry about the past have a hard time forgiving themselves. Here is the apostle Paul's solution to worrying about the past:

> *The one thing I do, however, is to forget what is behind me and do my best to reach what is ahead.*
>
> Philippians 3:13 GNT

If you worry about an event *in the future*, you are fearing a possibility. The French philosopher Montaigne said, "My life has been full of terrible misfortunes, most of which never happened." Whether you worry about the past or the future, your worry is keeping you from living in the present. Holocaust survivor Corrie ten Boom wrote, "Worry does not empty tomorrow of sorrows; it empties today of strength." Here is Jesus' advice to us about worry:

> *"So do not worry about tomorrow; it will have enough worries of its own. There is no need to add to the troubles each day brings."*
>
> Matthew 6:34 GNT

Next time you are gripped with worry about an event in the future, try using this Worry Worksheet to help you process your concerns:

Worry Worksheet

Worried about an event in the future? Answer the following questions:

1. What event am I worrying about? (Labeling it makes it more manageable.)

    Example 1: *I'm worried about my teenage son going to Africa.*
    Example 2: *I'm worried that I won't make my sales goals.*

    _____

    _____

2. What's the worst that could happen? If that happened, *then* what would happen?

    Example 1: *He could get malaria. If he got malaria, he might die.*
    Example 2: *I could lose my job. If I lose my job, then I could lose my house.*

    _____

    _____

3. What are the chances, according to the law of averages, that what I'm worried about will ever occur? (You could do a quick Internet search to check your facts.)

    Example 1: *His pills prevent malaria, but even if he gets it, malaria is a treatable disease, with only one of 300 malaria victims dying, usually children under five.*
    Example 2: *I have only missed my sales goals twice in the past five years, and neither time did I lose my job.*

    _____

    _____

4. What can I do about it?

    Example 1: *I can send him to Africa with extra-strength bug repellant and a mosquito net, just to be safe.*
    Example 2: *I can review my client list for additional leads. I can speak with my boss about other ways I can meet my goals.*

    _____

    _____

Give it to God — again and again throughout the day,
whenever worry rears its ugly head.

Anxiety

Anxiety is worry without boundaries. Worry is event-specific, but anxiety is a sense of foreboding or uneasiness, not necessarily associated with something in particular. Anxiety is just a general feeling of being upset over possible misfortune. Geri's description of anxiety is "being in a room where the walls are steadily moving in on you, closing you in until you cannot even breathe." That sounds like the source of the word *anxiety*, which is the term "to choke." Anxiety is being choked internally by apprehension when you are unable to control the uncontrollable. The apostle Paul offers the best defense against anxiety when he says to turn your anxious thoughts into prayers:

> *Do not be anxious about anything, but in every situation, by prayer and petition, with thanksgiving, present your requests to God. [7]And the peace of God, which transcends all understanding, will guard your hearts and your minds in Christ Jesus.*
>
> Philippians 4:6–7

Here's a worksheet to use the next time you feel a general sense of anxiety:

Anxiety Worksheet

Feeling generally anxious? Answer the following questions:

1. What is out of my control that is making me feel anxious?

   Example 1: *I can't keep people from criticizing me unjustly.*
   Example 2: *I can't make myself go to sleep.*

   _____

   _____

2. What's the worst that could happen?

   Example 1: *My reputation could be damaged.*
   Example 2: *I could feel tired and sick tomorrow.*

   _____

   _____

---

3. What is in my control?

   Example 1: *I can control how I react to unjust criticism.*

   Example 2: *I can rehearse my Scripture memory verses while I'm lying awake.*

   _____

   _____

4. How can I let God take control of everything else?

   Example 1: *I give God my reputation.*

   Example 2: *I'll ask God for strength to get through the day tomorrow.*

   _____

   _____

   Give God the control.

Lying

You may find it odd that I have included lying in the short list of fear's most common companions, but I think that some lying is very much a reflex of fear. If you'll recall, in an earlier section I pointed out that lying is not a solitary sin—it always pairs up with another sin, to cover it up. For instance, Pinocchio's initial lie had to do with skipping school; that lie dragged companion lies along with it, one after the other, like a parade of sin. That's where fear usually comes in. Lies cover up something you're afraid will be found out—afraid your shortcomings will be discovered, afraid your mistake will be criticized, or afraid of the consequences of your sin.

But here's the real truth about lying: Lying doesn't make things better; it makes things worse—like Pinocchio's growing nose. When you tell a lie, you are forming a web of deceit around the sin you're trying to hide, and the only person who gets caught in that trap is the liar herself. Even though it might not feel like it at the time, when you courageously speak the truth, you have opened the prison doors and set yourself free to be a real woman.

"Then you will know the truth, and the truth will set you free."

John 8:32

You obviously won't be able to run and get the Lying Worksheet (below) when you're in the middle of a conversation and tempted to lie, so try to memorize the three-point checklist, so you can quickly self-evaluate before you let a lie slip from your mouth.

Lying Worksheet

Tempted to tell a lie? Silently answer the following questions before you speak:

1. What am I trying to cover up?

   Example 1: *I'm afraid I'm not good enough.*
   Example 2: *I blew it.*

   _____

   _____

2. What's the worst that could happen *if I tell the truth*, and how long would the consequences last?

   Example 1: *I'll feel embarrassed, and that will stick with me for about a week.*
   Example 2: *My colleague will be angry, and he'll probably stay angry for about fifteen minutes.*

   _____

   _____

3. What's the worst that could happen *if I do lie* and it is discovered? (These consequences are usually worse than the consequences of the truth.)

   Example 1: *I could lose my job for faking my records.*
   Example 2: *He may have difficulty trusting me again.*

   _____

   _____

Tell the truth and let God take care of the consequences.

Lying vs. Truth-Telling

If lying is a real problem area for you, you might also want to memorize some of the many verses about lying and truth-telling in the Bible, for example:

The LORD *detests lying lips, but he delights in people who are trustworthy.*

Proverbs 12:22

The tongue that brings healing is a tree of life, but a deceitful tongue crushes the spirit.

Proverbs 15:4 NIV

The wisdom of the prudent is to give thought to their ways, but the folly of fools is deception.

Proverbs 14:8

Journal

Types of Fears

Select your top three fears from the following list:

☐ Fear of danger   "Something terrible will happen to me."
☐ Fear of ridicule   "They will laugh at me."
☐ Fear of criticism   "They will find something wrong with me."
☐ Fear of abandonment   "They will leave me here all alone."
☐ Fear of rejection   "They will not let me join them."
☐ Fear of embarrassment "They will whisper about me."
☐ Fear of attention   "I will stand out in a crowd."
☐ Fear of success   "I will have to live up to others' expectations."
☐ Fear of failure   "I will look like a fool—nobody will believe in me again."
☐ Fear of mistakes   "They will think I'm stupid because I can't get it right."
☐ Fear of being   "I am not really capable—I am an imposter."
    found out
☐ Other   _____

These next verses are worth stopping the clock a moment to digest. Pause long enough to read them through slowly. Whisper them aloud and just let them seep into your soul.

Be strong and courageous. Do not be afraid; do not be discouraged, for the LORD your God will be with you wherever you go.

Joshua 1:9

If God is for us, who can be against us?

Romans 8:31

For God has not given us a spirit of fear, but of power and of love and of a sound mind.

2 Timothy 1:7 NKJV

The one who is in you is greater than the one who is in the world.

1 John 4:4

Perfect love drives out fear.

1 John 4:18

In the following blanks, write out your top three fears from the Types of Fears checklist. Next, choose a verse for each fear. It's your option to use a different verse for each fear or the same verse for all three. Then, explain how that verse can help you overcome that fear.

Example: *I have a fear of abandonment, but Joshua 1:9 says not to be terrified because God will be with me wherever I go. So, even if everyone — absolutely everyone — walks out of my life, I've still got God!*

Fear #1

_____

_____

_____

Fear #2

Fear #3

PRAYER

Precious Lord,

Thank you that your perfect love for me drives out all my fears. I confess that at times I have succumbed to worry, and in doing so I'm saying I don't believe you will take care of everything that concerns me. Sometimes I feel anxious, and when I let anxiety govern my mind, I'm saying I can't release control to you. I have told lies, which means that I have deeper fears I'm trying to hide, and I'm not trusting you with the consequences of telling the truth. Jesus, you told a man who asked for your help that everything is possible to those who believe. And, like that man, I cry out with tears, "I do believe. Help me overcome my unbelief" (Mark 9:24).

In the name of Jesus, amen.

How to Be Daring

Far better it is to dare mighty things, to win glorious triumphs,
even though checkered by failure, than to take rank with those poor spirits
who neither enjoy much nor suffer much, because they live
in the gray twilight that knows neither victory nor defeat.

Teddy Roosevelt, 26th president of the United States

You've Got Mail

To:	"The Best You" Woman	Sent:	Day 3
From:	Katie Brazelton		
Subject:	Courage		

It's Day 3, so here is your weekly Email Message. Feel free to blog me a response at my website, www.LifePurposeCoachingCenters.com/CM, if you'd like. Enjoy the email-coaching and don't forget to open in prayer!

What We Can Learn
from Jael about Courage

Remember the story of Deborah and how she confidently inspired the Israelites to meet the Canaanite chariots in battle? Well, you might not be aware that Deborah's battle was capped off by another heroine named Jael, who actually killed the Canaanite general. You see, the general had escaped from the battle and hid in Jael's tent; and while he was sleeping, Jael pounded a tent stake through his head. (Gratefully, that doesn't happen on your average day in the suburbs!) Scripture is filled with remarkable profiles in courage such as Jael's and Deborah's. Let's look at several heroes of the Bible, as well as some everyday men and women who exhibit four different types of courage: courage for a cause, courage to make peace, courage to tell the truth, and courage to take risks.

COURAGE FOR A CAUSE

Courage for a cause is found in those who become impassioned about helping others, who attempt to do the right thing when no one else is doing it, or who take on a challenging project that seems impossible. When you know that you have God standing with you, it gives you courage to take an unpopular stand or start a God-sized project.

The courage to stand alone against the culture is seen in the Old Testament Scriptures when Shadrach, Meshach, and Abednego refused to worship the king's image and so were thrown into the fiery furnace. They faced their fate bravely, without backing down on their convictions—and God stood with them in the furnace (Daniel 3). Moses' sister Miriam, an enslaved Hebrew girl, bravely proposed to Egypt's princess a plan that saved her baby brother's life (Exodus 2:1–10). Solomon had the courage to take on a God-sized cause when he built the temple, because he knew that God was with him:

> *David also said to Solomon his son, "Be strong and courageous, and do the work. Do not be afraid or discouraged, for the LORD God, my God, is with you. He will not fail you or forsake you until all the work for the service of the temple of the LORD is finished."*
>
> 1 Chronicles 28:20

Dan and Kathleen are a married couple at my church, who in their own unassuming way, have shown courage for a cause. So frustrated was Dan about how fast their three kids outgrew their running shoes—barely used by the time they didn't fit anymore—that he felt there must be a way to get those shoes onto the feet of kids who didn't have any shoes at all. In researching the situation, he learned of the incredible need for shoes by the homeless and needy. Those feelings and knowledge birthed a ministry. He and Kathleen started casually asking their family and friends for their castoff shoes; then Dan figured out how to approach retailers and shoe manufacturers. For the past eighteen years their garage has been the collection center for over 200,000 pairs of shoes that have been donated to rescue missions and shipped to third world countries.

What's in your garage of ideas? Are there any simple steps you can take to help a cause, stand up for what's right, or tackle a big need? What kinds of pain exist in your local area that you could do something about? Where are you needed? Is it with ...

- Unemployed executives
- Elderly who have no family
- Dyslexic children
- New moms
- Sexually abused teens
- Developmentally disabled adults
- Cancer survivors who live in fear of recurrence

COURAGE TO MAKE PEACE

When there is conflict in your world, do you avoid or ignore it, hoping it will go away, or are you a peacemaker? A peacemaker is someone who cares enough about the people in conflict that she takes steps to create an environment conducive to reconciliation. This takes courage, especially if the conflict is volatile.

Such was the case for Abigail in the Scriptures. Her husband, Nabal, is described as a harsh and evil scoundrel who refused to give David and his band of men their due for the protection they had given his shepherds and flocks. David was so enraged by this affront that he set out to avenge himself and take what was due him. Abigail intervened, presenting David with bountiful provisions for his men. Then she humbly, yet boldly, spoke to him of God's destiny for him, and how he would not want to live the rest of his life with regret. Look at her wise words:

> When the LORD has fulfilled for my lord every good thing he promised concerning him and has appointed him ruler over Israel, [31] my lord will not have on his conscience the staggering burden of needless bloodshed or of having avenged himself.
>
> 1 Samuel 25:30–31

Abigail's courage had a healing, peacemaking influence on the men around her who were behaving wretchedly. David went away peaceably. And get this soap-opera plot twist: Nabal died of a stroke, David married Abigail, and they lived happily ever after! (The Bible doesn't actually say that last part, but it is fun to imagine, right?)

Consider too the twenty-first century example of Susan. She was elected mayor of her town when she was in her fifties, her first political role of any kind. On one occasion, a group of gay rights activists demanded that the school district start Gay Pride Month in all the elementary, middle, and high schools. Susan was in a difficult spot. If she lent support to the activists' proposal, she would be going against her personal belief and other constituents' wishes. She prayed for wisdom, and after their presentation, Susan said, "I recommend that we address the root problem here. I feel that the problem, at its core, is our students' lack of self-worth that prevents them from accepting others who are different than they are. If our students believed in themselves and accepted themselves, they would be less likely to ridicule others and exhibit prejudicial behaviors. So, I recommend we institute Self-Worth Month in our school district instead." And her recommendation was adopted!

Susan was a wise peacemaker, finding a mutually acceptable solution that acknowledged and resolved the needs of people on both sides of a potentially volatile issue. The courage to make peace is imperative when we attempt to address ...

- Racial injustice
- Religious discrimination
- Disagreements on school boards, town councils, city governments, or state legislatures
- Divorce issues
- Personal or family conflicts

COURAGE TO TELL THE TRUTH

We have already talked about how lying is a reflex of fear, and on the other side of the coin, truth-telling is an act of courage. It takes courage to be a truthful witness against a wrongdoer, to admit the truth when you have sinned, or to truthfully confront someone who needs correcting. In Scripture there are numerous instances of courageous truth-telling. For example, Peter reverted to Jewish legalism around fellow Jews, so Paul spoke the truth to him about his hypocrisy (Galatians 2:11 – 15).

Perhaps the most famous "truth reveal" in the Bible is when Nathan used a vivid word picture to confront David with his secret sins of adultery and murder. When David wanted to punish Nathan's fictional rich man who stole and killed a poor man's only lamb, Nathan thundered at David, "You are the man!" (2 Samuel 12:7).

There is nothing harder or more important than telling the truth about ourselves. Geri, who in Day 2 told us her story about her fear of sleeping alone, had to have courage to come forward as an adult and reveal the truth about her abuse. Secrets have power. Telling a shameful secret to a trustworthy person is the first step to ridding yourself of that shame, but let there be no doubt, it takes courage.

Brittany is another courageous truth-teller. I think what really impresses me the most about Brit is her age. She was only eighteen when she blossomed into a woman of integrity. As her high school's valedictorian, she was invited to give a commencement speech, but school officials, who review all graduation speeches before they are delivered, removed nine of her twelve references to God, Jesus, and salvation. Because Brittany believed in free speech, she delivered her speech in its original form, and her microphone was cut off by school leadership in the middle of it. She continued to deliver her speech without the microphone, as she was confronted by administrators on stage. The crowd responded with several minutes of jeering in objection to the censorship. The story hit the newswires, and although the graduates and their families didn't get to hear Brittany's testimony that day, the rest of the country did!

It takes courage to be truthful in the small events of our everyday lives:

- Correcting incorrect change given by a store clerk
- Paying the adult ticket price for your just-turned-thirteen-year-old child
- Purchasing a CD or video instead of illegally copying it
- Submitting an honest income tax return

The importance of truthfulness also extends to matters of public concern. Courageous Christian truth-tellers are needed who will arm themselves with supportable facts and proclaim them to others who do not understand or accept God's view about topics such as:

- Abortion
- Evolution
- Gambling
- Pornography

In addition, truth is important when there is a moral, ethical, or relational wrong that is being committed. That's not the time to keep secrets—that's the time to lovingly confront.

COURAGE TO TAKE RISKS

You miss 100 percent of the shots you don't take.

Wayne Gretzky, former National Hockey League all-star

The most dramatic form of courage is when someone performs an act of bravery, such as rescuing someone from a burning building, donating a kidney, going to prison for one's beliefs, or facing a tribe of headhunters armed only with a flannelgraph story about Jesus! Although such real life-threatening moments happen rarely these days, you *can* live courageously and stretch yourself by taking a risk. More on that in a moment.

In Scripture there are many stories of unlikely heroes who overcame their own issues and took a risk. David, the teenage shepherd, is pitted against the most fearsome giant ever seen and fells him with a sling and a rock (1 Samuel 17). Gideon, a lily-livered leader, is forced to face a massive army at night with only three hundred men and an inspired battle plan that panics the enemy into self-destruction (Judges 7). Oh—and there's also Peter, who sees Jesus walking on water, and on impulse decides to try it himself (Matthew 14:28–33). He's the modern-day equivalent of a stunt man! Each of these unlikely heroes took a big risk because of their faith in a bigger God. Some succeeded; some failed when their courage failed.

God is our refuge and strength, an ever-present help in trouble. ²Therefore we will not fear, though the earth give way and the mountains fall into the heart of the sea.

Psalm 46:1–2

I know of a woman who grew up in the foster care system and saw many of her foster girlfriends purposely get pregnant as they approached age eighteen. (It's a common practice that allows the girls to continue on government support.) But this woman chose a different path. She graduated from high school, worked her way through college, and now has a job working with children. Those youngsters are benefiting from the risk she took to forge an unmarked trail. Can you just imagine the strength of character that took?

Courage to risk is seen in many exciting endeavors:

- Moving to another city
- Making a friend
- Getting a new job
- Starting a business
- Taking a class
- Starting a new ministry
- Speaking in front of a group
- Doing a character makeover!

Journal

When I am afraid, I put my trust in you. ⁴In God, whose word I praise—in God I trust and am not afraid. What can mere mortals do to me?

Psalm 56:3–4

Read Psalm 56:3–4 aloud; then pray about each type of courage we discussed today. Ask God what he wants to do through you in each of these areas. Write out the impressions God lays on your heart about how he wants to develop each type of courage in your life.

Courage for a cause

_____

_____

Courage to make peace

_____

_____

Courage to tell the truth

_____

_____

Courage to take risks

_____

_____

PRAYER

Precious Lord,

Is there a cause you have placed in my path that you want me to take up? Give me courage. Am I to stand alone on an issue when everyone around me disagrees? Give me courage. Is there pain, conflict, arguing, or unfair treatment into which I can bring peace? Give me courage. Am I the one who has been prolonging a dispute when I should have been making peace? Give me courage. Is there a problem in my community about which you want me to tell the truth? Give me courage. Is there something immoral, unethical, or harmful being done that I need to stop keeping secret? Give me courage. Is there an adventure you want me to try, a risk you want me to take, or a thrill you want to give me? Give me courage. "When I am afraid, I put my trust in you ... what can mere mortals do to me?"

In the name of Jesus, amen.

Your Courage Coach

Courage is a character trait most oft attributable to men.
In fact, it is the universal virtue of all those who choose to do the right thing
over the expedient thing. It is the common currency of all those
who do what they are supposed to do in a time of conflict, crisis, and confusion.
Florence Nightingale, 1820–1910, pioneer of modern nursing

PERSPECTIVE-CHANGING OUTING

Today we're meeting at one of my favorite lookout spots on the coast. From here, we can pray to the Creator of the universe as we view grand vistas of sky and ocean and seashore and rocky cliffs. The breeze riffles our hair, scuttles the clouds along, and lifts the outstretched wings of the seagulls. And then, what we've been waiting for … a hang glider launches off the cliff. We hold our breath as that brave soul flings himself out over the open air, trusting the updraft to catch his wings and carry him on a soaring, winding journey back to solid earth. We have just seen a dramatic picture of courage. He faced the precipice with knowledge and preparation. He ran to gather speed, demonstrating conviction. He leapt out into the wind, which filled his sails, just as God's strength infuses us with courage. Yes, God *en-courages* us!

Until now we have been exploring different types of courage—standing up for a cause, making peace, telling the truth, and taking a risk. All these types of courage are noble-sounding, but maybe a bit out of reach for us most days. Today, we are going to talk about an everyday-reality type of courage—the courage to overcome. For many of us, there is a daily courage that we must find in order to have the stamina to keep tackling a solid obstacle in our life or to keep facing a recurring difficulty. The courage to overcome is something we can observe in people who face their phobias, function with a disability, or succeed despite a difficult childhood. So, let's sit here a while and talk about how you're doing at overcoming your past, your pain, and your failures.

COURAGE TO OVERCOME YOUR PAST

If you grew up in a dysfunctional home, suffered abuse, married an addict/alcoholic, had an abortion, dropped out of school, committed a crime, were a foster child, are a single parent, carry a secret shame, or ... you fill in the blank ... then you have a past to overcome. It can make you feel perpetually awkward if you think people associate you with your past and don't see you for who you are now. But sometimes, let's face it, the only person not letting go of your past is you!

The apostle Paul had a notorious reputation that took years to overcome. Before his dramatic conversion on the road to Damascus, he was a zealous religious bigot, intent on purifying his religion and eradicating it of all Jesus followers. It took people a long time to get over Paul's reputation as a bombastic murderer, even though he devoted three years to solitude and devout study prior to embarking on his new ministry. Paul overcame his past by relying on three important concepts that may be helpful in your own self-assessment.

1. Your past displays God's grace. Paul saw his past reputation as the picture frame God gave him to show off the perfect portrait of God's grace.

> *But for that very reason I was shown mercy so that in me, the worst of sinners, Christ Jesus might display his immense patience as an example for those who would believe in him and receive eternal life.*

> 1 Timothy 1:16

What is it about your past that God might want to use to show others that he has unlimited patience and mercy?

_____

_____

2. Your past must be released. The past can be a prison if you aren't letting it go. Paul knew he had to put his past behind him.

> *The one thing I do, however, is to forget what is behind me and do my best to reach what is ahead.*

> Philippians 3:13 GNT

How are you doing at overcoming your past by letting it go? If you need to release a person, an event, or a shame so that you can find courage to reach for what is ahead, consider prayerfully doing so on page 122.

I release *(name something in your past)*

_____

I reach for *(name something you hope for in the future)*

_____

3. Your past has been renewed. When Christ indwells you, your old self is exchanged for a new self. Paul was a living example of this miracle of new life.

Therefore, if anyone is in Christ, the new creation has come: The old has gone, the new is here!

2 Corinthians 5:17

How are you doing at overcoming your past by living like you're a new creation? Describe the old you that has gone and the new you that has come.

The old me was

_____

_____

The new me is

_____

_____

COURAGE TO OVERCOME PAIN

Pain comes in many forms. You might suffer from physical issues such as chronic pain, chronic fatigue, migraines, or cancer. You may be dealing with the anguish of psychological pain such as depression, mood swings, phobias, panic attacks, or emotional distress. Did you know that when you're physically or emotionally depleted, you are more likely to feel cowardly? The great football coach, Vince Lombardi, said, "Fatigue makes cowards of us all."

Ginny is an overcomer who has faced a lifetime of debilitating slavery to fear. She learned patterns of distrust and anxiety from her earliest childhood, and she lived her whole life afraid of literally everything. For her, just getting out of bed some mornings was an act of courage! Ginny defines her courage as stepping over the fear and living anyway. She has stepped over her fears and gotten Christian counseling, raised two children, led a Bible Study

Fellowship group, started a chronic pain support group, launched a greeting card business, and joined a healing prayer ministry. Ginny says, "I have learned firsthand the power of prayer, praise, and Scripture. I stand in my room and declare, 'I will not live this way any longer. I will not let fear ruin one more day. I am a child of the King. Greater is he who lives in me than the fear that lives in the world. God is for me, so who can be against me?' It takes courage to stand up and say these things out loud with conviction and authority, but I say them over and over until they penetrate my spirit, and then my soul and body line up with the truth."

There are three important principles in Scripture to understand about overcoming pain:

1. Sometimes illness is directly related to sin. You can be imprisoned by your illness if it is caused by unconfessed sin.

> *Because of your wrath there is no health in my body; there is no soundness in my bones because of my sin. ⁴My guilt has overwhelmed me like a burden too heavy to bear. ⁵My wounds fester and are loathsome because of my sinful folly.*
>
> Psalm 38:3–5

When you honestly search your heart, is there persistent sin that is causing illness in your life? It is very important that you do not take on personal blame if the Holy Spirit is not convicting you of sin. But some illnesses are triggered by failure to trust God, forgive yourself or others, tell the truth, live in purity, or resolve conflicts. If this is the case for you, describe what the Lord reveals to you that is causing your pain, and then ask God to forgive you and give you the power to overcome the sin pattern in your life.

_____

_____

_____

2. Sometimes illness has nothing to do with sin. Life happens. Birth defects, severe allergies, accidental injuries, and the like are life issues for many people who are not being punished by God for sin. Being an overcomer in the resulting illness or pain involves submitting to God's bigger plan.

> *His disciples asked him, "Rabbi, who sinned, this man or his parents, that he was born blind?"*
>
> *³"Neither this man nor his parents sinned," said Jesus, "but this happened so that the works of God might be displayed in him."*
>
> John 9:2–3

How are you doing at allowing the works of God to be displayed through your pain? Describe one way you see God using your pain to show himself to the world.

_____

_____

_____

3. Sometimes it's God's will to heal illness, and sometimes it's not. Paul's thorn in the flesh was never removed, despite his repeated appeals to God. Here's how Paul found the courage to face his pain.

> *But he said to me, "My grace is sufficient for you, for my power is made perfect in weakness." Therefore I will boast all the more gladly about my weaknesses, so that Christ's power may rest on me. ¹⁰That is why, for Christ's sake, I delight in weaknesses, in insults, in hardships, in persecutions, in difficulties. For when I am weak, then I am strong.*
>
> 2 Corinthians 12:9–10

How are you doing at boasting about your weaknesses and Christ's strength? Rewrite Paul's declaration in your own words.

_____

_____

_____

COURAGE TO OVERCOME FAILURE

There are two types of failure that require courage to overcome: (1) taking a risk but not succeeding, and (2) making a commitment but not keeping it. Examples of the first include losing money on a venture, starting a new business that fails, setting a goal and not reaching it, or entering a contest and losing. Examples of the second include breaking a promise, letting a friend down, failing a class, or getting a divorce. No matter if your failure happened because you went out on a limb and the branch broke, or because you blew it, it takes courage to come back from a failure.

One of Scripture's most spectacular failures is Peter's denial of Jesus to a servant girl (Luke 22:54–62). Peter had bragged to Jesus, "I will lay down my life for you," but a few hours later, Peter was denying that he even knew Jesus. After his resurrection, Jesus singled out Peter to restore his relationship with him (John 21:15–17), and Peter went on to become a humble, powerful leader of the fledgling church (Acts 2:37–41). That failure and subsequent restoration was a turning point in Peter's life. Note these lessons:

1. Failure is a good warning. Peter never repeated his mistake. The rest of his life was devoted to proclaiming Jesus' deity and resurrection to far more threatening audiences than a servant girl.

How have you been doing at learning from your mistakes? Describe an area where you seem to be repeating your mistakes, and think about how to overcome and break the cycle.

_____

_____

_____

2. Failure builds character. Peter's failure made him better prepared to lead. At the point where Peter used to feel the strongest and bragged about it (Luke 22:33), God showed him the truth about himself, and Peter now relied on God.

So, if you think you are standing firm, be careful that you don't fall!

1 Corinthians 10:12

Have you failed in the very area in which you felt the strongest? Explain how God has used that failure to build your character.

_____

_____

_____

3. Failure is not fatal. *After* Peter's denial, Jesus gave him a mission; "Feed my sheep." Jesus did not give up on Peter because he blew it. God is the God of second chances. It's up to us to accept the clean slate he offers us and to start over, trying again.

How are you doing at letting God release you from the prison of your failure? On the next page, write down the failure that has been on your slate; then cross it out and use your clean slate to write down a mission that God could be giving you as a result of your failure.

PRAYER

Precious Lord,

Make me an overcomer. Give me a daily dose of courage to face my everyday problems. Break me free from the prison of my past by using it to showcase your grace and daily making me a new creation. Break me free from the prison of my pain by using it to reveal your works and your power. If I have put myself in a prison of pain because of my own sin, convict me and help me turn from my sinful habits. Break me free from the prison of my failure by helping me to stop repeating my mistakes. Build my character upon the foundation of my brokenness, and write a new purpose on my clean slate that my failure now equips me to fulfill.

In the name of Jesus, amen.

Steps to Courage

We become brave
by doing brave acts.

Aristotle, 384–322 BC, Greek philosopher

SITTING QUIETLY WITH YOUR MAKER

Today is a time of reflection and solitude for you in the privacy of your own quiet-time space. You will be putting together a Courage Action Plan, working with God to further develop three types of courage: courage to take a risk, courage to take a stand, and courage to be of help.

Ask yourself how deeply you are able to focus on increasing your courage during this season of your life. Then select the appropriate action steps on pages 128–131, whatever you feel you can realistically experiment with this week. It's your plan, your life, and your prayerful decision—nobody else's. If you feel God impressing on you to concentrate on your courage right now, go for these exercises with gusto—without further ado or delay! I am confident that whatever effort you are able to devote to improving your courage will be richly rewarded by him on earth and in heaven.

Courage Action Plan

PRAYER FOCUS: Pray Jabez's prayer of risk: "Oh, that You would bless me indeed, and enlarge my territory, that Your hand would be with me, and that You would keep me from evil, that I may not cause pain!" (1 Chronicles 4:10 NKJV). Pray for government leaders, university professors, classroom teachers, social workers, police officers, and others, like yourself, who need courage to take a stand against the forces of evil and injustice in our culture. Then, ask God what he wants *you* to do about taking an action step yourself. Pray for the broken people in your community, whether they are hurting widows, orphans, elderly, disabled, addicts, abuse victims, pregnant teens, illiterate, lonely, prisoners, or prostitutes. Ask God what he wants *you* to do for them.

DEVOTIONAL FOCUS: Choose one of the following Scripture passages on the topic of courage: To focus on *taking a risk*, read about Abraham's obedience in Genesis 12:1–4 and Hebrews 11:8–10, and think about how the concepts of risk and faith are connected. To focus on *taking a stand*, read the story of Paul and Silas going to jail for helping a tortured slave girl in Acts 16:16–40, and find the attitudes they displayed during their ordeal. To focus on *being of help*, read about Barnabas (whose name means "son of encouragement") in Acts 11:22–30, and find the ways he encouraged people.

EXTRA PERSPECTIVE: Read *Good News About Injustice* by Gary Haugen to understand the shocking abuses going on in today's world and what Scripture demands of us in response. Or get creative and see how much good you can do with $10 in one afternoon!

Action Steps: Developing Courage to Take a Risk

Instructions: Prayerfully choose one or two action steps to experiment with this week.

Start Date

_____ ☐ **I will make a change.** I will make a change in my life to improve an unsatisfactory situation (i.e., change jobs, change my routine, remove stress). *(Identify the situation to improve.)*

_____

_____ ☐ **I will take a course.** I will sign up for a course to learn a skill I've always wanted to try or a subject I've always wanted to investigate. *(Name the course.)*

_____

_____ ☐ **I will try something new.** I will say "yes!" to a new experience that I would normally avoid (such as teaching a class, trying a specialty food from another country, or playing baseball). *(List the new experience.)*

_____

_____ ☐ **I will conquer a fear.** I will come up with a plan to conquer one major fear I have by doing something I'm afraid to do. (The plan might involve lessons, coaching, a support group, counseling, or medical advice.) I will take the steps necessary in order to finally do the thing that terrifies me. *(Identify the scary thing you will address, and how.)*

_____

_____

_____ ☐ **I will develop** courage to take a risk by *(add your idea here)*

_____

_____

Action Steps: Developing Courage to Take a Stand

Instructions: Prayerfully choose one or two action steps to experiment with this week.

Start Date

_____ ☐ **I will confront a wrong.** I will confront a moral, ethical, or relational wrong that has been going on by speaking the truth in love. *(Identify the wrong you will address, and how.)*

_____

_____ ☐ **I will stand up for myself.** I will stand up for who I am by defending my opinion, offering my ideas, verbalizing my preferences, and/or exerting my influence. (This is an important step if you are used to deferring to others or keeping your thoughts to yourself.) *(Identify one way you will stand up for yourself.)*

_____

_____ ☐ **I will join a cause.** I will begin to fight some form of social injustice, such as abortion, pornography, racial discrimination, or religious persecution. I will take action by raising money, raising awareness, or traveling to a location and helping victims. *(Identify the cause you will join, and how.)*

_____

_____

_____ ☐ **I will develop** courage to take a stand by *(add your idea here)*

_____

_____

Action Steps: Developing Courage to Be of Help

Instructions: Prayerfully choose one or two action steps to experiment with this week.

Start Date

_____ ☐ **I will support one person who's struggling.** I will offer comfort, help, and friendship to someone who is struggling or lonely (i.e., an unwed mother, military wife, shut-in, unemployed person, newly divorced woman). This could involve visiting, making a meal, teaching, or providing transportation or supplies. *(Identify who you will help, and how.)*

_____

_____

_____ ☐ **I will befriend someone.** I will be friendly to someone who looks like they need a friend. This could be a stranger I encounter during my day or someone I have been avoiding because they appear to be so needy. *(Wisely identify someone you could logically reach out to, and how.)*

_____

_____

_____ ☐ **I will start a ministry.** I will start a ministry or raise awareness on behalf of a group that is currently being ignored or victimized. This could mean launching a network for services: counseling, intervention, shelter, or medical help for single parents, children of prisoners, foreign exchange students, members of a mosque, or disaster victims. I will dream big! *(Identify who you will help, and how.)*

_____

_____

_____ ☐ **I will develop** courage to be of help by *(add your idea here)*

_____

_____

MASTER ACTION PLAN

Now, select only one major action step from this Day 5 exercise and record it on your Master Action Plan in appendix A on page 322. When you have finished reading this book, continue to refer to that one major action step on your Master Action Plan (as well as this Courage Action Plan, of course, as your season of life permits!). Remember, in order to become more like Christ in your character, you need to collaborate with God in three ways: preparation, prayer, and practice. You have done the work of preparation by learning God's truth about courage. Now, internalize it by praying for the Holy Spirit's help and practicing your action steps, one by one.

COURAGE PRAYER

Precious Lord,

You know that, alone, I would shrivel up on my bed into a ball of fear about, oh, so many things. Thank you that you never intended for me to be that fear-laden. Thank you that you have a better plan for me than cowering. Impress on me in a fresh, new, and bold way how your heart is glad when I walk in your power, protection, and provision. Grow in me the spirit of a mighty warrior who goes forth in your strength on your missions.

In the name of Jesus, amen.

PART 3

The Making
of a Right Relationship
to Others

Chapter 4

Self-Control

Like a city whose walls are broken through
is a person who lacks self-control.

Proverbs 25:28

Empowered by God

The greatest burden we have to carry in life is self;
the most difficult thing we have to manage is self.

**Hannah Whitall Smith, 1832–1911,
author of *The Christian's Secret of a Happy Life***

WELCOME BACK TO MY PLACE!

Come in! It is so good to see you again. I hope you had a great week and that you are pacing yourself on every aspect of your character renovation. Why don't we sit here today at my dining room table? You mentioned that you loved flowers, so I thought you would enjoy the color and fragrance of this arrangement that my daughter, Stephanie, brought over. How does iced tea sound to you today? I just brewed a fresh pot of tea that we can pour over ice, if you like. But before we get carried away having too much fun, why don't we bless our time together in prayer:

God of All Truth,

Amaze us with your ability to increase our self-control. As we discuss and study this important topic this week, and as we pray our way through the exercises, stay by our side shedding light on the areas that will cause us to be more like you. We live only to please you.

Amen.

Is anyone ever really ready to handle today's topic: self-control? Shall we buckle our seat belts, figuratively speaking, and just start at the beginning?

AN OUT-OF-CONTROL ME

For years, I crippled my family's finances in the months before and after Christmas. I shopped till I dropped with money I didn't have. I would frantically wrap and exchange gifts and then end up paying for my actions, literally, through March of the next year via my credit card payments. One time, I even had to wait for our income tax refund check to arrive in May to bail us out of debt. Yes, I was out of control. I'm pleased to be able to say that the Lord has helped me to break free from that compulsion. What was I trying to prove? That is no way to live, and it was definitely not God's plan for my life.

Self-control is a character quality with many facets and far-reaching implications for several areas of our lives. For instance, you exercise self-control when you ...

- Regularly put money into your savings account
- Resist the impulse to buy something you don't need
- Discipline yourself to get up early and exercise every day
- Think before you speak
- Say no to an unnecessary commitment
- Decline a second serving of an entrée

Some of the concepts that are inherent in self-control include moderation, self-discipline, willpower, and restraint. On the other hand, ideas that are contrary to self-control include being overindulgent, impulsive, overreactive, or lazy. And here comes another paradox for practicing Christians: The strongest self-control is not self-control at all, but God-control. In and of ourselves, we don't have the willpower, strength, or virtue to exercise consistent self-control. But when we put our self under *God's* control, then we will find the power we need to exercise *self*-control.

DAVID'S EXAMPLE OF SELF-CONTROL

For thirteen long years, Israel's future king, David, was a shining example of self-control. These were the years between when God told him he would be the next king and when Saul, the current king, died. During that time, Saul grew more and more insanely jealous of David's popularity. And right up until Saul's death at the hands of the Philistines, Saul kept David on a run for his life. (To understand the intensity of this unfair manhunt, think of any scene in *The Fugitive* with Tommy Lee Jones chasing Harrison Ford!) Yet, even though David had repeated opportunities to retaliate and kill Saul, he resisted time after time, believing that it was not his place to lift his hand against God's anointed king (1 Samuel 26:23).

David's restraint demonstrates an important aspect of self-control, which is this: Restraint gives you personal mastery over your own impulses and reactions. There are things in life you can't control, such as the actions of an angry, sick man who is out to get you. But you can control your response to such people. When you have the power of God in you to restrain yourself, you don't have to react *to* anger *with* anger. A self-controlled person is able to let go of the uncontrollables and unchangeables in her life, and focus on what is controllable and what is changeable, namely, her own attitude.

> *Those who live according to the sinful nature have their minds set on what that nature desires; but those who live in accordance with the Spirit have their minds set on what the Spirit desires. 6The mind controlled by the sinful nature is death, but the mind controlled by the Spirit is life and peace.*
>
> Romans 8:5–6

Here are some ways that healthy God-control helps you draw the right kinds of boundaries:

- I can't change others, but I can change myself.
- I can't control certain situations, but I can control my attitude.
- I can't look to others to keep my controls in place; I must really desire to control myself.
- I can't depend on others to fix me; I am responsible for my own growth.

A *self-under-control* person takes ownership for what she can control in God's power, and does not abdicate personal responsibility by relying on others for boundaries or controls.

SAMSON'S LIFE OF SELF-INDULGENCE

At the opposite end of the self-control spectrum is David in his later years, but instead let's pick on Samson today, who was also the epitome of self-indulgence. His was the original entitlement mentality! Whenever he saw a pretty girl, he wanted her; and then he whined, wheedled, and terrorized people until he got her. It didn't matter to Samson whether or not the girl shared his faith, desires, or wedding bed.

Samson was not the big, strong hero he imagined himself to be. Rather, he was a weakling, controlled and manipulated by his appetites, impulses, and feelings. Samson's life took an extra tragic turn when he succumbed to Delilah's wiles and gave away the secret of his strength. Captured, blinded, tortured, and imprisoned, he ended his life with a final burst of strength that brought down a temple upon himself and the three thousand Philistines in it. (See Judges 14–16.)

Our society panders to self-indulgence. We are encouraged to give ourselves a break, do ourselves a favor, and have it our way. It is assumed that our pleasures, prestige, power, and passions drive us, not our principles. Yet, even the good things in life will hurt us if we overindulge in them. Food, sex, exercise, sleep, money—all these are not inherently bad, of course, but uncontrolled indulgence in any of them can be harmful. Aided by God's power, we need to exercise a fair amount of self-discipline instead of self-indulgence.

> *You too must strengthen yourselves with the same way of thinking that [Christ] had.... ²From now on, then, you must live the rest of your earthly lives controlled by God's will and not by human desires.*
>
> 1 Peter 4:1–2 GNT

This translates into some life principles that we tell our children, but to which we should pay attention as well:

- Just because it's fun doesn't make it right.
- Just because everyone is doing it doesn't mean you have to.
- Just because you want it doesn't mean you should get it.
- Just because you can afford it doesn't mean you should buy it.

A *self-under-control* person, in God's power, exercises restraint, moderation, and willpower, and makes decisions based on principles, not pleasures.

MARTHA'S ATTEMPT AT OTHER-CONTROL

Let's step aside and look at self-control from an entirely different angle. We've looked at self-control as restraining your impulses and disciplining your appetites. But another aspect of self-control is that it is *myself*-control, not *other*-control. When it comes down to it, I am the only person who can change me, and you are the only person who can change you. When I cross that boundary and start trying to change you, that becomes *other*-control.

In the Bible, one person with a notorious reputation for trying to use other-control is Martha. She operated under the mistaken notion that her sister Mary should be doing what she [Martha] was doing, and she tried to enlist Jesus' help to get her sister to change. But Jesus didn't take the bait. Instead, he released Mary to keep doing something that typically only the males in that society would do—sit at the feet of a teacher and learn.

But Martha was distracted by all the preparations that had to be made. She came to him and asked, "Lord, don't you care that my sister has left me to do the work by myself? Tell her to help me!"

[41]"Martha, Martha," the Lord answered, "you are worried and upset about many things, [42]but few things are needed — or indeed only one. Mary has chosen what is better, and it will not be taken away from her."

Luke 10:40–42

The principle we can glean from this story is that self-control limits your desire to be an other-controller:

- It is healthy to be in control. It is *not* healthy to be controlling.
- It is healthy to fix, change, improve, and develop yourself. It is *not* healthy to overprotect, dominate, manipulate, or micromanage others.

A *self-under-control* person, in God's power, resists the urge to cross boundaries and exercise control over someone else's life.

It's time now to see how you are doing in all areas of self-control. Remember to take a deep breath and be kind to yourself, so you don't feel "lowlier than a worm." Wormliness is not the goal here; godliness is! God will lovingly help you, if you focus on him!

Self-Control Checklist

The following is a list of issues that can result from a lack of self-control. Check the problem areas you are currently dealing with in your life.

Personal Life
- ☐ Habitual self-indulgence
- ☐ Negative self-talk
- ☐ Overindulgence in fantasies
- ☐ Overspending
- ☐ Perfectionism
- ☐ Unbalanced diet

Relationships with Others
- ☐ Compromise of values in order to be accepted
- ☐ Need to be a caretaker—attracted to needy people
- ☐ Need to be a people-pleaser
- ☐ Need to fix, change, or improve others
- ☐ Need to overprotect, dominate, manipulate, or micromanage others
- ☐ Overdependence on others to be your control mechanism
- ☐ Sexual immorality

Verbal/Emotional
- ☐ Anger that harms self or others
- ☐ Criticism
- ☐ Cruelty
- ☐ Gossip
- ☐ Habitually finishing people's sentences
- ☐ Judgmental spirit
- ☐ Lying
- ☐ Negativity

- ☐ Uncontrolled words
- ☐ Unreasonable fears
- ☐ Withholding of praise

Time Management
- ☐ Excessive activities
- ☐ Frequently stressed
- ☐ Habitual lateness
- ☐ Overwork
- ☐ Procrastination
- ☐ Reactive time management
- ☐ Unbalanced schedule

Compulsive and/or Addictive Behaviors
- ☐ Alcoholism
- ☐ Body image obsession
- ☐ Caffeine addiction
- ☐ Compulsive cleaning
- ☐ Drug addiction
- ☐ Eating disorder
- ☐ Exercise obsession
- ☐ Gambling addiction
- ☐ Pornography
- ☐ Religious legalism
- ☐ Sexual addiction
- ☐ Shopping addiction
- ☐ Smoking addiction
- ☐ Sugar addiction
- ☐ Workaholism

As you prepare to work on your journal exercises beginning on page 142, prayerfully reflect back on this self-assessment and ask God to breathe insight from it into your answers.

Journal

Read the following passage about the attributes we are supposed to develop as Christians:

> *For this very reason, make every effort to add to your faith goodness; and to goodness, knowledge; ⁶and to knowledge, self-control; and to self-control, perseverance; and to perseverance, godliness; ⁷and to godliness, mutual affection; and to mutual affection, love. ⁸For if you possess these qualities in increasing measure, they will keep you from being ineffective and unproductive in your knowledge of our Lord Jesus Christ.*
>
> 2 Peter 1:5–8

Now color in the appropriate number of squares on each line of the chart below according to how strong you feel you are in each attribute. One box means you feel very weak in that area and five boxes means you feel very strong in that area.

Attributes Assessment	Weak				Strong
Example: Faith					
Faith					
Goodness					
Knowledge					
Self-control					
Perseverance					
Godliness					
Affection					
Love					

How do the attributes in which you are strongest help you exercise self-control? (You can even mention how self-control helps you exercise more self-control.)

Example: *I am strong in <u>knowledge</u> because I try to pick up ideas from efficient people I know, and thus I have learned how to control my schedule and don't get stressed out too often.*

_____

_____

_____

Next, look at your weakest areas on the Attributes Assessment. How would you say your weaknesses are contributing to your difficulties with self-control?

Example: *I am weak in <u>kindness,</u> so I lash out at people with my mouth very easily and hurt people without thinking.*

_____

_____

_____

PRAYER

Precious Lord,

Thank you for your power. I know that when I place my self under control—your control—you give me your power to exercise self-control. Where I am struggling with self-control, I pray that you would help me develop the Christian attributes that will strengthen my resolve to lean on you more. Help me not to be reactionary, self-indulgent, or controlling. Instead, give me your power to restrain my impulses, discipline my desires, and control my own self and not everyone else.

In the name of Jesus, amen.

Anger:
Exposing Your Inner
Fred Flintstone

Speak when you are angry and you will make
the best speech you will ever regret.

Ambrose Bierce, 1842–1914, American satirist

A VIRTUAL MESSAGE

 NOTE: It's Day 2, so you have the option of listening to today's message by downloading it from my website, www.LifePurposeCoachingCenters.com/CM, or reading the message text below. Enjoy the virtual coaching and don't forget to open in prayer!

THE FLIP SIDE OF SELF-CONTROL

"Willllmaaaaa!" Whenever I think of the classic cartoon character Fred Flintstone, I immediately hear in my mind that Stone Age holler of frustration. Fred was a bombastic, overreactive master of melodrama, who was badly in need of a good dose of self-control. He went through life yelling about everything and at everyone he loved. He yelled when he was frustrated; he yelled when he was hurt; he yelled when he was embarrassed; he yelled when he was disappointed; he even yelled when he was afraid.

One area over which it is most difficult to exercise self-control is our words, and some of the most difficult types of words to control are angry words. I'd like you to meet my friend Jan, who has battled with her own eruptions of anger. Read the story of how she overcame her rage problem.

JAN'S STORY OF RAGE

Fourth grade was a pivotal year for Jan. It was then that several pieces of her self-concept formed that took years to undo. She moved to a new town and was behind her new class in every subject, so she decided she was not smart. Because she was the only new student, she also felt like a misfit. Her family members were dealing with their own issues and didn't give her the support she needed during this traumatic adjustment, so she felt alone. Jan was unaware of her father's alcohol addiction until she was an adult, but she knew he was regularly absent and she often felt abandoned. Her mother didn't talk about feelings, and rather than using words to express herself, she'd slam doors and bang things, which made Jan feel afraid and isolated.

Fast-forward to Jan's mid-twenties. She married a kind, generous, thoughtful man named Tim (to whom she has been married for thirty-four years), but she had not overcome her feelings of insignificance and worthlessness. Because she did not know how to use words to express her concerns, she resorted to rage whenever the smallest event triggered her subliminal fear of being rejected or abandoned. In her rage she would throw things, slam doors, and yell whatever hurtful words came to her mind. As a Christian, she felt defeated and ashamed by her cycles of anger, but it seemed like no matter how Tim tried to pacify her and shield her from things that could set her off, she was becoming more and more out of control.

Now, you might think that Jan found relief by working out her frustrations through gardening, going on a walk, counting to ten, or memorizing Bible verses about self-control and anger. But, no. Trying harder to fight her urge to rage never worked for Jan. When she cried out to God in desperation for help, God surprised her with the answer. The answer to releasing Jan from her rage trap was to understand God himself. The more Jan learned about God's true character, the more her fear of rejection diminished, and as her fear diminished, her rage diminished. Put yourself in Jan's place and imagine how it felt to her when she discovered God's ways and started writing them in her journal:

Jan's Escape from Rage

Psalm 3:3	*God is a shield and he protects me.*
Psalm 3:4	*God listens to me and talks to me.*
Psalm 3:5	*God is with me while I am sleeping.*
Psalm 16:7	*God counsels me.*

(cont.)

Psalm 34:17	*God hears my cry for help.*
Psalm 34:18	*God knows when I am sad.*
Psalm 37:4	*God cares about what I want.*
Psalm 54:4	*God is my helper.*
Psalm 139:18	*God is with me when I awaken.*

Jan spent months dwelling on the Psalms and discovering God. The more pages she filled with notes about God, the more secure she felt with him. This, in turn, gave her a feeling of being surrounded by his protection, love, and comfort. Once she didn't fear anymore, she didn't rage anymore.

Jan's experience brings to mind a progression of spiritual growth that the apostle Peter describes. Look closely at the steps he lists that lead to godliness:

> *Knowing God leads to self-control. Self-control leads to patient endurance, and patient endurance leads to godliness.*
>
> 2 Peter 1:6 NLT

ANATOMY OF SOME UNCONTROLLED EMOTIONS

Emotions such as anger, rage, harshness, and irritability cannot always be blamed on a "bad temper." Consider the following sources of negative emotions. Are you susceptible to any of these?

Fatigue: We've all experienced being short-tempered and irritable when we're at the end of the day and exhausted. A pastor's wife once warned, "Don't bring me your problems between five and seven p.m. — that's when I feel like everybody's got a straw stuck in me and they're all sucking hard!" When you don't have any physical reserves left, it's much harder to prevent harsh words from slipping out.

Embarrassment: Have you ever seen those television shows like *Candid Camera*, *Punk'd*, or *America's Funniest Home Videos*, in which an unsuspecting subject is embarrassed or humiliated in some way? Some people react to being embarrassed by lashing out with angry words, by attacking, or by running away, in order to get the attention off themselves.

Frustration: This type of anger is sometimes directed inwardly. For example, have you ever been frustrated by having to tear out incorrect rows of knitting (aargh!)? You can also direct your frustration at others, which is something for which Job's wife is famous. After enduring many of the same losses as her husband and seeing her husband in abject misery as he scraped his boils, she lashed out in frustration, "Are you still maintaining your integrity? Curse God and die!" (Job 2:9).

Rejection: Being deeply wounded by rejection can also cause you to lash out. This is what happened to Cain when God rejected his sacrifice. Jealousy over God's acceptance of Abel's sacrifice drove him into a rage that spawned the world's first murder (Genesis 4:1–8).

Righteous Indignation: If you feel wronged, offended, or cheated, it can be natural to react in anger. For instance, when someone blames you for something you didn't do, it's easy to blurt out angry words. Think about the righteous indignation that must have been simmering inside Peter before he lopped off the ear of the guard who came to arrest Jesus in the garden (John 18:10–11). Because Jesus had predicted Peter's denial only hours earlier, he was probably just looking for a chance to prove Jesus wrong. And, he was likely still embarrassed that he had fallen asleep while praying and incurred Jesus' gentle rebuke. So, when that soldier closed in, Peter lost his cool and let loose with his sword. It could have been an "I *told* you I would defend you to the death, Jesus, so there!" sort of move.

Vengeance: Sometimes anger comes from wanting to punish someone in return for a wrong they committed. We see this time and time again in the life of Samson, whose main motive in life was to get even. When he was cheated on a bet, he killed thirty men. When his girlfriend married someone else, he retaliated by burning crops and killing a thousand men. He was known for comments like: "This time I have a right to get even with the Philistines; I will really harm them.... Since you've acted like this, I swear that I won't stop until I get my revenge.... I merely did to them what they did to me" (Judges 15:3, 7, 11). In these three statements Samson is saying, "Vengeance is mine; it's all their fault; they started it." Does that sound like anybody you know?

DEALING WITH UNCONTROLLED WORDS

Scripture is very clear about how potentially dangerous our tongue is.

> *The tongue is a small thing, but what enormous damage it can do. A great forest can be set on fire by one tiny spark....* [6]*The tongue ... can turn our whole lives into a blazing flame of destruction and disaster.*
>
> James 3:5–6 LB

Dangerous as the tongue can be, the Bible says it is possible to control our speech. It seems that our speech is the barometer of how well-controlled we are in every other area of life:

We all make many mistakes, but those who control their tongues can also control themselves in every other way.

James 3:2 NLT

When you get angry, your body involuntarily launches a physiological response to the anger that you can't ignore. You've got to do something about the alarms going off in your heart, face, and tingling nerves. But here's an important distinction to understand: Although you may not initially be able to control your body's reaction to anger, you *can* control your response to those feelings—which will calm you down physiologically. We are not victims of our own anger; we choose our response. We can choose to succumb to our anger and explode; we can choose to shut down if our anger scares us; or we can choose a healthy response to anger, which involves the following four steps:

1. Check your heart. Jesus said, "But the things that come out of the mouth come from the heart" (Matthew 15:18). Before you can deal with your words, it is critical to deal with the source of those words: your heart. This is exactly what Jan found to be true. She couldn't make any progress with her anger until she had dealt with her heart of fear. When you're gripped with anger, stop and ask yourself: What am I afraid of right now? If you don't deal with what you're afraid of, it will be useless to try the other steps.

2. Get heart surgery. You can't control your words by your own power. Why? Because your mouth isn't the problem—your heart is. Your mouth is just a window into what's in your heart. So, if you want to change what comes out of your mouth, you need to ask God to change your heart. And fortunately, God is in the heart transplant business.

Rid yourselves of all the offenses you have committed, and get a new heart and a new spirit.

Ezekiel 18:31

Create in me a clean heart, O God.

Psalm 51:10 NKJV

3. Ask God for long-term help. True self-control does not come when your *self* is in control, but when your self is under *God's* control. So, place yourself under God's long-term control; then, like the Psalmist, ask him for the ongoing power to control your mouth.

Set a guard over my mouth, LORD, keep watch over the door of my lips.

Psalm 141:3

4. Think first; speak later. Remember: You're not a victim of your impulses. You have a choice as to how you will respond to your feelings of anger. If you can make a choice to rein in your tongue around your boss or your church friends, you can make the same choice around your family and your secular bowling league.

Those who consider themselves religious and yet do not keep a tight rein on their tongues deceive themselves, and their religion is worthless.

James 1:26

Intelligent people think before they speak; what they say is then more persuasive.

Proverbs 16:23 GNT

Is There a Fear at the Heart of Your Anger?

- Anger when you don't get invited to join a group might signal a fear of rejection.
- Anger and defensiveness when you're criticized might indicate a fear of failure.
- Anger when you've been caught doing something wrong may be triggered because you're afraid someone will abandon you.
- Anger and retaliation when someone wrongs you might come from a fear they won't get properly punished.
- Anger and criticism when someone fails to live up to your standard might come from your own fears of not being "good enough."
- Anger and a judgmental attitude over someone's sin may signal your own guilt and fear that you will be found out too.

Journal

Check your heart. Do you see a correlation between the things that make you angry and your fears? If so, explain.

_____

_____

_____

Get heart surgery. Have you given your heart to God? Have you asked him for a heart transplant? Write out a prayer that gives God your heart of fear and asks him to replace it with his new heart of love.

_____

_____

_____

Ask God for long-term help. What are some of the differences it would make in your life to place yourself under God's ongoing control, rather than trying to be self-controlled?

_____

_____

_____

Think first; speak later. Reconsider this statement: "If you can make a choice to rein in your tongue around your boss or your church friends, you can make the same choice around your family and secular bowling league." Are there any changes you need to make in this area of reining in your tongue, even if that means finding a different circle of friends?

_____

_____

_____

PRAYER

Precious Lord,

I confess that my heart has been harboring some things that are being revealed by my mouth. I have had fury, retaliation, envy, hatred, and spite in my heart, so I've had a cruel mouth. I have had hurt, misery, loneliness, depression, and ugliness in my heart, so I've had a negative mouth. I have had guilt, shame, remorse, blame, and hopelessness in my heart, so I've had a judgmental mouth. I have had anxiety, insecurity, tension, pressure, and panic in my heart, so I've had a critical mouth. Create in me a clean heart, O God, and replace my self-control with your control. Then, set your guard over my mouth, and give me your power to choose my reactions—every time—on all fronts.

In the name of Jesus, amen.

How to Reduce Stress

Beware of the "shoulds" other people assign to your life,
and learn to say no. Remember:
Just because you can, doesn't mean you have to.
Lisa Ryan, author, broadcaster

You've Got Mail

To:	"The Best You" Woman	Sent:	Day 3
From:	Katie Brazelton		
Subject:	Self-Control		

It's Day 3, so here is your weekly Email Message. Feel free to blog me a response at my website, www.LifePurposeCoachingCenters.com/CM, if you'd like. Enjoy the email-coaching and don't forget to open in prayer!

Stress from a Coach's Perspective

One of the most stressful experiences of my life happened years ago when I was teaching my son, Andy, to drive. Because his father had passed away years earlier, I became my kids' designated, behind-the-wheel coaching mama. May I hasten to point out that Andy wasn't stressed at all. He was blithely making lane changes and blazing through intersections without a moment's concern. I, on the other hand, was nothing but a blob of quivering nerves by the time he lurched back into our driveway after each session. The time he took me for a spin uphill in heavy, city traffic—armed with a newly acquired stick shift—still gives me nightmares. Now, do I get that stressed when *I'm* behind the steering wheel? No! And why is that? Because when I'm behind the wheel, I'm in control. Stress is directly related to how out-of-control we feel. The more self-controlled we are, the less stressed we feel.

TOP FIVE STRESSORS

When your life is out of balance, you have stress. Stress isn't the same as anxiety. Stress can *lead to* anxiety, but stressed-out people aren't necessarily worried about it—they're just overloaded. Stress is basically a problem of too much: too much to do, too many people to take care of, too many conflicting priorities, too many problems to solve.

From a stress survey conducted in 2006 by the American Psychological Association, here are the top five stressors:

• Sick family member
• Money
• Your own health
• Children
• Work

If you're in the growing population of people caring for aging parents, you could write a book on stress! Money is a stressor, both when you don't have enough and when you have too much. Your health is a stressor, whether you're trying to maintain a healthy lifestyle or deal with an illness. Children are a stressor, both to a married couple and to a single parent. Work may have stress inherent in it, or it might simply add stress because it doesn't leave you enough disposable time in a day.

TOP TEN DE-STRESSORS

Stress is part and parcel of life on earth. Yes, specific examples may vary, but the realities are the same. So, how did Jesus handle stress? Mark 6 depicts both the types of stress Jesus encountered as well as how he responded. His responses to stress provide ten solid principles as to how we can de-stress in healthy ways.

1. Don't add to your stress; start eliminating.

According to Mark's gospel account, Jesus went to Nazareth and tried to teach. After the townspeople listened to their hometown boy for a while, they were "offended at him" because he sounded so authoritative. Jesus knew he would be unable to do any major work among his own people, so he didn't force the issue. "He could not do any miracles there, except lay his hands on a few sick people and heal them" (Mark 6:5).

Think about how much of your own stress is self-inflicted when you continue to do things you should be eliminating. Have you overcommitted to something that will take more effort than it's worth? Are you demanding too much of yourself by trying to do more than one person's work? If you are expending a lot of effort on a losing cause, or if you are trapped in a project that's sapping all your energy, maybe it's time to put yourself out of your misery and release it to God.

Conclusion: *It takes self-control to resist overcommitment.*

2. Remove some stress by delegating.

Jesus didn't try to do everything himself. Look at Mark 6:7–13 where we see Jesus sending out the twelve disciples to preach and heal:

> *Calling the Twelve to him, he began to send them out two by two and gave them authority over evil spirits.*
>
> *[8]These were his instructions: "Take nothing for the journey except a staff—no bread, no bag, no money in your belts. [9]Wear sandals but not an extra shirt. [10]Whenever you enter a house, stay there until you leave that town. [11]And if any place will not welcome you or listen to you, shake the dust off your feet when you leave, as a testimony against them."*
>
> *[12]They went out and preached that people should repent. [13]They drove out many demons and anointed many sick people with oil and healed them.*

Jesus equipped his disciples, prepared them, and then released them to go and share his workload. Think about people in your life to whom you can delegate: coworkers, committee members, husband, children, and friends. In order to delegate effectively, you must give up your need to have things done exactly the way you would do them. Other people may not operate in the same way as you (or as well as you do!), but until you say, "So be it," and allow them to step in and take care of some things on your behalf, you could be hanging on to some unnecessary stress.

Conclusion: *It takes self-control to resist overcontrolling.*

3. Release your stress by rejuvenating.

After the disciples returned from their journeys, Jesus said, "Come with me by yourselves to a quiet place and get some rest" (Mark 6:31). Something else very significant had just happened: Jesus' good friend, John the Baptist, had been beheaded by King Herod. With the news of that tragedy, coupled with the exhaustion of their mission trips, it was important to rejuvenate. During stressful seasons, inject calming, soothing experiences. Be sure to get daily rest by sleeping well and weekly rest by taking a Sabbath. You can get other periodic rest by going on a retreat, spending time with friends, or scheduling enjoyable activities.

Conclusion: *It takes self-control to resist overactivity.*

4. Refocus on your passion when stress is escalating.

As you read what happened next in Jesus' long day, put yourself in his place and think of how you would react when your stress escalates.

> *For there were many coming and going, and they did not even have time to eat.... ³²So they departed to a deserted place ... ³³and many knew him and ran there on foot.... ³⁴And Jesus, when he came out, saw a great multitude and was moved with compassion for them.*
>
> Mark 6:31–34 NKJV

Some people thrive on pressure; they are adrenaline junkies. They love being busy and feel best when they're active. But even those folks need time to eat! It would be doubly frustrating to arrange for a break, only to have people chase you down and want more from you. Yet, when the stress escalated, Jesus didn't get frustrated. Instead, he was "moved with compassion." (Notice the word "passion" tucked inside "compassion"!) When stress is closing in on you and you feel all used up, pierce through the frustration by remembering why you're there, who you love, and what you're passionate about.

Conclusion: *It takes self-control to resist frustration and focus on your passion.*

5. Don't avoid your stress; it will be waiting for you.

As the day grew late, the disciples grew nervous, because they were in a deserted place where the crowds would not be able to buy food. The disciples wanted to get rid of the problem and let someone else deal with it, but Jesus wanted them to face it.

"Send the people away so that they can go to the surrounding countryside and villages and buy themselves something to eat." [37] *But he answered, "You give them something to eat."*

Mark 6:36–37

When you're stressed out by a problem, do you try to duck out of solving it or to somehow ignore it? Avoiding your problem may delay the pain, but it doesn't solve it. In fact, your problem will probably wait for your return, and avoidance could make it worse. When faced with a problem, own it and deal with it.

Conclusion: *It takes self-control to resist avoiding your problem.*

6. Don't increase your stress by exaggerating.

When the disciples heard that Jesus expected them to face their problem, instead of simply acknowledging it, they reacted by catastrophizing it.

They said to him, "That would take almost a year's wages! Are we to go and spend that much on bread and give it to them to eat?"

Mark 6:37

The disciples looked to themselves to be the solution to the problem, and so they immediately panicked. In their minds—from their human perspective and ours—the problem was indeed unmanageable and impossible to remedy. Facing your problem doesn't necessarily mean solving the problem yourself—it means giving it to God to solve, and not resorting to panic.

Conclusion: *It takes self-control to resist overreacting.*

7. Address your stress by prioritizing and evaluating.

Jesus calmly dealt with the problem by giving the disciples a simple task with which to start. He basically told them to evaluate their situation. " 'How many loaves do you have?' he asked. 'Go and see.' When they found out, they said, 'Five—and two fish' " (6:38). When you have a daunting problem, evaluate it and break it down into smaller tasks; then start with the simple ones you can accomplish quickly. Or, another school of thought says to handle the most difficult tasks first, when your energy may be highest. You decide.

Conclusion: *It takes self-control to resist getting overwhelmed.*

8. Get help with your stress by organizing and coordinating.

Another way Jesus dealt with the stress was to get organized. "Then Jesus directed them to have all the people sit down in groups on the green grass" (6:39). He coordinated his team and got everyone involved in sorting out the situation. When I have an unmanageable problem, I have noticed that getting myself organized helps, whether that means dividing my papers into piles, sorting my list into topics, or deciding my first step. On particularly large projects, it also helps to get more people involved in accomplishing the goal.

Conclusion: *It takes self-control to resist overworking.*

9. Manage your stress by not deviating.

Jesus didn't let the turmoil of that moment deter him from keeping to his regular habit of giving thanks for his food and of eating at the proper time. (I'm so glad he finally ate—at least we presume he ate!)

> *Taking the five loaves and the two fish and looking up to heaven, he gave thanks and broke the loaves....* [42]*They all ate and were satisfied.*
>
> Mark 6:41–42

Here are three basic habits that will see you through the stressful times, if you do not deviate from them:

Stay praying. After this crisis, Jesus departed to the mountain to pray (6:46), and we are told elsewhere that he often withdrew to pray (Luke 5:16). How do you do at continuing your prayer habit when you're stressed? Is that the time you pray even more, or does prayer go by the wayside when you have too much to do?

Stay healthy. How do you do at maintaining healthy eating habits when you're stressed? That's the time you most need a balanced diet, right? So don't succumb to the temptation to skip meals or subsist on junk food because you're in a rush.

Stay on a schedule. Your stress level and that of your entire family will go down if you stick to a regular schedule. The predictability of family meals, for example, anchors your home life and contributes to a sense of security and discipline. If your mealtimes need to vary daily in order to work around different commitments, consider posting a schedule so that everyone can plan to eat together.

Conclusion: *It takes self-control to resist slipping away from good habits.*

10. Deepen your faith, when stress turns to crisis.

At the end of their very stressful day, Jesus sent the disciples off in a boat while he went to pray. They had certainly had enough stress for one day, but look at what happens next:

> *He saw the disciples straining at the oars, because the wind was against them. Shortly before dawn he went out to them, walking on the lake.... [49]They cried out, [50]because they all saw him and were terrified. Immediately he spoke to them and said, "Take courage! It is I. Don't be afraid." [51]Then he climbed into the boat with them, and the wind died down. They were completely amazed.*
>
> Mark 6:48–51

When your stressful day takes on crisis proportions, remember that Jesus cares deeply about you and your stress level. It takes faith to believe that you're not going to capsize and that Jesus is always with you in the proverbial boat or at least walking on the water nearby! Having eyes to see him in the midst of your crisis is all you need to reclaim peace and security.

Conclusion: *It takes self-control to resist becoming overanxious.*

Journal

Choose three of the following statements taken from Mark 6 and explain how they can help you with your stress:

He could not do any miracles there. (v. 5)—See #1

_____

_____

Calling the Twelve to him, he began to send them out two by two. (v. 7)—See #2

_____

_____

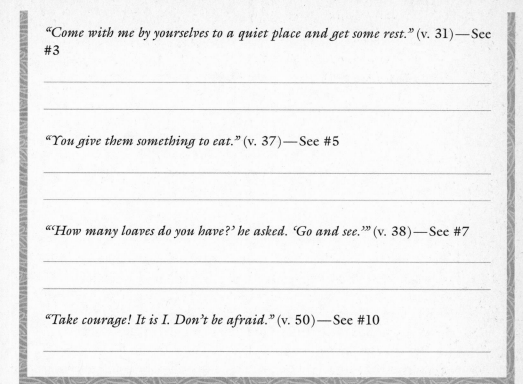

"Come with me by yourselves to a quiet place and get some rest." (v. 31) — See #3

"You give them something to eat." (v. 37) — See #5

"'How many loaves do you have?' he asked. 'Go and see.'" (v. 38) — See #7

"Take courage! It is I. Don't be afraid." (v. 50) — See #10

PRAYER

Precious Lord,

Thank you that you care about the things that stress me out. Thank you for modeling how to deal with stress. You didn't hang onto a hopeless cause. Then, you delegated to people who couldn't possibly teach or heal as well as you, and they got to experience the blessing of being stretched and rewarded for their service. You took a break, renewed your passion, faced your problems, set priorities, and got organized. You didn't stop praying. And when stress erupted into a crisis, you climbed into the boat and brought peace along with you. Thank you that your very presence soothes my stress.

In the name of Jesus, amen.

Your Self-Control Coach

The only conquests which are permanent,
and leave no regrets, are our conquests over ourselves.
Napoleon Bonaparte, 1769–1821, French emperor

PERSPECTIVE-CHANGING OUTING

Today we're meeting at an awesome place—a local frozen yogurt shop! In this week when we're discussing self-control, this seems like the perfect place for us to practice this character quality. You order Irish cream frozen yogurt with fat-free, sugar-free marshmallow crème, topped with fresh strawberries. I am doing some self-controlled indulging in Belgian chocolate frozen yogurt with sugar-free fudge sauce and carob chips to top it off. Wow! I love self-control! Let's find a spot under an outdoor umbrella and open our time together with a prayer. We can savor our nearly fat-free treats and talk about how you're doing with self-control in the areas of your habits and your schedule.

SELF-CONTROL OF YOUR HABITS

You're more likely to act yourself into feeling
than feel yourself into action. So act!
Whatever it is you know you should do, do it.
Anonymous

No matter what kinds of habits you have developed over the years, good or bad, they all have one thing in common: they give you some form of pleasure, which reinforces the habit. The difference between good and bad habits is that the reward for a bad habit is temporary and is often followed by negative consequences, and the reward for a good habit can be more long-lasting and is often followed by positive results.

For instance, a gambler's habit is reinforced by an emotional rush of winning, but that is quickly followed by financial and relational fallout. On the other hand, a walker's habit is rewarded with extra energy and lowered stress, and over the years of practiced discipline, the positive results of walking can include health, fitness, and longevity.

The key to breaking bad habits and foregoing their addictive rewards is to replace them with good habits, which carry more significant rewards. So, while we enjoy our healthier-than-ice-cream yogurt, let's talk about how you are doing at replacing your bad habits with good ones.

Seek God's Power

Bad habits and temptations have a strong pull. The first step to break their power is to *admit your powerlessness* to overcome them (sound like an AA meeting?) and to *seek God's power* over your habits.

> *For when I tried to keep the law, I realized I could never earn God's approval. So I died to the law so that I might live for God. I have been crucified with Christ. ²⁰I myself no longer live, but Christ lives in me. So I live my life in this earthly body by trusting in the Son of God, who loved me and gave himself for me.*
>
> Galatians 2:19–20 NLT

What habit or temptation has power over you?

_____

From Galatians 2:19–20, find one phrase that you need to apply to your temptation. What phrase did you choose, and why?

_____

_____

Show No Mercy

Bad habits don't deserve one iota of mercy from you. Temptation is your enemy, and you can't afford to say: "I'll give in, just this once." Instead, you need to declare to your temptations: "I am not your slave!"

> *Just as you used to offer yourselves as slaves to impurity and to ever-increasing wickedness, so now offer yourselves as slaves to righteousness leading to holiness.*
>
> Romans 6:19

Describe any situation, place, or person you need to stay away from—in order to prevent yourself from slipping back into slavery to your temptation.

_____

_____

Just avoiding temptation is not enough. Although it is important to set boundaries on your Internet browser if you are tempted by pornography, or stay out of shopping malls if you overspend, or avoid bars if you're an alcoholic, those choices don't solve the root cause of your habit. You will still have a broken place inside you that draws you to that temptation or a new one.

What is broken inside you that is at the root of your attraction to this temptation? (This could be low self-esteem, fear of abandonment, need for acceptance, greed, etc.)

_____

_____

_____

Scripture tells us to kill temptation!

So put to death the sinful, earthly things lurking within you. Have nothing to do with sexual sin, impurity, lust, and shameful desires. Don't be greedy for the good things of this life, for that is idolatry.

Colossians 3:5 NLT

If you were to stop living as though that temptation were alive in you, and instead live as though it were dead to you, how would that change things?

_____

_____

_____

In with the New

Once you clean house by avoiding your temptations and "killing" your old self, fill that empty space with positive, new habits, or your old habits will return worse than before (see Luke 11:24–26). So, it's out with the old and in with the new. The following passage is an awesome description of how to build new habits, so we'll look at it in its entirety. As you read it aloud, notice the action verbs like *clothe* and *bear* and *forgive*, words that tell you how to build new habits.

> *Therefore, as God's chosen people, holy and dearly loved, clothe yourselves with compassion, kindness, humility, gentleness and patience. [13]Bear with each other and forgive whatever grievances you may have against one another. Forgive as the Lord forgave you. [14]And over all these virtues put on love, which binds them all together in perfect unity.*
>
> *[15]Let the peace of Christ rule in your hearts, since as members of one body you were called to peace. And be thankful. [16]Let the word of Christ dwell in you richly as you teach and admonish one another with all wisdom, and as you sing psalms, hymns and spiritual songs with gratitude in your hearts to God. [17]And whatever you do, whether in word or deed, do it all in the name of the Lord Jesus, giving thanks to God the Father through him.*
>
> Colossians 3:12–17 NIV

Let's ponder the habits that this passage suggests. For each of the following daily habits, what bad habit can it replace?

What's the new daily habit?	What old habit can this replace?
v. 12 Get dressed in ...	
v. 13 Bear with ...	
v. 13 Forgive ...	
v. 14 Put on love which ...	
v. 15 Be ruled by ...	
v. 16 Fill up with ...	

(cont.)

What's the new daily habit?	What old habit can this replace?
v. 16 Spend time with …	
v. 17 Speak and act in …	

SELF-CONTROL OF YOUR SCHEDULE

Most people are so busy knocking themselves out trying
to do everything they think they should do,
they never get around to what they want to do.

Anonymous

When someone asks you how you're doing, have you ever answered: "too busy," "too much to do," or "overwhelmed"? Well, join the club. But being too busy is not a badge of honor. It's an area in which we need a reminder to exercise self-control.

Use every chance you have for doing good, because these are evil times. [17]So do not be foolish but learn what the Lord wants you to do.

Ephesians 5:16–17 NCV

This Scripture should not be misunderstood. "Use every chance you have for doing good" does not imply that we should fill our schedules with every good thing that comes along. No. Rather, the passage continues by telling us that we are not to be foolish about our choices, but instead, stop and ask God what he wants us to do with our time. He wants us to have space in our schedule to take on the good things he has for us to do. If we fill our calendar with activities that seem good, without running them through his filter, we will have no margin left to be interrupted, have our plans changed, stop and spend time with an unexpected visitor, listen to someone who's hurting, or do something about a need we come across. Being able to respond to the surprises in our day requires margin, yet so many of us are operating on no margin at all.

It's time for another self-check.

Schedule Self-Test

Use the following chart to evaluate your schedule, including your children's activities.

Optional Activities. List all your optional activities in a week or a month, including things like seminars, ministry, lessons, sports, and fitness.

Costs. Then, figure out how much each activity costs you in terms of time and money. This means totaling the fees involved to participate and the time it takes per week or month, including travel time to get there and back.

Benefits. Next, identify the benefit of keeping each activity on your calendar. Does it serve someone? Meet a need? Further your career? Complete your education? Teach your child a life skill? Improve your health? Inspire you to excellence?

Motive. Now, drill down further. What is your true motive for doing it? Love of God and obedience to him? Ego? Meeting someone's expectations? Materialism? The need to be needed? Desire to achieve? Living out your dreams through your child? Be honest with yourself as you think through why you have each activity on your schedule.

Optional Activities	Costs		Benefits	Motive
	Money	Time		

Congratulations! That was probably a little tough to complete. But let's not stop there. We're going to take a deeper look and see what this schedule evaluation is telling us.

First, look over your Optional Activities column. Do you need to include any activities that would help you to observe a regular Sabbath? Do you need to add anything to your list that you could do purely to relax, rest, or take a break? If so, write your ideas here:

_____

_____

Let's look next at the two Cost columns. Are you spending too much money to stay involved in certain activities? What total time per week or month do you invest in your optional activities? Do you have enough margin in your schedule to allow for God-ordained interruptions and detours?

_____

_____

Next, evaluate the Benefits column. When you look at what each activity is doing for you, what trends do you see? Are there any activities on your schedule that do not have enough God-desired benefits to justify the costs of time and money?

_____

_____

Finally, let's review the Motive column. Again, look for themes. Does a repeated theme drive you? Are there activities on your schedule that you should remove because they are there for the wrong reasons?

_____

_____

Build In a Sabbath Rest

The Hebrew word *shabath* means "to stop," "to desist," "to cease from doing." Do you have regular time built into your schedule to "cease from doing"? Observing a Sabbath doesn't just mean going to church and sitting still to read your Bible. When you see what the Father and the Son did on the Sabbath, you get a picture of what the fifth commandment ("Remember the Sabbath and keep it holy") really means.

- **God enjoyed his accomplishments.** You can look back and find something to celebrate in your achievements of the week.
- **God delighted in creation.** You can go on a picnic or a hike and enjoy nature. You can create something—do a craft, bake a pie, or paint a picture.
- **Jesus healed people physically and spiritually, bringing them joy.** Make your Sabbath a day of joy (see Isaiah 58:13–14) by planning activities of refreshment, rest, relaxation, renewal, and personal healing. Do a fun project with others, start a tradition of giving affirmations to people over Sunday lunch, hold a weekly family talent show, or spend some extended time writing in your spiritual journal.
- **Jesus pointed people to God.** You can focus on God by telling others about him and by dedicating part of every day to him as a mini-Sabbath.

PRAYER

Precious Lord,
    There are some habits that have power over me, and I have been powerless to overcome them. Give me your power, I pray, to break free from them. Give me the willpower to avoid situations that will lead to temptation, and help me to start living like my broken places are dead, because they are. Replace my bad habits with good ones, such as filling myself every day with your Word, and spending regular time with like-minded friends who can encourage me and hold me accountable. And, Lord, I turn over my schedule to you. I confess that I have taken on some things that you never intended for me to do, and as a result, my days are too full to stop, rest, have fun, bring joy to someone, listen to you, and respond to divine interruptions. Help me to make some tough decisions about my activities, because I do not want to be foolish, but to learn what you want me to do.

                                                 In the name of Jesus, amen.

Steps to Self-Control

I count him braver who overcomes his desires
than him who conquers his enemies;
for the hardest victory is over self.

Aristotle, 384–322 BC, Greek philosopher

SITTING QUIETLY WITH YOUR MAKER

Today is a time of reflection and solitude for you in the privacy of your own quiet-time space. You will be putting together a Self-Control Action Plan. What a tough, but important task: to work on developing self-control over your mouth, developing self-discipline, and developing good habits.

Ask yourself how deeply you are able to focus on increasing your self-control during this season of your life. Then select the appropriate action steps on pages 169–172, whatever you feel you can realistically experiment with this week. It's your plan, your life, and your prayerful decision—nobody else's. If you feel God impressing on you to concentrate on your self-control right now, go for these exercises with gusto—without further ado or delay! I am confident that whatever effort you are able to devote to improving your self-control will be richly rewarded by him on earth and in heaven.

Self-Control Action Plan

PRAYER FOCUS: Pray that God will give you his power to control your words and become someone who consistently uses her mouth to deliver good, not evil. Pray that you will be sensitive to the conviction of the Holy Spirit when you are being too self-indulgent, and that you will enlist the power of the Holy Spirit to deny yourself every pleasure that is not healthy. Pray for all your choices in the upcoming day. You probably make hundreds of choices in any given day, and they form the basis of your attitudes, perspectives, and habits. Ask God to remind you to consult with him about even your smallest decisions throughout the day.

DEVOTIONAL FOCUS: Choose one of the following Scripture passages on the topic of self-control: To focus on *developing more control over your mouth*, read about the fruit of the Spirit in Galatians 5:22–23 and meditate on how these nine characteristics apply to your speech. To focus on *developing more self-discipline*, read 1 Corinthians 9:24–27 to see how to practice self-discipline and learn about its rewards. To focus on *developing more good habits*, read Galatians 6:7–10 and apply the principles of sowing and reaping to the process of developing good habits. Pay special attention to the benefits.

EXTRA PERSPECTIVE: Read books about controlling emotions, like *Make Anger Your Ally* by Neil Clark Warren, or *Emotions, Can You Trust Them?* by Dr. James Dobson. Or get creative and fine yourself a quarter every time you lose control!

Action Steps: Developing Self-Control Over My Mouth

Instructions: Prayerfully choose one or two action steps to experiment with this week.

Start Date

_____ ☐ **I will give a blessing.** I will make it a habit not to leave a conversation without blessing the other person by saying something encouraging or affirming.

_____ ☐ **I will stop and think.** I will work on not talking too much or speaking foolishly. I will pause before I speak, evaluating what I'm about to say, and deciding whether or not it is really necessary or wise to say it.

_____ ☐ **I will stop gossiping.** If someone around me is gossiping, I will have the courage to find something positive to say about the object of the gossip, or at minimum, I will change the subject or excuse myself from the conversation.

_____ ☐ **I will be gentle.** I will be kind, not wounding with my words. With God's power, I will consciously avoid negativity and harsh words, because that disposition stirs up anger (Proverbs 15:1) and is discouraging to be around.

_____ ☐ **I will be thankful.** I will be marked by thankfulness. For those I live with, I will find at least one thing to thank them for daily. I will write thank-you notes for favors received. I will not let an act of kindness go unacknowledged.

_____ ☐ **I will guard my mind.** What I store in my mind spills into my words. Therefore, I will guard my mind from the senseless gossip of tabloids, the provocative stories in romance novels, the trash topics of soap operas and certain talk shows, and the conversations of people who are dwelling on such things. With God's power, I will relentlessly keep my filters on, not even saying, "Just this once" about one television show, one magazine, one book, or one conversation that I know is headed in an unwholesome direction. I will fill the space in my mind with positive, uplifting input.

_____ ☐ **I will work** on developing control over my mouth by (add your idea here)

_____

_____

Action Steps: Developing Self-Discipline

Instructions: Prayerfully choose one or two action steps to experiment with this week.

Start Date

_____ ☐ **I will start exercising** at least three times a week, doing something manageable that I can keep up. (Identify the exercise here.)

_____

_____ ☐ **I will eat a balanced diet.** I will, with God's power, not let food control me. I will find other God-inspired ways to reward or comfort myself when I would normally turn to food. I will acknowledge my emotions and not use food as a substitute. I will eat only when I'm hungry, and only what I need, not as much as I want.

_____ ☐ **I will take a Sabbath.** I will clear enough commitments from my schedule, so I can devote one day a week to God and rest.

_____ ☐ **I will be punctual.** I will stop trying to squeeze too much into my preparation time before leaving one location and going to another. I will walk out the door in time to be ten minutes early to my appointments. When I arrive ten minutes early, I will use that time to organize my thoughts and pray for what's about to happen. Or, I can use that time to take care of a phone call or thank-you note on my to-do list. Or (here's a wild idea for Type A personalities): I will use that time to get to know someone better.

_____ ☐ **I will stop procrastinating.** I will ask myself, "What is the best thing I could be working on right now, and what is keeping me from doing it?" I will stop letting endless errands, perpetual housecleaning, or one of my many moods keep me from finishing that which is most important to do at the time.

_____ ☐ **I will try some advanced self-control.** I will try a spiritual discipline such as fasting or solitude, to stretch myself in a way of connecting with God that requires more advanced self-control. (For guidelines on fasting and having a spiritual solitude retreat, go to www.LifePurposeCoachingCenters.com/CM.)

_____ ☐ **I will work** on developing self-discipline by *(add your idea here)*

_____

_____

Action Steps: Developing Good Habits

Instructions: Prayerfully choose one or two action steps to experiment with this week.

Start Date

_____ ☐ **I will keep a journal.** I will keep a written record of my life lessons, prayers, dreams, and important events, which is a great way to track my spiritual progress and recall God's work in my life.

_____ ☐ **I will find a mentor.** I will partner with someone (or join a group) for study and prayer, so I will be challenged in my Christian walk. *(Identify one or two potential mentors.)*

_____

_____

_____ ☐ **I will worship.** I will develop a habit of weekly worship in a congregation of believers, daily worship when I honor God in a scheduled time of prayer, and moments of worship when I see something that reminds me to praise God.

_____ ☐ **I will have a daily mini-Sabbath.** I will commit the *first fruits* of my day to a time of renewal by connecting with God through worship, prayer, Scripture reading, meditation, and/or journaling. (For ideas on how to have a mini-Sabbath, go to www.LifePurpose CoachingCenters.com/CM.)

_____ ☐ **I will find an accountability partner.** I will find an accountability partner and meet with her regularly. Knowing that I have to be honest and tell a trusted friend how I am doing with developing self-control will help me in those moments when I'm tempted to tell myself, "Just this once." I will give my accountability partner permission to reprove me when I slip up. (For a list of accountability questions to ask each other during your meetings, go to www.LifePurposeCoachingCenters.com/CM.) *(Identify potential accountability partners.)*

_____

_____ ☐ **I will work** on developing good habits by *(add your idea here)*

_____

_____

MASTER ACTION PLAN

Now, select only one major action step from this Day 5 exercise and record it on your Master Action Plan in appendix A on page 322. When you have finished reading this book, continue to refer to that one major action step on your Master Action Plan (as well as this Self-Control Action Plan, of course, as your season of life permits!). Remember, in order to become more like Christ in your character, you need to collaborate with God in three ways: preparation, prayer, and practice. You have done the work of preparation by learning God's truth about self-control. Now, internalize it by praying for the Holy Spirit's help and practicing your action steps, one by one.

SELF-CONTROL PRAYER

Precious Lord,

I'm not doing so well with my self-control. It seems like every time I turn around, I'm "blowing it" again. When I lose control, sin is evident or close on its heels. Help me pay special attention to the action steps I marked, concentrating on them not only this week for homework, but for a lifetime. Hear my request. Send me an accountability partner who will check in with me regularly for prayer and discussion about how I am doing. I need an extra measure of grace to help me implement this character trait into my life, and I am grateful you have already made that deposit in my spiritual bank account. Thank you.

In the name of Jesus, amen.

Chapter 5

Patience

Love is patient.

1 Corinthians 13:4

Waiting on God

I believe in the sun, even when it's not shining.
And I believe in love, even when I don't feel it.
I believe in God, even when he's silent.
Inscription on a wall in Nazi Germany

WELCOME BACK TO MY PLACE!

Hello! Come in ... but don't take off your sweater. I have a surprise for today's adventure that delves more deeply into your character reformation. I've packed a picnic and thought we would walk down my street to that park you keep admiring. I'll bring a blanket in case the picnic tables and benches are all taken. Does that sound like a plan? Before we head out, though, let's ask the Lord to join us on our outing:

Wonderful Counselor,

Go with us today as we investigate the topic of patience. You know that this character trait is not such an easy one for us to grasp. Greatly increase our awareness of what you want for us in this area of our lives. And thanks for being so patient with us.

Amen.

PATIENCE IS NOT MY STRONG SUIT

I think what wears down my patience the most is waiting in line at the bank, post office, or local coffee house. No ... wait a minute, I think what irritates me most is being put on hold by a computer repair person or utility company. No, I change my mind ... it's waiting for a waitress to bring a long-overdue meal. Do you see a pattern here? Basically, I hate disorganization or poor planning that inconveniences me, the all-important consumer.

Okay, before you panic that your Character Coach is hopelessly impatient, I will tell you that I've come a long way, baby! I still hate all those things, and it will never make sense to me why all companies don't hire efficiency-expert consultants to help them, but I can honestly say that what has helped me improve ever so gradually is that I now realize that God *expects* me to be patient. That little "aha" began to change my life. Hey, last Christmas, I even caught myself silently praying for those in a long line at a shopping mall—and I didn't even have the Christmas spirit yet! God is good. All the time.

PATIENCE IS WAITING

Patience is an outwardly displayed character quality that results from the inward character quality of self-control. In fact, Scripture directly links these two qualities together:

> *Knowing God leads to self-control. Self-control leads to patient endurance, and patient endurance leads to godliness.*
>
> 2 Peter 1:6 NLT

The Bible uses two different words for "patience." One refers to the patience of waiting under difficult circumstances, and the other is more of a long-suffering type of effort with difficult people. For today, we're going to concentrate on the first area: the one that will take us into the waiting . . . waiting . . . waiting room of patience.

THE BIBLE IS ALL ABOUT WAITING

So many of our Bible stories have an aspect of waiting in them. In fact, the Bible is all about waiting! See if you can spot a type of waiting on this chart that is close to your heart:

Waiting for healing	• Naaman waited for healing from leprosy (2 Kings 5). • A woman waited twelve years for healing from her bleeding (Mark 5:25). • Lazarus waited four days to be raised from the dead (John 11). • Paul waited in vain for relief from his "thorn in the flesh" (2 Corinthians 12:7).
Waiting to fulfill a vision	• David waited thirteen years to become king (2 Samuel 3:1; 5:4). • Nehemiah prayed for four months before approaching the king about rebuilding Jerusalem's walls (Nehemiah 1–2).

(cont.)

Waiting to start a ministry	• Moses waited and waited in the wilderness (Deuteronomy 31:2). • Jesus waited thirty years in a carpenter's shop (Luke 3:23). • The disciples waited ten days in the upper room (Acts 1–2). • Paul waited for years in exile until the Jews stopped fearing him (Galatians 1:18).
Waiting to be vindicated	• Noah waited for rain after being ridiculed for building a boat in a waterless land (Genesis 7). • Joseph waited in prison after being unjustly accused (Genesis 39–41). • Jesus' mother, Mary, waited for the Messiah to be made known when everyone assumed she was an adulteress (John 2:1–11).
Waiting to be rescued	• Joseph waited in a pit, then in a prison, and then in a famine-torn land (Genesis 37:24–28, 41:1). • Rahab waited on the Jericho wall (Joshua 2; 6:22). • Daniel waited in the lion's den (Daniel 6:16–24). • Jonah waited in the belly of a whale (Jonah 1:17). • Jesus' father, Joseph, waited with his wife and child in Egypt until it was safe to return to Nazareth (Matthew 2:13–15).
Waiting for a spouse	• Jacob waited and worked for fourteen years to marry Rachel (Genesis 29:20–30). • Ruth waited for Boaz (Ruth 3).
Waiting for children	• Abraham and Sarah waited for Isaac (Genesis 21:5). • Rachel waited for Joseph and Benjamin (Genesis 30:22). • Hannah waited for Samuel (1 Samuel 1). • Zechariah and Elizabeth waited for John the Baptist (Luke 1:18–25).

Were you able to find any examples of the types of waiting that you have experienced? You won't find many biblical characters who have not at some point had to wait for something in their lives. God's timetable is definitely different from ours, and the process of waiting is a God-ordained experience that he uses to prepare us for what he has in store.

WILDERNESS WAITING

Any type of waiting can turn into what is often called "waiting in the wilderness." Have you ever experienced wilderness waiting: an illness that isn't going away; a financial circumstance that is burying you; a family member who is rebelling; an unendurable job situation; or a dream that is turning to disappointment? When you're in a wilderness, it can seem like God has deserted you. You're confused, unsure of what to do next, and probably experiencing deep anguish in your soul. Let's see why God takes us through times of wilderness waiting.

Interestingly, times of wilderness waiting can occur after both terrible lows (crises or tragedies) or great highs (spiritual victories). For example, Moses went into his own personal time of wilderness after a crisis—he had just murdered someone and he fled to the mountains to hide for an entire season of his life. On the other hand, years later, he and the Israelites started their forty-year journey through the wilderness on the heels of two huge victories—the Passover and the parting of the Red Sea. In either case, once you're in a wilderness of waiting, you have two choices about how to respond—you can resist or you can relax.

You Can Resist the Wilderness

Wildernesses are not pleasant places! The natural reaction to finding yourself in the wilderness is to complain, get confused, and lose faith. But if you insist on resisting, and get mired in your bad attitude and selfish perspective, your resistance will make the wilderness experience that much more difficult, and possibly even more prolonged.

Complaining makes you more miserable. Why is it that the minute things get a little uncomfortable, we whine? Yes, the wilderness has its drawbacks. It's dry, barren, deserted, ugly, and there are no good sushi restaurants! But complaining about it only makes you feel more miserable. When the Israelites complained, they lost sight of their blessings.

> *"But now we have lost our appetite; we never see anything but this manna!"* ... [10]*Moses heard the people of every family wailing at the entrance to their tents.*

> Numbers 11:6, 10

Confusion leads to despair. You can also get confused in the wilderness. You may ask: Why did God allow this? Where did I go wrong? Why is this happening to me? Did I misunderstand God? Am I sinning? Am I not spiritual enough? Has God forgotten me? Does God even care? When you get confused, it's easy to despair and lose hope. Watch what happened to Israel when they despaired:

> *All the Israelites grumbled against Moses and Aaron, and the whole assembly said to them, "If only we had died in Egypt! Or in this wilderness!*

³Why is the LORD bringing us to this land only to let us fall by the sword? Our wives and children will be taken as plunder. Wouldn't it be better for us to go back to Egypt?"

Numbers 14:2–3

In their confusion, they actually considered going back to slavery in Egypt instead of proceeding to the Promised Land! What were they thinking? They had been promised a new home, but they wanted to return to their old hovels, their familiar surroundings. When the situation looks grim, don't look back and try to reclaim that from which God has delivered you.

Losing faith gets you stuck. God may be asking you to trust him and step out in faith, but if you refuse and lose sight of his power to overcome what you fear, you might never leave the wilderness. This is precisely what happened to a whole generation of Israelites whose fear not only trapped them on the wrong side of the Jordan, but eventually led to their death in the wilderness. They were prevented from going into the Promised Land because they believed the bad report of the spies and would not step out in faith.

"Not one of those who saw my glory and the signs I performed in Egypt and in the wilderness but who disobeyed me and tested me ten times—²³not one of them will ever see the land I promised on oath to their ancestors. No one who has treated me with contempt will ever see it."

Numbers 14:22–23

You Can Relax in the Wilderness

The alternative to resisting the wilderness is to relax in it. It may seem counterintuitive, but let's face it, what else is there to do in a dry and dreary land? Actually, once you decide to embrace the wilderness and match your pace to that of your surroundings, you open yourself up to what God wants to do for you in this place. And believe it or not, God can use the wilderness as a place of nurturing. There are three ways God nurtures us in the wilderness:

God meets you. The wilderness is not a place where great deeds are done for God. No, instead it's a place where God meets people. Consider these two examples: God followed Elijah to the wilderness, fed him, and whispered to him there. And Jesus himself regularly went to the wilderness when he wanted to commune with his Father.

Then there were the Israelites, who didn't conquer any cities or build any temples in the wilderness. They just did laps around Mount Sinai, and as they walked, God went with them. He fed them every morning, gave them water, guided them with a cloud, protected them at night, and spoke to them. He treated them with loving care as a measure of his affection for them, even though they usually just took it for granted. Theirs was not a lifestyle of achieving something new every day. Rather, the wilderness was where their major tasks were on hold and they got to know God in a deeper, more intimate way than ever before. The moral of the story: Relationships take time, and the wilderness is a great place to build a relationship with God.

God refreshes you. When you come out of a great crisis or descend from a spiritual mountaintop, you can be exhausted. Sometimes, in those instances, God ushers us right into the wilderness in order to give us a break, slow things down, give us space to restore our souls, or get back on our feet again. His waiting room forces us to stop so he can recharge our spiritual batteries.

But those who wait on the LORD shall renew their strength; they shall mount up with wings like eagles, they shall run and not be weary, they shall walk and not faint.

Isaiah 40:31 NKJV

God grows you. In the wilderness, something is going on that you rarely notice while it's happening, but it's one of the purposes of the waiting. God is growing something in you. He is trying to show you that he is more concerned with your character while you wait in the desert than in expediting the end of the situation. When Israel emerged from the wilderness, they were going to have a huge job to do: possess the Promised Land. But as their failed expedition with the spies proved (Numbers 13–14), their faith was very, very tiny. So, God took forty years to raise a new generation of Israelites who would trust him enough to step into the rushing Jordan River and conquer a city of supposed giants by marching around the walls of Jericho seven times.

I think that's why wilderness waiting takes longer than we think it should. Because God wants to prepare you for what's next after the wilderness, he needs to let you stay there long enough to grow your trust in him. It's like when a seed germinates and sprouts below the earth, long before there is any evidence of growth above the earth. If God knows you need to grow into an oak tree for your next challenge, he won't move you out of his wilderness hothouse if you've only just sprouted a tiny leaf. Oak trees take time to grow.

Journal

Let's study a few of those who had wilderness experiences. Choose one or two (or more if you have time) of the following Bible characters who spent time in the wilderness, and fill in the blanks:

	What crisis or victory happened beforehand?	How did God strengthen him/her in the wilderness?	What was the outcome of his/her time in the wilderness?
Moses Exodus 2:11 – 3:12			
Elijah 1 Kings 18:21 – 19:18			
Hagar Genesis 21:9 – 21			
Jesus Matthew 3:13 – 4:17			

If you are experiencing (or have experienced in the past) a wilderness wait, answer these questions for yourself:

What crisis or victory preceded your journey through the wilderness?

_____

_____

_____

_____

In what areas is God strengthening you (or has he strengthened you) through your time in the wilderness?

_____

_____

_____

_____

What are you praying will be the final outcome of this experience?

_____

_____

_____

_____

PRAYER

Precious Lord,

I wasn't sure I would ever say this, but thank you for the wilderness. I admit I've complained, despaired, and even lost faith during my time of waiting. But you've been patient with me. Thank you. Help me to keep waiting patiently, knowing that this quiet time is both healing and restorative, a time when you and I can just meet together and be together, without too many expectations. Thank you that while I wait, you are working in ways I cannot see, leaving me here as long as it takes to grow me into the oak tree I need to be for the next thing you have in store for me.

In the name of Jesus, amen.

Impatience: Exposing Your Inner Shrek

Seek first to understand, then to be understood.

Dale Carnegie, 1888–1955, author

A VIRTUAL MESSAGE

 NOTE: It's Day 2, so you have the option of listening to today's message by downloading it from my website, www.LifePurposeCoachingCenters.com/ CM, or reading the message text below. Enjoy the virtual coaching and don't forget to open in prayer!

THE FLIP SIDE OF PATIENCE

In *Shrek*, the 2001 animated movie, we meet the title character (voiced by Mike Myers), a big, green ogre, seething with impatience while on a mission to regain his swamp. In that now-classic tale, an obnoxiously annoying donkey (voiced by Eddie Murphy) attaches himself to Shrek for the journey. Being a prickly kind of guy, Shrek gets pretty irritated with Donkey, who tries to get too personal all the time. Take this conversation, for example:

SHREK: Ogres are like onions.
DONKEY: They stink?
SHREK: Yes ... no!
DONKEY: Oh, they make you cry.
SHREK: No.
DONKEY: Oh, you leave 'em out in the sun, they get all brown, start sproutin' little white hairs.
SHREK: NO! Layers. Onions have layers. Ogres have layers. Onions have layers. You get it? We both have layers.

DONKEY: Oh, you both have layers. Oh. You know, not everybody likes onions. But everybody like parfaits. Have you ever met a person, you say, "Let's get some parfait," they say, "No, I don't like no parfait"? Parfaits are delicious.

SHREK: NO! You dense, irritating, miniature beast of burden! Ogres are like onions! End of story. Bye-bye. See ya later.

DONKEY: Hey, what's your problem, Shrek? What you got against the whole world anyway, huh?

Some people are irritating like Donkey, and some people are irritable, like Shrek. What kinds of people trigger your impatience? An incompetent clerk? A cantankerous relative? A messy roommate? A boisterous child? A talkative airplane passenger? Or how about some of the more deeply frustrating relationships, such as an aging parent who is growing increasingly dependent and argumentative; a daughter who is making poor choices; a husband who is not willing to work on the marriage; a longtime neighbor with whom you have a serious disagreement. These difficult relationships are the breeding ground for impatience, which is a characteristic we can see in the life of Moses.

THE IMPATIENCE OF MOSES

Moses had a problem controlling his temper. Granted, he was working with a group of very irritating people. Nonetheless, he was prone to zing people when he got frustrated. In one particular example, you can just hear the impatience oozing from him as he deals with yet another round of complaints. Let's set the stage.

First off, his sister, Miriam, has just died, so he's emotionally depleted. Right on the heels of the burial, the Israelites ganged up on Moses and his brother Aaron to complain about not having any water. In Moses' defense, their timing was unfortunate. Plus, they ought to have known by now that God wouldn't let them go thirsty. But here they are complaining and playing the "Egypt card":

> *"Why did you bring [us] into this wilderness, that we and our livestock should die here? ⁵Why did you bring us up out of Egypt to this terrible place? It has no grain or figs, grapevines or pomegranates. And there is no water to drink!"*

> Numbers 20:4–5

Can't you just hear their whiny boo-hooing? Nevertheless, Moses and Aaron do the right thing. First, they pray about the complaint, and receive instructions from the Lord to speak to the rock and bring forth water. So, off they trot to speak to a rock! But by the time they get back to the people, Moses has had enough of their dissension. He not only calls them a name—in anger—but he hauls off and strikes the rock. Counting to ten to cool his anger was *not* his strong suit.

> *"Listen, you rebels, must we bring you water out of this rock?"* [11]*Then Moses raised his arm and struck the rock twice with his staff.*
>
> Numbers 20:10–11

Moses never got to enter the Promised Land because of that little eruption of impatient disobedience. God had clearly said: "Speak to the rock." He had not said: "If you happen to become really impatient, it's okay to strike the rock."

ANATOMY OF IMPATIENCE

How do you demonstrate your impatience? Here are some positive and negative ways Moses dealt with his impatience. Can you relate to any of these?

- *Do you stop and pray?* After Moses and Aaron had heard the complaints of the people, they "fell facedown, and the glory of the LORD appeared to them" (Numbers 20:6).
- *Do you blame and label the person who is irritating you?* Moses accused the Israelites: "Listen, you rebels ..." (v. 10), as if to say, "If you weren't such rebels, I wouldn't have to get impatient."
- *Do you feel sorry for yourself?* Moses asked, "Must we bring you water out of this rock?" (v. 10), as if to say, "I'm so fed up with all your demands, I can't take it anymore."
- *Do you hit or throw or shake something?* "Moses raised his arm and struck ..." (v. 11), as if to vent his frustration on an inanimate object.

If we were to dissect impatience, we would find that it's rooted in blocked desires. It rises to the surface most readily when someone disagrees with us (getting at our pride), when we don't get our own way (which is self-centeredness), when we're too tired or hungry (that's fallout from lack of self-control), and when we're oversensitive (that's back to ego).

How to Be Patient
with Irritating People

How do we deal with those people in our lives who just get on our nerves? Scripture tells us to give them understanding *and* give them a break.

Give Them Understanding

Those who are patient have great understanding, but the quick-tempered display folly.

Proverbs 14:29

The people with whom we get most impatient are those we don't understand. Can you relate? For instance, I found myself getting irritated with a noisy child, until I figured out he suffers from some type of disorder. Once I understood a little more about the child's situation, I was embarassed at my impatience. I also recall dealing with a sales clerk who was so slow in responding that I wondered why they hired her. But when I found out she was worried about her mother in the hospital, my irritation dissipated.

Here are some reasons that misunderstandings crop up between people:

You think you can figure out someone else's motives. You can't.

No one can know what anyone else is really thinking except that person alone.

1 Corinthians 2:11 NLT

You think someone's words mean the same thing you would mean if you said them. They don't. In the English language, for example, five hundred of the most common words have an average of twenty-eight different meanings each. People don't always mean the same thing, even when they use the same words.

The more you understand, the more patient you become. In order to really understand someone else, the first order of business is to stop assuming you understand them! You can't know others' motives until they reveal them, and you can't know what they mean until they clarify them. There are two steps to understanding people better: (1) Ask clarifying questions, such as: What did you mean by that? How are you feeling? Is there something else you're wanting me to hear? What do you need from me right now? Why do you feel that way? (2) Listen to the answers. Really listen. Don't speak before the other person has had a chance to clarify his or her motives and meaning.

To answer before listening—that is folly and shame.

Proverbs 18:13

Once you understand the other person better through clarifying and listening, go to the next level and try to put yourself in that person's place. When your perspective is one-sided—your side—it's easy to be impatient. Try mentally changing places, and look at things from the other person's perspective—it will do wonders for your patience.

Give Them a Break

Be patient with each other, making allowance for each other's faults because of your love.

Ephesians 4:2 NLT

Sometimes people simply have a bad day; they are just not at their best for whatever reason. Perhaps they don't feel well, or they lost their job, or their bank account is overdrawn, or their washing machine overflowed. Realize two things:

You have bad days too, and God accepts you.

I was shown mercy so that in me, the worst of sinners, Christ Jesus might display his immense patience.

1 Timothy 1:16

When you stop to think about it, God has had to exhibit far more patience with you over your lifetime than you have to show to the person you're irritated with at the moment. Think of what you're like on your bad days; then give them a break.

Sometimes good relationships need good ignoring.

A person's wisdom yields patience; it is to one's glory to overlook an offense.

Proverbs 19:11

Don't pick up on every little thing that someone does wrong. Let some things slide. Overlook an insult. Don't keep a record of wrongs done.

Journal

Thinking of times you get impatient with people, rank yourself on a scale of 1–5 in each area, with 1 indicating you rarely use the noted response and 5 indicating you frequently use that response.

Rarely Use		Frequently Use			
1	2	3	4	5	When I feel impatient, I try to remember that I probably don't know the person's motives.
1	2	3	4	5	When I feel impatient, I try to assume that I probably don't know what the person means.
1	2	3	4	5	When I feel impatient, I seek first to understand.
1	2	3	4	5	When I feel impatient, I ask clarifying questions.
1	2	3	4	5	When I feel impatient, I listen before I speak.
1	2	3	4	5	When I feel impatient, I give the person a break.
1	2	3	4	5	When I feel impatient, I remember God accepts me.
1	2	3	4	5	When I feel impatient, I ignore small insults.

What one response do you need to work on the most? Why?

PRAYER

Precious Lord,

Thank you for showing me patience, even on my bad days. In the Bible's "love chapter" (1 Corinthians 13), patience ranks first on the list of how to love, so if I want to love people better, I'll need more patience. Help me seek to understand those who irritate me. Help me to clarify their motives and their meanings. Help me to stop assuming that when everyone finally grows up, they will be just like me. Help me not to be so judgmental toward people who disagree with me. Remind me, Lord, that I am not always right about everything. Teach me to be gracious to people who ignore me, disapprove of me, or hurt me, even when I think it was done deliberately. I want to lighten up, show more love, and give to others the patience you have so generously shown to me.

In the name of Jesus, amen.

How to Slow Down

Whoever is in a hurry shows that the thing
he is about is too big for him.
Lord Chesterfield, 1694–1773, British statesman

YOU'VE GOT MAIL

To:	"The Best You" Woman	Sent:	Day 3
From:	Katie Brazelton		
Subject:	Patience		

It's Day 3, so here is your weekly Email Message. Feel free to blog me a response at my website, www.LifePurposeCoachingCenters.com/CM, if you'd like. Enjoy the email-coaching and don't forget to open in prayer!

THE LANGUAGE OF OUR LIFESTYLE

I couldn't say it any better than Rick Warren did in a sermon a few years back: You *leap out* of bed, *zip* in and out of the shower, *bolt* down your breakfast, *gulp* down your coffee, and *rush* off to work. Your boss tells you to *hustle* on that report, *get in gear* on those changes, and *step on it* to complete that project. You *dash out* to lunch where you *wolf* down a sandwich, *hurry* back to the office, *dash off* some emails, *whip* through your voice mails, and *get cracking* on those assignments. At five, you *hotfoot* it out of there, *race* home in *rush-hour* traffic, and *dart* in the front door. You *throw* dinner on the table, *run* through everyone's report about their day, *scramble* to get the kids to their lessons, and *fall* into bed after doing *instant* messaging and paying some bills on *Quicken*®. And at night you pray, "Lord, I need patience, and I need it now!"

Our culture has certainly coined a lot of words to describe hurry! We can be harried-sounding when it comes to our pace of life. What does it take to get our foot off the accelerator, slooooooow down, and keep from impatiently pushing our way through life? For Lisa, it took a catastrophe.

LISA'S MULTITASKING

Lisa's catastrophe was caused by multitasking. As a special birthday treat for her husband, she thought she'd try recreating one of those deep-fried onions, such as you would find as an appetizer at some steak restaurants. She didn't own a deep fryer, so she poured half of a bottle of oil into a fry pan, set the plastic jug next to the stove, and turned on the burner. Lisa says, "Now, being the queen of multitasking, I couldn't just stand there waiting for the oil to heat up, could I? I had too much I needed to do . . . I mean, good grief, we women can do the laundry, make a scrapbook, write thank-you notes, clean the bathrooms, and wipe a nose in the time it takes for the oil to heat up, right?" She went upstairs for a quick minute to make a dent in a work project she had going and, of course, she lost track of time. When the smoke alarm went off, she ran downstairs to find flames as high as the upper cabinets. Her efforts to extinguish the blaze only made things worse, and she got burned badly, especially on her right arm. The fire department came, but not before the kitchen was destroyed and smoke damage pervaded the entire house.

In the aftermath of the fire, Lisa went through extensive treatments and therapy, and she required help with the simplest of functions, such as dressing, getting a glass of water, and holding a fork. She had to learn a whole new pace of life, a change that required an intense dose of patience, especially for the driven multitasker she was. Just prior to the fire, Lisa and her husband had bought this house that was proving to be too big, and then she made some career moves that were too demanding. The stress of over-commitment combined with her forced slowdown triggered a major time of surrender for Lisa. She realized she had been going too fast, jumping into decisions too quickly, trying to do too much on too many fronts, and not going deep enough with her husband, children, and ministry. A year after the fire, after much soul-searching and surrender, Lisa left the corporate world, downsized their home, and now heads up women's ministries at her church with a much more peaceful attitude.

Has your multitasking ever gotten you into trouble? Do you get moving so fast you lose track of where you're going? We need to learn to slow down, breathe deep, and develop a lifestyle of patience, calm, serenity . . . What?!

Do we even know what those words mean anymore? We're more likely to specialize in activities like *Jumping the Gun* and *Indulging Pet Peeves*.

JUMPING THE GUN

Lisa made a few impulsive decisions that she regretted. Has that ever happened to you? You took a job that wasn't right for you? Enrolled in a course that took too much time away from your family? Tried to solve a problem only to make it worse? Committed to a debt you couldn't afford? Sometimes, our impatience to get moving sucks us into Jumping the Gun. Jumping the Gun is what we do when delays are making us nervous or the decision isn't clear. We get antsy and feel like we should be making something happen. We rush to fill gaps, make snap decisions, or go with what feels good. The motto of Jumping the Gun could be, "Don't just stand there; do something —anything!" Instead, we should adopt the opposite tactic when faced with this temptation.

"Don't Just Do Something; Stand There!"

Be still before the LORD and wait patiently for him; do not fret.

Psalm 37:7

In Genesis 15 God promised Abraham that he would have numberless descendents, more than the stars in the heavens. But how could that happen when he and his wife, Sarah, were childless and getting on in years? Not a problem for Sarah, being the take-charge woman that she was. According to Genesis 16, she decided to speed up the process by setting up a surrogate arrangement between Abraham and her servant Hagar, who gave birth to Ishmael. Sarah subscribed to the "Don't just stand there; do something!" school of decision-making.

Usually, though, when God delays, we're better off to adopt an upside-down approach: "Don't just do something; stand there!" Delays and road-blocks are often there for a reason. Use the delay to pray. Don't steamroller over the roadblock. Invite God to stand there with you and learn not to make a move until he releases you to do so.

Another strategy to keep you from jumping the gun is counting the cost.

Count the Cost

But don't begin until you count the cost.

Luke 14:28 LB

Most likely, Sarah didn't think through what her decision might cost her. After Ishmael's birth, Sarah blamed Abraham for going along with her plan (he should have known she would!). Hagar and Sarah were locked in bitter jealousy, and the feud of the mothers was passed down to their sons, a fight that continues to this day between the Arabs and Jews.

Scripture says, "Count the cost." In the case of Sarah's jumping ahead to take care of God's promise, it caused relational breakdowns, marital discord, family rifts, living arrangement issues, and jealousy. We should not commit to a course of action without thoroughly thinking through the possible ramifications.

The last way to keep from jumping the gun is to evaluate whether or not you're in a state of confusion about your course of action.

God Is Not a God of Confusion

For God is not the author of confusion, but of peace.

1 Corinthians 14:33 NKJV

Try reflecting on your course of action before forging ahead.

- Feeling confused?
- Receiving conflicting advice?
- You and your husband don't agree?

Our first impulse to act can sometimes be seriously flawed, and it is waiting that clarifies what we should do. Consider the illustration from *God's Little Devotional Book for Women* (Honor Books, 2001) about the speedboat driver who was involved in a serious accident. Thrown from her seat and propelled so deeply into the water that she could not see any light from the surface, she had no idea which direction was up. But rather than panic, the woman remained calm and waited for the buoyancy of her life vest to begin pulling her up. Then she swam in that direction.

If you're panicking and thinking you don't have peace about a decision, just pause, ponder, and pray. Follow the old adage: "When there's confusion, we wait." Wait for God's gentle tug that pulls you closer to him. The wait could take a few minutes, hours, or even months, but the tug will come — clarity will come out of the chaos.

Patient people stop before they Jump the Gun, and they rely on God. Patient people also go slow enough to love others along the way, so they're less likely to Indulge Their Pet Peeves.

INDULGING YOUR PET PEEVES

Impatient people tend to let certain things peeve them or *get to them* instantaneously. Pet peeves are really nothing more than minor, unannounced inconveniences and annoyances that are beyond our control. These irritations block our agenda, causing us to get easily irked. The more impatient you are, the more pet peeves you will notice in your life, and the more willing you are to indulge them—to give in to being agitated by them.

Oh yes, I admit that I have had my fair share of peeves over the years and that they have at times been allowed to reign supreme in my life! My pet peeves would most commonly erupt whenever I felt overly tired, hungry, or cold; or my expectations got blocked; or I was frustrated by something beyond my control. Here are just a few things that can still get my goat:

- Losing my keys
- Tight waistbands
- Dirty dishes in the sink
- Teenagers' messy bedrooms
- All telemarketers
- School magazine drives (*Not ... I repeat ... not Girl Scout cookie sales drives! Bring 'em on.*)
- Traffic getting out of the church parking lot
- Charities that I'm not sure are legitimate, knocking at my door
- Neighborhood rock 'n' roll groups rehearsing their music in a nearby garage

In her book *Parent Warrior* (Victor Books, 1993), Karen Scalf Linamen told this story of a young mom who was instructing her five-year-old in patience. "Kaitlyn," she said, "you have to learn to be patient. If you don't, it'll cause you problems all your life."

"You don't understand," Kaitlyn sincerely replied. "It's like I have twenty *patiences*. And when they're gone, they're gone!"

Do you have so many pet peeves on any given day that you use up all your *patiences* before lunch? The secret to not indulging them is to learn to let go of your agenda, your preferences, and your expectations—yes, at a moment's notice—so you can sail more selflessly through a frustrating circumstance. We just make ourselves miserable when we insist on grabbing all the happiness of heaven right here on earth right now. Learn to see your pet peeves as God's reminder signals—his little nudges to get you to love someone who doesn't deserve it, to do something kind, to learn patience, or (if all else fails) to get you to talk to him about your attitude!

[Love is] never haughty or selfish or rude. Love does not demand its own way. It is not irritable or touchy. It does not hold grudges and will hardly even notice when others do it wrong.

1 Corinthians 13:5 LB

Journal

"Don't Just Do Something; Stand There!"

Be still before the LORD and wait patiently for him; do not fret.

Psalm 37:7

How does this verse help you have an attitude of rest instead of Jumping the Gun?

_____

_____

_____

Count the Cost

But don't begin until you count the cost.

Luke 14:28 LB

Are there any decisions you have made where you Jumped the Gun and did not count the cost? What happened as a result?

_____

_____

_____

God Is Not a God of Confusion

For God is not the author of confusion, but of peace.

1 Corinthians 14:33 NKJV

How does this verse help you in making decisions?

_____

_____

Indulging Pet Peeves

[Love is] never haughty or selfish or rude. Love does not demand its own way. It is not irritable or touchy. It does not hold grudges and will hardly even notice when others do it wrong.

1 Corinthians 13:5 LB

What are some of your favorite pet peeves? How can this verse help you deal with them?

_____

_____

_____

PRAYER

Precious Lord,

When I read Lisa's story of multitasking, I think, "There but for the grace of God go I!" Thank you so much for protecting me from my own catastrophic results during the many times I have been trying to do too much too fast. Please continue to protect me. I don't want to hurt people because of my impatient lifestyle. And help me not to Jump the Gun. When I encounter roadblocks, give me the patience to just stand there; I invite you to stand there with me. When I am facing a decision, help me to count the cost and not move ahead until you have given me peace. And help me not to Indulge My Pet Peeves, but to show patience and love when things irritate me. Slow me down; give me a spirit of calm, and yes, even serenity.

In the name of Jesus, amen.

Your Patience Coach

Bumper Sticker:
A man without patience is like a car without brakes.

PERSPECTIVE-CHANGING OUTING

It's a beautiful day for a nature walk in the local mountains. We amble slowly into the redwoods on a well-maintained path, our footsteps crunching on the bark. As we go, we leave civilization behind and start to speak in hushed tones, as if not to disturb nature with our voices. Light filters down on us in holy beams. Birds twitter, leaves rustle, and we drink in the invigorating scent of pine, bark, and leaves. We finally come to the little clearing I had in mind, and we settle on a fallen log, silent together as we whisper a private prayer and savor nature's cathedral. Looking down, we see why we came here. At our feet sprout tiny, miniature redwood trees, bravely peeking above the soil. These little living buds remind us of the purpose of God's waiting room. It's where he shelters us, feeds us, and gives us time and protection to grow strong enough to withstand storms and fires—and to flourish.

Today we're going to step it up a notch with a patience reality check. We've been learning about the patience it takes to wait in the wilderness, to understand people, and to slow down. Now, we're going to see how you're doing in *extreme* tests of patience: patience when the wilderness remains silent; patience when we just can't wait; and patience when people won't change.

PATIENCE WHEN THE WILDERNESS REMAINS SILENT

Often, in the wilderness, the only result we get from all our prayers is God's silence, which can be rather unnerving. Sometimes, God is silent because he is quietly waiting until we're ready for his answer. And he might not necessarily be waiting to give us exactly what we asked for; he may be waiting to give us more than we could ever imagine!

Let's recall how this worked for Mary and Martha in John 11:1–44. When Jesus received word about the illness of their brother, his friend Lazarus, he purposely delayed going to heal him. He remained silent throughout the final throes of Lazarus' illness, death, and burial. He even stayed silent for four more days after that. When Jesus finally showed up, Mary and Martha were heartbroken and questioned him about not healing their brother. I love how Henry Blackaby and coauthor Claude King portray Jesus' response in their book *Experiencing God* (Broadman and Holman, 1994):

> If I had come when you asked me to, you know that I could have healed him because you have seen me heal many, many times. But, you would have never known any more about me than you already know. I knew that you were ready for a greater revelation of me. I wanted you to know that I am the resurrection and the life. My refusal and my silence was not rejection. It was an opportunity for me to disclose to you more of me than you have ever known.

Describe the most revolutionary personal discovery you have made about God. You might begin with a sentence something like this: "I discovered God wasn't like my earthly dad when ..." or "I experienced God's direct leading when ..." or "God did a miracle in my life by ...."

_____

_____

_____

Describe a time you were most disappointed in God, because it felt like he was being silent. For what specific thing(s) were you praying at the time?

_____

_____

_____

Have there been any connections for you between the silences of God and your discoveries about God or his best intentions for you?

_____

_____

_____

"These things I plan won't happen right away. Slowly, steadily, surely, the time approaches when the vision will be fulfilled. If it seems slow, do not despair, for these things will surely come to pass. Just be patient! They will not be overdue a single day!"

Habakkuk 2:3 LB

How does this passage make you feel about your wilderness experience?

_____

_____

PATIENCE WHEN WE JUST CAN'T WAIT

Many people don't know how to wait anymore. We shift from line to line at the grocery store to keep from waiting. We dread pauses in a conversation. We honk if a car in front of us delays a little at a green light. We strap the mattress to the top of our Jetta instead of waiting for the delivery truck the next day. We get the flat-screen television on a buy-now, pay-later plan. And if a certain friend doesn't have email (which must be a cardinal sin!), forget it—who wants to find paper, an envelope, and a stamp, and wait days for the letter to be delivered?

In order to be a good wait-er, we need to get our theology straight. Those who are good at waiting are those who are convinced that God will provide, that he is on schedule, and that he is in control.

God Will Provide

One person in the Bible who couldn't wait was Esau. He was so hungry he gave his birthright to his brother in exchange for a bowl of stew. Esau thought at the time he was going to "die from hunger," so his need for instant gratification cost him heavily (see Genesis 25:29–34).

The obvious lesson here is to not make life-altering decisions on an empty stomach! Or, better yet, I think what we can gather from Esau's mistake is that we should not let our natural desires drive us to meet our own needs, independent of the provision that God is ready to offer us. The irony of Esau's story is that he wasn't going to have to go hungry for very long. His food was on the stove, simmering. He just didn't have the willpower to wait for the proper mealtime.

I wait expectantly, trusting God to help, for he has promised.

Psalm 130:5 LB

"I am the Lord; no one who waits for my help will be disappointed."

Isaiah 49:23 GNT

What is a genuine need you have that you don't think you can wait for? How do these Scriptures apply to your impatience?

_____

_____

_____

God Is on Schedule

There's also the story of King Saul, who got nervous when the prophet Samuel failed to show up on time to offer a sacrifice to the Lord, so Saul went ahead and prepared his own burnt offerings. Samuel later admonished Saul for not following the Lord's command, warning the king that his impatience was an act of presumption and disobedience that would cost him his crown (see 1 Samuel 13:5–14).

God makes everything happen at the right time.

Ecclesiastes 3:11 CEV

In what situations have you felt like God was late? In what ways are you tempted to be presumptuous and do things yourself? How does this verse help you be patient at times like that?

_____

_____

_____

God Is in Control

Recall Scripture's account of the giving of the Ten Commandments, when Aaron was waiting below Mount Sinai for Moses to return to camp. Well, time started to drag and the people complained (surprise, surprise). Convincing Aaron that Moses was never coming back, the Israelites wore him down to the point that he finally made a golden calf to take God's place (see Exodus 32:1–6). Moral of the story: If you've gotta wait, try not to listen to ungodly counsel.

Entrust your ways to the LORD. Trust him, and he will act on your behalf.

Psalm 37:5 GWT

But as for me, I watch in hope for the LORD, I wait for God my Savior; my God will hear me.

Micah 7:7

Was there a time when you thought God had lost control of the situation? How did you feel during that time? How can these Scriptures give you patience during such times?

_____

_____

_____

PATIENCE WHEN PEOPLE WON'T CHANGE

Some people are never going to change for the good. Think about such a person in your life while completing the following exercise. Mark the place on each scale that reflects how you most frequently interact with that person.

I am irritable   I am accepting
1   2   3   4   5   6   7   8   9   10

I get more intense   I back off
1   2   3   4   5   6   7   8   9   10

I exhibit impatience   I exhibit patience
1   2   3   4   5   6   7   8   9   10

I am rigid in my expectations   I have flexible expectations
1   2   3   4   5   6   7   8   9   10

I get pushy   I am relaxed
1   2   3   4   5   6   7   8   9   10

I smother with affection   I give affection occasionally
1   2   3   4   5   6   7   8   9   10

I try to control   I offer advice when asked
1   2   3   4   5   6   7   8   9   10

I have a tendency to exasperate him/her   I am encouraging
1   2   3   4   5   6   7   8   9   10

I am rules-oriented   I am grace-oriented
1   2   3   4   5   6   7   8   9   10

I express strong beliefs and principles						I allow for differing opinions			
1	2	3	4	5	6	7	8	9	10

I put on pressure						I let God have space to work			
1	2	3	4	5	6	7	8	9	10

I expect behavior like mine						I encourage individuality			
1	2	3	4	5	6	7	8	9	10

I feel miserable when I think about him/her						I let go and move on			
1	2	3	4	5	6	7	8	9	10

From this quiz, what was the most revealing scale for you and why?

_____

_____

_____

PRAYER

Precious Lord,

Thank you for the discoveries I have made about you during my life. Thank you for your silences, and how they have prepared me to receive a new truth or enter into a new experience with you. Help me to grow up, Lord, in the area of waiting patiently. Sometimes I can be like a child who wants what she wants when she wants it, but I want to grow beyond that stage. Help me not to jump ahead of your provision, not to be presumptuous when I think you're late, and not to take over when I think you've lost control.

I want to pray now about my situation with an unchangeable person. Father, tell me, am I the unchangeable person in this relationship? I pray that you would help me to look honestly at how I have been dealing with this person. Show me where I can back off, lighten up, show more grace, and frankly, be more like you are with me. I release this person to you, as I stayed focused on you.

In the name of Jesus, amen.

Steps to Patience

Have patience with all things, but chiefly have patience with yourself.
Do not lose courage in considering your own imperfections,
but instantly set about remedying them — every day begin the task anew.
Francis de Sales, 1567-1622, bishop of Geneva

SITTING QUIETLY WITH YOUR MAKER

Today is a time of reflection and solitude for you in the privacy of your own quiet-time space. You will be putting together a Patience Action Plan. It's your private day to work on developing patience in the wilderness, patience in relationships, and patience every day.

Ask yourself how deeply you are able to focus on increasing your patience during this season of your life. Then select the appropriate action steps on pages 204–207, whatever you feel you can realistically experiment with this week. It's your plan, your life, and your prayerful decision — nobody else's. If you feel God impressing on you to concentrate on your patience right now, go for these exercises with gusto — without further ado or delay! I am confident that whatever effort you are able to devote to improving your patience will be richly rewarded by him on earth and in heaven.

Patience Action Plan

PRAYER FOCUS: Shift the focus of your prayers from asking for a solution to your problems to asking God to meet you in a deeper way. Pray, "Lord, I am waiting on you." Pray for people with whom you tend to be impatient. Consider especially including all your family members, since it can be hard to be patient with those to whom you are supposed to be closest. Pray for their blessing and pray that God will give you a new understanding of them. Pray specifically for everyday patience. That's one of the scariest prayers ever!

DEVOTIONAL FOCUS: Choose one of the following Scripture passages on the topic of patience: To focus on *patience in the wilderness*, read about the four-month waiting experience of Nehemiah (Nehemiah 1:1–2:8) to see what the young visionary did during God's silence. To focus on *patience in relationships*, read 1 Corinthians 13 and think about why patience is first on the list of characteristics talking about love. To focus on *everyday patience*, read Romans 8:28 and apply it to the things that make you impatient during the day.

EXTRA PERSPECTIVE: Read John Ortberg's excellent book on how to love difficult people, called *Everybody's Normal Till You Get to Know Them*. Or get creative and walk in somebody else's shoes for a few hours—someone whose life role calls for patience (i.e., shadow a kindergarten teacher, caregiver of an elderly person, receptionist, or sight-impaired individual).

Action Steps: Developing Patience in the Wilderness

Instructions: Prayerfully choose one or two action steps to experiment with this week.

Start Date

_____ ☐ **I will make an encouragement card** to read whenever I need it. On one side I'll write out what I'm waiting for or struggling with. On the other, I'll write the text of Isaiah 64:4: "Since ancient times no one has heard, no ear has perceived, no eye has seen any God besides you, who acts on behalf of those who wait for him."

_____ ☐ **I will change my pace.** I will try to get more rest and allow myself more recreation. I will think about whether or not God may want me to change my pace permanently.

_____ ☐ **I will meet God outdoors.** I will find somewhere in nature to have a special time of reading my Bible, praying, singing, and journaling. If it's too hot or too cold to be outdoors, I will park my car at a scenic place and look at the scenery from inside a cozy getaway.

_____ ☐ **I will pray in a new way.** I will find a way to refresh my connection with God. I will choose a new place in which to pray (i.e., my children's bedroom when they are at school, a nearby hill, on my porch). I will adopt a new body position for prayer — open hands, kneeling, face down, standing, looking up. I will sing my prayers and read my prayers directly from Scripture. I will pray out loud and write out my prayers.

_____ ☐ **I will keep a wilderness record.** Every day during a wilderness time, I will write down three things: a prayer, one thing I am thankful for, and one way I saw God that day. This is my record that God is with me and working for my good, even though it may not feel like it. I will look for and expect connections between what I prayed for and what God is actually doing.

_____ ☐ **I will develop** patience in the wilderness by *(add your idea here)*

_____

_____

Action Steps: Developing Patience in Relationships

Instructions: Prayerfully choose one or two action steps to experiment with this week.

Start Date

_____ ☐ **I will get to know someone.** Because I am habitually impatient with a few people, I will find out their top three interests and their top three pet peeves. I will see if I can learn what irritates them, what has hurt them in the past, and what makes them happy and fills them with passionate purpose. *(Identify two people you will get to know.)*

_____

_____ ☐ **I will pray.** During conversations when I am feeling impatient, I will send up quick prayers for the other person, including prayers for their blessing and for joy to come to them during their day.

_____ ☐ **I will listen.** Patient people listen; impatient people interrupt. I will try not to interrupt during any of my conversations. I will allow others to speak more than me. I will ask questions that indicate an interest in the other person, and then listen to their complete answer, following up with more questions instead of my own story.

_____ ☐ **I will be flexible.** Rigid people tend to be more impatient than flexible people so I will find one area in which I am typically rigid, such as being on time, or how the dishwasher is loaded, or where things belong, or what people eat, and try relaxing on that issue for an entire week. At first it will probably be stressful, but I will stick with the exercise and watch how the people around me react when I am consistently not showing impatience about that issue. _(Identify one area in which you will be more flexible.)_

_____

_____

_____ ☐ **I will be interruptible.** I will view interruptions as divine appointments. I will put down what I'm doing, look the interrupter in the eyes, and be welcoming. (If interruptions are a frustration for you because they keep you from getting everything done, then add a few items called "Unknown Interruption" to your to-do list, so that you can rejoice with each one you get to check off!)

_____ ☐ **I will develop** patience in my relationships by _(add your idea here)_

_____

_____

_____

Action Steps: Developing Everyday Patience

Instructions: Prayerfully choose one or two action steps to experiment with this week.

Start Date

_____ ☐ **I will practice waiting.** Purposely choose the longer line at the grocery store or the slower lane on the freeway. (Okay … just try it a few times, or at a minimum, don't plow mindlessly past people and cars to avoid waiting!) I will consciously breathe deeply while waiting, slow down my pulse rate, and mentally engage with what is going on around me. I will look at the people near me, and even though I don't know them, I will pray about the things God brings to mind for them.

_____ ☐ **I will practice going slower.** I will eat my meals more slowly — actually chewing my food thoroughly and really tasting it. I will start things with more grace by talking to God for the first thirty seconds of everything I do (i.e., driving, meeting, cooking, studying, playing a board game, or even taking a nap). I will be more relaxed when I say hello to someone — focus on people's arrival; give eye contact; genuinely ask about them before moving on to whatever task is at hand. I will adopt a slower pace to say good-bye to people — give a hug, give a blessing, say a prayer together.

_____ ☐ **I will practice being there.** I will stop multitasking. When I'm talking on the phone, I won't answer emails — focusing on the person with whom I'm speaking. When I'm having a conversation, I won't watch television or do any other activity; instead, I will give the person direct eye contact and keep my hands still. When I'm driving, I won't change radio channels constantly — choosing silence or a soothing station, so I can look around me and thank God for whatever beauty I see.

_____ ☐ **I will be serene.** I will memorize 1 Peter 3:4 (NLT): "You should be known for the beauty that comes from within, the unfading beauty of a gentle and quiet spirit, which is so precious to God." I will repeat it whenever I feel impatient. I will ask God to transform me into a woman marked by peace and serenity.

_____ ☐ **I will develop** everyday patience by *(add your idea here)*

_____

_____

_____

_____

MASTER ACTION PLAN

Now, select only one major action step from this Day 5 exercise and record it on your Master Action Plan in appendix A on page 322. When you have finished reading this book, continue to refer to that one major action step on your Master Action Plan (as well as this Patience Action Plan, of course, as your season of life permits!). Remember, in order to become more like Christ in your character, you need to collaborate with God in three ways: preparation, prayer, and practice. You have done the work of preparation by learning God's truth about patience. Now, internalize it by praying for the Holy Spirit's help and practicing your action steps, one by one.

PATIENCE PRAYER

Precious Lord,

I sit before you humbled that you have always been patient with me. After all, you know how often I've moved forward spiritually only to take my eyes off you ... time and time again. Yet, you always wait patiently for me to look toward you once more. I want you to be my role model in this do-over of my character, especially my patience! I marvel at how patient you were when you were wrongly accused, beaten nearly to death, and sent to the cross to die. Thank you for having such enormous patience, even during the worst of situations. It's well past time that I ask you for some of your patience to rub off on me. Thank you in advance for continuing to help me.

In the name of Jesus, amen.

PART 4

The Making of a Right Relationship to Things

Chapter 6

Contentment

I know what it is to be in need, and I know what it is to have plenty.
I have learned the secret of being content in any and every situation,
whether well fed or hungry, whether living in plenty or in want.

Philippians 4:12

Thanking God

Contentment makes poor men rich;
discontentment makes rich men poor.
Benjamin Franklin, early American statesman

WELCOME BACK TO MY PLACE!

I would love for us to meet in my "tidy" office today—the one I actually invite clients into, not the messy one with the closed door! (Talk about major makeover needed—don't venture behind any woman's closed door, right?!) I love the desk in the clean office; it's from India where they weren't afraid to add blue and green paint tones and old-world stenciling. You get the leather chair with the footstool, so you can kick up your feet and relax to the hilt. I'll take this lattice-woven chair across from you. You had mentioned that you would like to learn to pray aloud more, so why don't you voice our prayer today:

King of All,
  We bow before you to tell you that we adore you. Forgive us for any discontentment that might be blocking your abundant blessings from our lives. Even though it's a little scary, we ask for your honest insight into our character during this coaching session. We thank you for being everything we need.
                                            Amen.

Thank you for praying. I think we are ready to cover today's topic: contentment.

A COACH WHO HAD WANING CONTENTMENT ISSUES

I used to say, "Life doesn't get any better than this" in regard to my utter joy in eating a meatloaf sandwich with mustard! That luncheon specialty must remind me of my mom's cooking or something, because I really enjoy one of those delightful feasts. But one day at work many years ago, just after I had said those very words about a sandwich I had ordered in (and as I was still wiping the mustard from the sides of my mouth), a florist delivered a bouquet of roses for one of my coworkers. It was literally the size of her large desk! I stood in the hallway gawking at the gorgeous arrangement as it floated down the corridor, and out of my mouth I heard these words: "Well, maybe there is something better than a meatloaf sandwich with mustard!" How quick was that shift in my loyalty and contentment!

CONTENTMENT: WHY IS IT SO ELUSIVE?

Here's a fascinating comment from John Gardner in his book *Self-Renewal: The Individual and the Innovative Society* (W. W. Norton & Company, 1981): "If happiness could be found in having material things and in being able to indulge yourself in things you consider pleasurable, then we ... would be deliriously happy. We would be telling one another frequently of our unparalleled bliss, rather than trading anti-depressant prescriptions." So, if contentment can't be found in material blessings, where can it be found?

That's a great question that I know is only confounded by our own unreasonably high expectations of what it means to be happy. Have you ever felt duped by the fairy tales that built such high expectations into us from the time we were little girls? Granted, we all grew up and realized that the odds were high we might not experience a romantic, "happily-ever-after" rescue by Prince Charming on his white horse. Yet I see rampant evidence these days of a "fairy tale mentality" which tells us, "If I can get _____ perfect, I will live happily ever after," then we fill in the blank with things like:

- **Perfect beauty:** There is a newly diagnosed addiction called body dimorphic disorder; it's an addiction to plastic surgery due to a never-ending dissatisfaction with one's appearance.
- **Perfect body:** Our cultural glorification of thinness, combined with poor self-esteem or a psychological need for control, drives an increasing number of women to anorexia, bulimia, laxative abuse, diet pill abuse, or exercise addiction.
- **Perfect house:** Some women are perpetually cleaning, arranging, decorating, redecorating, overspending, and underenjoying their homes in their quest for the perfect house.

- **Perfect children:** Many mothers push their unwilling children into overinvolvement in dance, theater, music, academics, or athletics, subconsciously trying to realize their own dreams through their children.

The Paradox of Our Age

"We spend more but have less; we buy more but enjoy it less; we have more conveniences, yet less time; more leisure and less fun; we have more knowledge but less judgment; we have more gadgets but less satisfaction; more medicine, yet less wellness. We spend too recklessly; laugh too little; drive too fast; get angry too quickly; stay up too late; get up too tired; read too little; watch TV too much, pray too seldom.

"We have multiplied our possessions, but reduced our values; we talk too much, love too little and lie too often. We've learned to rush, but not to wait; we have more parties, but less fun; more acquaintances, but fewer friends. These are times of fancier houses, but broken homes; higher incomes, but lower morals. We've learned how to make a living, but not a life; we've added years to life, not life to our years" (Bob Moorehead, *Words Aptly Spoken*, Kirkland, Wash.: Overlake Christian Bookstore, 1995).

The Truth about Contentment

Should it really be that hard to be content? Eve was not contented—and she lived in paradise; some of the angels were not contented—and they lived in heaven; King Solomon thought life was a waste—and he was the most wildly wealthy, indulged, powerful man of his day. So we can safely say that ideal circumstances, heavenly mansions, and extravagant possessions don't produce contentment. According to the apostle Paul, contentment is not earned; it's *learned*:

> *I have learned to be content whatever the circumstances.* ^{12}*I know what it is to be in need, and I know what it is to have plenty. I have learned the secret of being content in any and every situation, whether well fed or hungry, whether living in plenty or in want.* ^{13}*I can do all this through him who gives me strength.*

Philippians 4:11–13

Any one of us can be content, because contentment is a state of satisfaction that is *independent* of circumstances, and we learn contentment by trusting in Christ, who gives us strength. So, you may ask: Are you telling me my house doesn't have to be organized before I can be content? That's right. And my kids don't have to be successfully employed before I can be content? You bet. And I don't have to wait until we're on a Hawaiian island before I can sigh in contentment? Well ... that does sound awfully nice, but it's true, you can sigh in contentment right where you are. Well, what about the tough situations, like my financial loss? Can I be content after that? Certainly. Is contentment conceivable sitting by a hospital bed? Absolutely. Is it possible to be content if my child has a learning disability, or if I struggle with infertility, or if I lose my husband? Yes, it's possible—and attainable. Contentment is a sense of satisfaction in God that doesn't go away because of what you lack, how you're hurt, or where you're stuck.

I don't want you to think I am saying that contentment is complacency. Complacency says, "Don't bug me; I'm just fine where I am." And, let's go one step further and say that contentment is also not fatalism, which says "I'm trapped" or "Why try?" or "It's no use." That kind of thinking does not line up with the "holy discontent" that comes when God is perfecting us or moving us to make a difference in the world. Fatalistic thinking can also talk us out of listening when the Holy Spirit is convicting us. Don't stay stuck in a stagnant place of no growth, or a dangerous situation, by chalking it up to "I'm just being content." No, no, no!

Contentment is also not denial. There are some women who overspiritualize their problems and live in denial of their very real wounds. That's not healthy, and that's not being content. Real contentment is perspective. It is the perspective that says, "God knows my pain, and he knows my needs. God is a pain-healer and a need-meeter. He has been faithful to take care of me in the past. He will take care of my todays. He will keep his promises in my tomorrows. I can trust his voice and follow his guidance."

THE PRACTICE OF CONTENTMENT: THANKFULNESS

When you're struggling with being content, try being thankful. It's the best way to practice contentment when you don't feel content. If anyone has ever known how to be thankful in dire circumstance, it's—you guessed it—the apostle Paul. He seemed to delight in finding impossible situations in which to be thankful. With memories of imprisonment, shipwrecks, beatings, and hunger fresh on his mind, Paul wrote:

- **Give thanks for what you have:** "Always giving thanks to God the Father for everything" (Ephesians 5:20).
- **Give thanks for what occupies your time during the day:** "And in all you do, give thanks to God the Father" (Colossians 3:17 NCV).
- **Give thanks for your circumstances:** "Rejoice always, pray continually, give thanks in all circumstances; for this is God's will for you in Christ Jesus" (1 Thessalonians 5:16–18).

That pretty much covers everything, doesn't it? There is not much I can think of that is *not* included in that list. And thankfulness is not conditional. Paul doesn't give us an "out" to be ungrateful when we don't get what we want, when we're feeling unfulfilled in our work, or when our circumstances are painful. We're just supposed to give thanks, because thankfulness signals to God that we trust him completely, even when life doesn't make sense. And in that moment, when you have found some way to thank God or express your trust in him, you can truly say with contentment, "Life doesn't get any better than this."

Journal

Use the following categories to make lists of things for which you are thankful. (You may need to get creative in a category where you have experienced pain or where you are currently struggling with contentment. Ask God to show you some genuine ways you can thank him for that difficulty, or simply express your trust that you will be able to thank him in the future.)

I am thankful for the following things in my ...

Family:

_____

_____

Marital state (whether I'm married or single):

_____

_____

State of motherhood (whether I have my own children, or nieces, nephews, students, or neighbor's children in my life):

_____

_____

Occupation:

_____

_____

Home:

_____

_____

Hobby:

_____

_____

Health:

_____

_____

Church:

_____

_____

Friendships:

_____

_____

Possessions:

_____

_____

Imagine that you must choose between a million dollars and contentment. Which would you choose and why? (Don't cheat and say: "Well, if I had a mil, I'd be content!")

_____

_____

PRAYER

Precious Lord,

THANK YOU! Thank you that contentment is the realization of how much I already have. (Go back through today's journal and thank God specifically for each thing you listed.) *As I pray through the lists I have just made, I thank you for each blessing you have given me, even the ones for which I had to get creative. Please fill me afresh with the realization of how much I already have. Life doesn't get any better than this.*

In the name of Jesus, amen.

Envy: Exposing Your Inner Veruca Salt

What makes us discontented with our condition
is the absurdly exaggerated idea
we have of the happiness of others.
French proverb

Lots of people know a good thing the minute
the other fellow sees it first.
Charlie "Tremendous" Jones, motivational speaker

A VIRTUAL MESSAGE

 NOTE: It's Day 2, so you have the option of listening to today's message by downloading it from my website, www.LifePurposeCoachingCenters.com/ CM, or reading the message text below. Enjoy the virtual coaching and don't forget to open in prayer!

THE FLIP SIDE OF CONTENTMENT

I secretly relate to Veruca Salt, the self-centered girl who was never satisfied in *Willy Wonka and the Chocolate Factory*, when she sings, "I want the works/I want the whole works/Presents and prizes and sweets and surprises/Of all shapes and sizes/And now/Don't care how/I want it now." And, please don't tell me that you haven't hummed that tune at times in the quiet of your own soul! We women do tend to want *the works*, especially if someone else got the works first. If you see another person's good fortune and Veruca's song starts up in your mind, you've got envy, my friend.

> Greed, jealousy and envy are akin to each other.
> Greed wants more. Jealousy hoards what it already has.
> But envy wants to have what someone else possesses.

Charles Swindoll, pastor, author

ENVY IN SHELLEY'S WEEK

During the week we were writing this chapter, Shelley had her own run-in with envy! Read about it in her words:

Let me begin with this: When our children were little, one of my pet peeves was when they whined, "That's not faaaair!" whenever one of them got to lick the icing bowl and the other only got the spoon and beaters, or one got to play outside but the other had to stay in and do homework. It became a mission of mine to stamp out those words from their vocabulary. So, my husband and I had them memorize Romans 12:16, "Rejoice with those who rejoice, and weep with those who weep," and we chanted that verse whenever they slipped into rejoicing over a brother's pain, or weeping about a sister's good fortune.

Sounds good, doesn't it? Fast forward to this past week.

Envy Episode #1: Monday we took muffins to the new young couple moving in across the street, and they showed me all the work they're doing on their house. They've got to be *at least* twenty years younger than me, and they are doing all the renovating that *I've* been wishing for. She's getting the carpet I want, the swimming pool I'll never get, even the deep kitchen sink I want that could actually fit my frying pan in flat. That's *so* not fair.

Envy Episode #2: This gorgeous friend of mine is getting her already beautiful teeth straightened with those invisible braces. Well, *I* want straight white teeth without unsightly braces, so Tuesday I marched into my orthodontist's office, figuring he'd give me a great discount since I'm already paying him to fix four of my five kids' teeth! But, *no*. Invisible teeth straightening will cost more than carpet for my entire house! Plus, I have absolutely no health reason to justify braces. Phooey. There's nothing fair about that.

Envy Episode #3: On Wednesday, I saw a coworker wearing the exact green shoes for which I've been shopping. Six months I've been looking for that shade of green! I dashed to the store, but *of course* they don't have the green shoes anymore, nor do any of their other locations within a fifty-mile radius. That is *beyond* not fair. That's a shoe travesty. I told her I was green with envy.

I don't know about you, but I can certainly relate to Shelley's week! I am embarrassed to admit how often I have envied someone's house, appearance, or accessories! Envy is defined as "a feeling of discontent and resentment aroused by the desire to have the possessions or qualities or success of another." Is this your battle?

We humans are prone to envy. In fact, envy is such a common, pervasive problem that God started and ended the Ten Commandments on this critical theme:

- **Commandment #1:** "You shall have no other gods before me" (Exodus 20:3).
- **Commandment #10:** "You shall not covet your neighbor's house. You shall not covet your neighbor's wife, or his male or female servant, his ox or donkey, or anything that belongs to your neighbor" (Exodus 20:17).

You may not have a problem coveting oxen or donkeys, but how about your neighbor's SUV or convertible? Your neighbor may not have maidservants to covet, but what about her house cleaning service? Do you imagine that your neighbor's marriage is what you want for yourself? If you have broken the tenth commandment by envying what your neighbor has, chances are pretty good that you may have also broken the first commandment and made that thing a god. For example, if you covet your friend's career success, it may be best to investigate what related idol (money, recognition, travel, freedom, clothes, creative outlet, affirmation, perceived value, or power) is a craving in your life.

ENVY'S HALLMARKS

In case you're not sure if you have the envy bug, here are a few hallmarks of envy for which you can be on the lookout: making comparisons, being ego-driven, and coveting what others have.

Envy's Favorite Sport: The Comparison Game

Whenever you catch yourself comparing your lot in life to someone else's, watch out! Envy could be brewing. When you compare and fret about something lacking in your life, you may be tempted to say, along with Shelley, "I didn't get what she got—that's not fair!" Or, when you compare, you could begin to feel boastful that you did, indeed, come out ahead. In that case you're saying, "She doesn't have what I have—la-de-da!" Pride is the evil sister of envy, and both are germinated in the soil of comparison.

The comparison game is divisive. When you want what someone else has, it puts a wedge between you and that person. Just look at what happened between two friends, Saul and David. When King Saul heard the comparison between David and himself (as put to music: "Saul has slain his thousands, and David his ten thousands"), his searing envy ignited an all-out manhunt that capsized their friendship and lasted thirteen long years (1 Samuel 18).

How do you stop the comparison game? Try Romans 12:15 (NASB): "Rejoice with those who rejoice." Why is it so much easier to do the rest of this verse—"and weep with those who weep"? Oh sure, if my girlfriend gains ten pounds, I can weep with the best of them. But if she *loses* ten pound, it's a little harder to "rejoice with those who rejoice."

Envy's Ego-Driven Bumper Sticker: "It's All About Me"

Here's how envy would sum up her life philosophy on a bumper sticker: "It's all about me." Envy is definitely ego-driven. But what happens when your ego gets all that attention it wants? Instead of feeling confident, you start feeling insecure—literally afraid that you can't keep up the facade. The "it's all about me" person tries to prove herself to other people, and in doing so, she only reinforces a feeling of inferiority.

When my eyes are looking inward, I can't simultaneously look outward. So an inward focus keeps me from focusing on the needs of others, the worth of others, or even the sufficiency of Christ. This is dramatically illustrated in the story of Joseph's jealous brothers, who watched their father, Jacob, lavish Joseph with attention, praise, and favor. Imagine the damage to the brothers' self-esteem to have to compete for their father's love. Their envy of Joseph fed their anger, and eventually, it led to the plot to eliminate Joseph from the family (Genesis 37).

What's the cure for the "it's all about me" disease? Love others. First Corinthians 13:4 says that love "does not envy." You see, love cancels out envy. Envy is inward-focused; love is outward-focused. Love gets your eyes off yourself and onto someone else. If Joseph's brothers had chosen to love him (the object of their envy), they might have even gained the very thing they desired most—their father's approval. It is important to realize that often what you really long for when you envy someone is not the things the other person has but what those things represent—affection, approval, acclaim, affirmation, accolades. These are all image-driven needs, which envy is trying desperately to meet.

Envy's Theme Song: "I Want It All"

Veruca Salt's rendition of "I Want It All" reminds me of Aesop's fable entitled "The Dog and the Shadow." In that story, a dog is carrying a piece of meat in his mouth while he crosses over a brook. He looks down and sees his own reflection in the water. Thinking it is another dog with another piece of meat, he decides that he also wants what that dog has. So he snaps at the shadow in the water, but as he opens his mouth, his piece of meat drops into the water and is lost. The moral of the story: If you covet all, you may lose all.

The grasping of envy can cost you what you already have. Take Adam and Eve, for example. They were given only one rule in their paradise: Do not eat the fruit of the tree of the knowledge of good and evil. But Satan got them to focus on the one thing they couldn't have, and they risked everything they did have. When Eve reached out for that fruit, she was deciding to reach for something of God's that she didn't have—God's knowledge about evil. She knew about good, but up until then, there was no evil in Eden. So her decision to become like God and learn about evil ushered in the very thing she probably would not have chosen, had she known. The result was that Adam and Eve were banished from the garden. They got the apple, but they lost Eden.

Will your envy cost you the very things you most treasure? The cure for the "I want it all" syndrome is a thinking adjustment. Try these "thinking steps" to get you from the *state of wanting* to the *practice of trusting*:

1. God is *able* to give me anything I ask.

"I am the LORD, the God of the whole human race. Is anything too hard for me?"

Jeremiah 32:27

2. So, I ask.

You do not have because you do not ask God.

James 4:2

3. Now, there are three possibilities that can occur:

- If I get it, it's because God knows it would be good for me to have.

  "How much more will your Father in heaven give good gifts to those who ask him!"

  Matthew 7:11

- If I don't get it, it's because God knows it wouldn't be good for me to have.

  Every good and perfect gift is from above, coming down from the Father of the heavenly lights, who does not change like shifting shadows.

  James 1:17

- If I get something different, it's because God knows what I need better than I do.

  "As the heavens are higher than the earth, so are my ways higher than your ways and my thoughts than your thoughts."

  Isaiah 55:9

4. So, I can trust God to give me what I need.

And my God will meet all your needs according to the riches of his glory in Christ Jesus.

Philippians 4:19

ENVY BUSTERS

To recap, if you are marked by any of the hallmarks of envy—playing the comparison game, saying "It's all about me," or singing "I want it all" —remember these envy busters: (1) If you are caught up in comparing yourself to others, try rejoicing with those who rejoice. (2) If you feel insecure to the point of needing to get attention, try focusing on others by loving them. (3) If you are grasping for so much that you stand to lose what you really value, try a thinking adjustment and trust God to give you what you really need.

Journal

If you are playing the "That's Not Fair" comparison game, what do you find yourself comparing most frequently? And, what is one way you can "rejoice with those who rejoice" in this regard?

_____

_____

_____

BONUS QUESTION: What is the underlying need you have that causes you to compare (i.e., a need for approval, affirmation, credit, or respect that the other person is getting instead of you)?

_____

_____

_____

If you have the "It's All about Me" disease, in what area are you feeling inferior? What is one way you can get your attention off yourself when you're feeling ego-driven?

_____

_____

_____

BONUS QUESTION: What is the underlying issue you have that causes you to be insecure (i.e., low self-esteem, fear of abandonment, need for acceptance)?

_____

_____

_____

If you are caught in the "I Want It All" syndrome, refer back to the "thinking steps" and identify where you may be stuck (i.e., "I don't believe God is able"; "I don't ask"; "I don't usually understand what happens as God answers"; or "I don't trust God to give me what I need").

_____

_____

_____

BONUS QUESTION: What is the underlying reason that causes you to want what others have (i.e., fear of the future; ungrateful for what you do have; pent-up anger at the cards you've been dealt in life; tired of sharing)?

_____

_____

_____

PRAYER

Precious Lord,

Forgive me for acting like Veruca Salt sometimes when I demand, "I want the works/I want it now." Only you can supply all my needs and wants, Lord. So, the next time I feel inadequate in comparison to my coworker or jealous of someone's good fortune, remind me that getting what they have will not increase my trust in you. You know the deeper needs, wants, issues, and reasons beneath my envy. Only you can help me feel the respect I wish I had when I'm envious of my coworker's promotion. Only you can give me the affirmation that I think would come with a nicer house. Only you can reassure me that I am desirable when I wish I had a different body. Help me to start receiving your provision for my true, underlying needs by rejoicing with others, loving others, and trusting you.

In the name of Jesus, amen.

How to Have Joy and Peace

To experience happiness we must train ourselves to live in this moment,
to savor it for what it is, not running ahead in anticipation
of some future date nor lagging behind in the paralysis of the past.
Luci Swindoll, author, speaker

The mother of excess is not joy but joylessness.
Friedrich Nietzsche, 1844–1900, German philosopher

YOU'VE GOT MAIL

To:	"The Best You" Woman	Sent: **Day 3**
From:	Katie Brazelton	
Subject:	Contentment	

It's Day 3, so here is your weekly Email Message. Feel free to blog me a response at my website, www.LifePurposeCoachingCenters.com/CM, if you'd like. Enjoy the email-coaching and don't forget to open in prayer!

THE PARTNERS OF CONTENTMENT

Ironically, amusement parks are often places of great discontentment. It seems as if the more rides you take a child on, the less satisfied he gets. Pretty soon, he doesn't even say, "That was fun!" anymore. He just bounces off at the end and asks, "What's next?" Then he wants cotton candy and money for the arcade games, as if a seventy-five dollar admission to the happiest place on earth wasn't enough for one day!

Now, let's imagine an ideal (obviously make-believe!) child going through the same experience with contentment. He jumps off a roller coaster and says, "Wow! I just want to sit here for a minute and remember that ride. It was so much fun!" When he passes the cotton candy vendor he says, "That reminds me — I sure enjoyed those snacks you brought today." At the arcade, he remarks, "It seems silly to waste more money on those games when the rides are so much more fun."

That is a great, but highly unlikely, picture of contentment. The contented child in the amusement park savors each experience and is not driven by some inner demon to get to the next ride and the next ride, without ever really enjoying the ride he's on. He has *joy*. Plus, he is grateful for what he receives and is not demanding or anxious when he sees something he has not received. He doesn't fear that there is more fun or more satisfaction in what other kids have than in what he has. He has *peace*. Joy and peace are the partners of contentment — when one shows up, the other shows up too.

CHRIS:
AN UNLIKELY EXAMPLE OF CONTENTMENT

Chris does not live the typical life that we would assume one needs to have in order to be content. Chris was diagnosed with multiple sclerosis in 1981 when she was in her late twenties, and within a year, this young mother of three was in a wheelchair. From day to day, her symptoms are unpredictable and ugly. One day she might have to deal with seizures. Another day, she is unable to feed herself. At another time, she might be unable to open her eyelids, which triggers the fear that she's losing her eyesight.

How did Chris, like Paul, learn to be content in whatever state she's in? Chris likes to say, "I have MS — MS doesn't have me." She has learned to draw the fine line between contentment and compliance. Contentment accepts what she can and cannot do, but compliance caves in and lets the disease rule her life. Compliance is when Chris gave in to frustration because other people had to do the little things for her children that she wished she could do herself. But in her contentment she found things she could still do for her children, such as giving them hugs and cheering their successes. Compliance is when she feels sorry for herself, which happens at times, certainly. But contentment is when she seeks to be controlled by thankfulness instead of grief. If she gave in to compliance, she would give up completely on all her dreams for her life. But contentment defines a "new normal," one in which she adjusts her dreams and plans for the future, and rejoices in the fact that she does have a future!

Chris has a friend with MS who is *not* content. While Chris was enjoying the fact that she was still able to hug her children, he was reading incessantly about MS and getting more and more negative in his outlook. When she planned a family trip to Disney World, he tried to talk her out of going, saying "How can you enjoy anything from a wheelchair?" While she was doing her leg exercises in hopes of restoring some usefulness to her muscles, he had settled into his chair and given up trying. While she was persisting in being a wife and mother, he had given up on living.

Chris credits her contentment to her trust in God. "Today I have the courage to face new challenges and try new things, getting out of my comfort zone, because I know in whose hands my life is, and I trust him completely. I am determined to enjoy life and be as active as I can be. Because of the ways God has cared for me in the past, and knowing that I am his, I can face today and all that comes with it."

Chris's story shows us that contentment is not a lifestyle but a choice; and it is up to us whether or not we will allow our contentment to be stolen from us by wishful thinking or feeling sorry for ourselves.

JOY THIEF: THE DAILY DRUDGE

There is a joy thief called *The Daily Drudge* lurking, threatening to steal your joy. This thief saps the meaning out of your life and makes your daily duties feel like a chore. To some degree, everyone has drudge in their days. The administrative assistant has filing. The teacher has grading. The doctor has charting. The lawyer has briefings. The athlete has training. The musician has practicing. The computer technician has ... um, uh ... I don't think many of us can explain what the computer technician has! But, I do know that the homemaker has housecleaning, and I love what this mom tried:

> One mother of young children, tired of feeling insignificant, decided to prove to her husband that what she did mattered by simply not doing it for one whole day. "What happened here today?" he asked when he walked into a kitchen strewn with dirty dishes, half-eaten sandwiches, and spilled cereal. Sitting on a couch amid the clutter of toys and newspapers, she replied, "You're always asking me what I do all day, so I decided not to do it" (Elisa Morgan and Carol Kuykendall, *What Every Mom Needs*, Grand Rapids, Mich.: Zondervan, 1995).

Now, I'm not advocating going on strike, even though some days that would feel downright delightful. I'm simply pointing out that everyone has to deal with activities that are draining, demotivating, or dull. If you start to focus on the dullness and the drudgery, it will zap your joy! If, instead, you see your work as a holy calling, not a daily grind, you'll rediscover the joy and meaning in your tasks.

> *Whatever you do, work at it with all your heart, as though you were working for the Lord and not for people.*
>
> Colossians 3:23 GNT

PEACE THIEF: THE GREENER GRASS

In addition to the joy thief, there is also a peace thief called *The Greener Grass.* This thief tries to keep you unsettled with restless ambition, feeling unsatisfied, never able to enjoy what you're doing now. This thief uses the words "if only" (and other dastardly phrases with the same meaning) to get you to put your contentment on hold until certain conditions are met. Do any of these expressions sound familiar? "I would be happy if only ..." or "I can't wait until ..." or "I'll be fulfilled when ..." or "It will be much better after ..."?

What are you and I waiting for? Must we continually put off contentment until we have attained a particular achievement? Look over these clusters of statements, and see how The Greener Grass can keep you from being content in each season of your life:

The Career Season

"I can't wait until I finish my degree and get a good job."
 She doesn't appreciate a student lifestyle. She endures school and graduates.

"I'll be fulfilled when I have achieved my career goals."
 Her great salary somehow doesn't satisfy. And now her job is frustrating.

"If only I could get a promotion, I'd be happy."

The Marriage Season

"I'll be fulfilled when I find a husband."
She gets married. Reality hits.

"I would be happy if my husband were different."
She tries to change him. He withdraws.

"If only I was more attractive, he'd love me more."

The Motherhood Season

"I'll be happy after we have our first baby."
She has a baby. Three years later ...

"If only my child would obey."
She feels inadequate as a mother, so she escapes into her hobbies. Five years later ...

"I can't wait until my kids grow up."

If you have found yourself caught in a cycle of dissatisfaction in your season of life, guess what? Two things are true: (1) You are not alone; we all do it. (2) You are missing the journey; we all have! Don't wait until you reach your next goal to let yourself be content. Remind yourself that it does not take a particular status or thing or person or achievement before you "earn" contentment.

King Solomon, despite his vast wealth, struggled with being content. He came to the conclusion that the only source of contentment is God's gift of being able to do some good with your life and knowing that your work was worth it.

> *I know that there is nothing better for people than to be happy and to do good while they live.* [13]*That each of them may eat and drink, and find satisfaction in all their toil—this is the gift of God.*
>
> Ecclesiastes 3:12–13

Don't skim over the fact that this is a gift from God. Imagine that God is holding out the gift of contentment to you right now. He's not waiting for you to have "arrived"—it's there for the taking right this minute. Receive his contentment in the climb. Delight in today's adventure. Savor the struggle of now. Don't wait until you get to the next ride to celebrate or relax. When you hop off the roller coaster, just sit there for a while and say, "Wow! That was fun!"

Journal

Are you bored with your life, struggling to see any meaning or find joy in your daily tasks? Are you perpetually on hold, waiting to reach the next stage before you feel content? Describe an area in your life where you need more joy, peace, or contentment.

_____

_____

_____

Here is one of our key contentment passages again:

> *I have learned to be content whatever the circumstances.* [12] *I know what it is to be in need, and I know what it is to have plenty. I have learned the secret of being content in any and every situation, whether well fed or hungry, whether living in plenty or in want.* [13] *I can do all this through him who gives me strength.*
>
> Philippians 4:11–13

Rewrite Philippians 4:11–13 in your own words, filling in your situation when the passage references "things" or "everything."

Example: *I have learned to be satisfied with the town we have moved to and the fact that we had to move before Jesse's senior year. I know how to live when I don't like the town, and I know how to live when I love my home. I have learned the secret of being happy, whenever and wherever I move. I can be content in this move through Christ, because he gives me strength.*

_____

_____

_____

_____

_____

PRAYER

Precious Lord,

I sure feel assaulted sometimes by joy thieves and peace thieves. I'm missing out on the joy in my daily chores, because I'm not doing them as if I'm working for you. I'm missing out on the peace in my journey, because I'm not receiving your gift of satisfaction in the milestones. Instead, I'm scrambling from ride to ride, anxious about what I might be missing, thinking everyone else must be having a better time than me. Help me to just sit down for a minute, look at where I have just come from, and say to you: "Thanks for that ride. That one was really great. I got on; I held on for dear life; I screamed; I made it to the end; and I have a fun photo to prove it." I claim your gift of contentment, right now.

In the name of Jesus, amen.

Your Contentment Coach

*If I find in myself desires which nothing in this world can satisfy,
the only logical explanation is that I was made for another world.*
C. S. Lewis, 1898–1963, author, scholar

PERSPECTIVE-CHANGING OUTING

Today you and I are going to meet in a place that might give us some real evidence of what contentment looks like — the modest living room of my Bible Study leader, Sally. She welcomes us at her front door and shows us inside. When you say, "What an inviting room!" Sally doesn't get embarrassed and point out that she doesn't have any curtains hung yet. She shows us to comfy chairs and brings in the tea, but she doesn't apologize for the chipped saucer. She just pours the tea, and we chat about her memories of the grandmother who left her a few pieces of treasured china. When her young daughter interrupts us, she doesn't get irritated. She pulls her onto her lap for a minute, gives her child her full attention, and then reminds her firmly that she is to be helping Daddy in the garage. As her daughter skips off, we catch each other's eyes, enjoying the tender moment that just happened. Well, so far, Sally has passed our contentment test with flying colors.

Let's dig a little deeper now and check on her contentment close up!

How Content Are You with What You Have?

Choose rather to want less, than to have more.

Thomas à Kempis, 1380–1471, Dutch monk and author

I ask Sally: "How content are you with what you have?"

She replies: "I look around at the furniture we've acquired. I look at the pictures on the walls and the decorative touches we've added. I think about things in our closets and kitchen and garage (way too much stuff in that garage!). Then, I just pause and thank God for all we have. I thank him for those basics that are easy to overlook, such as our water heater that allows us to have hot showers and our screen door that keeps out bugs. I thank him for our insulation that keeps us warm in the winter and our medicine chest full of vitamins and remedies. I thank him for our telephone, so we can receive calls from telemarketers during dinner ... okay, maybe not that. I thank him for those things that took a long time to get, but now we might be taking for granted, such as our minivan to haul the children (and neighbor's children!) around. I don't know if I'm content because I'm blessed, or if I'm more blessed because I'm content."

Then Sally says, "Enjoy the living room for your coaching session. I'm heading to the garage to help my family give away what we don't need anymore! Bye."

So, let's read this passage together as our opening prayer, and then launch into our important discussion about how content you are with what you have:

> *Since we entered the world penniless and will leave it penniless, ⁸if we have bread on the table and shoes on our feet, that's enough. ⁹But if it's only money [we're] after, [we'll] self-destruct in no time. ¹⁰Lust for money brings trouble and nothing but trouble. Going down that path, some lose their footing in the faith completely and live to regret it bitterly ever after.*
>
> 1 Timothy 6:7–10 MSG

1. If you were able to sit on God's knee and tell him all the things you are wishing for right now, what would be on your list? (Use the space at the top of page 236.) Be exhaustive, not shy. Remember, God knows the desires of your heart already. Include anything physical you want, and don't forget services like getting your hair colored or hiring a housekeeper. Trust me on this for a moment, rather than trying to figure out what the purpose of the exercise is, okay? Don't sneak a peek ahead!

----

2. Now, review your list and place an "N" next to items that represent genuine needs and a "W" next to items that are wants. What do you observe about your list when you identify your needs versus your wants? (By the way, I will never forget the day in 1991 that a woman-friend was talking about her needs versus wants as a single mother trying to raise three teenage boys in a small condo. I looked at her like she was speaking a foreign language. My brow was furrowed and my mouth was turned up at the corners in utter confusion. The concept was ludicrous to me. I had only known the mind-set of "You want it; you get it." I just thought you should know how shocked I was when I was first introduced to this idea!)

3. Finally, circle the items that seem to be causing you anxiety, conflict, or envy. If you are sacrificing peace of mind, forfeiting relationships, forgoing giving to others, or focusing your thoughts and energy on those things, then they could be enslaving you.

How Content Are You with What You Do?

Any child who is anxious to mow the lawn is too young to do it.
Charlie "Tremendous" Jones

Have you ever noticed how attractive an activity looks, until you actually have to do it day after day? For example, did you ever run for a position in student government, only to find out you had to make a lot of posters, but not a lot of decisions? Did you yearn to get pregnant without taking into account the brain-fuzzing, nerve-jangling ordeal that a colicky, sleepless newborn can put you through? How about that dream job you applied for, not realizing how much of your day you'd be sitting at a desk?

No matter whether the activities of your day energize you or irritate you, fascinate you or frustrate you, you can be content in what you do by changing why you do them, and for whom you do them.

Whatever you do, work at it with all your heart, as though you were working for the Lord and not for people.

Colossians 3:23 GNT

1. In the past week, what are some things you did that were meaningful or fun? What was it about those activities that made them fulfilling? Describe your state of contentment or discontentment during those activities.

_____

_____

_____

2. In the past week, what are some things you did that were monotonous or irritating? What is it about that type of activity that you do not enjoy? Describe your state of contentment or discontent during those activities.

_____

_____

_____

3. What percentage of your week is meaningful, and what percentage is monotonous?

Meaningful: _____%   Monotonous: _____%

How do you feel about your answer? What can you do to transform your monotonous activities into meaningful ones?

_____

_____

_____

HOW CONTENT ARE YOU WITH WHAT HAPPENS?

> Happy the man who can endure the highest
> and the lowest fortune. He who has endured such changeability
> with calmness has deprived misfortune of its power.
>
> **Marcus Annaeus Seneca, 4 BC – 65 AD,**
> **Roman statesman, philosopher**

Have you experienced misfortune in your life? Sometimes, the very thing that causes your pain can be the greatest trigger of contentment in your life. Suppose, for instance, that you had a financial reversal and had to sell your furniture and eat off packing crates. How do you think you would feel about your first table and chairs after that? You might enjoy the simple pleasure of eating at a table far more than you ever did before the crates, right? Or, say you went through a time of illness during which you lost your hair and were violently ill. Afterward, wouldn't you be far more grateful than ever for little things like eyebrows and keeping down breakfast?

We can see how loss would trigger contentment after the fact, when the loss is restored. But what about when the pain is still fresh and the loss is too real? Are we expected to experience contentment right away? Read this prayer of thanksgiving that the English minister Matthew Henry (1662 – 1714) prayed when his wallet was stolen:

I thank Thee first because I was never robbed before;
second, because although they took my purse they did not take my life;
third, because although they took my all, it was not much;
and fourth because it was I who was robbed, and not I who robbed.

1. Could you have prayed that prayer if you were robbed? Think of a minor or major catastrophe you have experienced this month (choose anything from your toddler pouring honey on your sofa, to you backing the car into a fire hydrant, to getting bad news from the doctor) and write down two or three things you could have been thankful for right away.

---

2. Describe an ongoing circumstance in which you feel discontented. This could be a financial, social, medical, or self-image issue; marital concern; relocation; tragic death; painful addiction; or childhood memory. Write down two or three things to be thankful for about that situation.

_____

_____

_____

3. How does it feel to focus on the positive side of this circumstance? Do you need to make an overall shift in the way you talk about this situation, moving from negative to positive?

_____

_____

_____

Want more assessment questions on contentment? Go to www.LifePurposeCoachingCenters.com/CM.

PRAYER

Precious Lord,

I have been going through my days whining about things I have no right to be upset about. I have become a slave to some things that I have been wanting. But you have given so much to me. You have met my physical needs and taken care of so many of my wants too. Thank you for all I have; I release to you my anxiety over the things I don't have. I also want to confess my griping about some of the dailyness of my days. You have given me meaningful work, yet I lose perspective and focus on the drudgery. Increase my contentment by helping me work as if I'm working for you. And finally, Lord, my circumstance has been such that I felt I had a right to complain. Heal me of resentment and worry in this situation, and help me to trust you and to stop dragging down myself and others by the way I speak about it. Reveal to me new things I can be thankful for in this situation; and I thank you right now for the things I already thought of today.

In the name of Jesus, amen.

Steps to Contentment

Contentment is not the fulfillment of what you want,
but the realization of how much you already have.
Author unknown

SITTING QUIETLY WITH YOUR MAKER

Today is a time of reflection and solitude for you in the privacy of your own quiet-time space. You will be putting together a Contentment Action Plan. I am your biggest cheerleader in this area. Dig down! Action steps for this week are built on your attitudes, thoughts, and emotions: ideas for developing an attitude of thankfulness, ideas for developing a mind of peace, and ideas for developing a heart of joy.

Ask yourself how deeply you are able to focus on increasing your contentment during this season of your life. Then select the appropriate action steps on pages 241–243, whatever you feel you can realistically experiment with this week. It's your plan, your life, and your prayerful decision—nobody else's. If you feel God impressing on you to concentrate on your contentment right now, go for these exercises with gusto—without further ado or delay! I am confident that whatever effort you are able to devote to improving your contentment will be richly rewarded by him on earth and in heaven.

Contentment Action Plan

PRAYER FOCUS: Make prayer your first activity in the morning when you wake up. Immediately give God your day, your self, your schedule, and your concerns. Pray daily during one of your regular tasks, such as your commute, your walk, or putting on your makeup. Spend that time thanking God for as many things as you can recall. Pray a rejoicing psalm daily, such as Psalm 98, 100, or 103 — to focus on God's power, protection, and provision.

DEVOTIONAL FOCUS: Choose one of the following Scripture passages on the topic of contentment: To focus on *developing an attitude of thankfulness*, read the "thankful" passages — Ephesians 5:20, Philippians 4:6 – 7, and 1 Thessalonians 5:16 – 18. To focus on *developing a mind of peace*, read Psalm 34 to discover how God is all you need. To focus on *developing a heart of joy*, read Philippians 4:4 – 19 to delve into the practices of a joyful person.

EXTRA PERSPECTIVE: Read *Don't Sweat the Small Stuff — And It's All Small Stuff*, by Richard Carlson, to get perspective on things that can steal your gratitude, peace, and joy. Or get creative and count the number of times you actually smile or laugh this week!

Ideas for Developing an Attitude of Thankfulness

Instructions: Prayerfully choose one or two action steps to experiment with this week.

Start Date

_____ ☐ **I will be thankful.** I will make a conscious effort to look for things for which to be thankful, especially in situations that normally trouble me. I will keep updating the Day 1 list of things for which I am thankful, and I will refer to it when I feel discontented.

_____ ☐ **I will observe contentment.** I will find a contented person and observe how he or she finds contentment. *(Identify a contented person with whom to connect.)*

_____ ☐ **I will redefine my "needs."** I will gain more satisfaction in life by redefining some of my unmet "needs" and seeing them for what they really are — "wants."

_____ ☐ **I will have a "stay-at-home" celebration** to counteract the "buy more, but enjoy it less" syndrome (mentioned in Day 1).

> INSTRUCTIONS: *Instead of going out for recreation, entertainment, and dinner, go through your house and find things you haven't been using—books you haven't read, kitchen gadgets you haven't tried, games you haven't played, crafts you haven't done, food you haven't cooked. Try them out and enjoy what you already have.* (Adapted from Luci Swindoll's story told in *Joy Breaks*, by Patsy Clairmont, Barbara Johnson, Marilyn Meberg, and Luci Swindoll, Zondervan, 1997.)

_____ ☐ **I will go on a "spending fast,"** where I try going a whole week without buying anything, not even groceries, and then give the money I save to a special project. (For the story of how Shelley Leith's family of seven went on a spending fast *for a month* and survived, go to www.LifePurposeCoachingCenters.com/CM.)

> INSTRUCTIONS: *Make do with supplies you already have; get creative and repurpose things for new uses; and pray about needs that arise throughout the week. Keep a record of the ways God supplies your needs, so you can look back on his provision when you're feeling discontented and recall your newfound satisfaction with what you already have.*

_____ ☐ **I will develop** an attitude of thankfulness by *(add your idea here)*

Action Steps: Developing a Mind of Peace

Instructions: Prayerfully choose one or two action steps to experiment with this week.

Start Date

_____ ☐ **I will genuinely compliment someone** who has more than me.

_____ ☐ **I will develop myself.** I will expand not what I have, but who I am, by cultivating friendships; enjoying conversation, music, and art; savoring reflection and solitude; or exploring hobbies and interests.

_____ ☐ **I will engage in recreation** that does not involve an admission ticket or sitting in bleachers. I will walk, ride a bike, play games, go camping, explore a trail, or have a picnic.

_____ ☐ **I will rest.** I will plan some leisure time into every day. I will give myself a short break at least once a day where I do something I enjoy, such as read a book, crochet, or take a catnap. I will sit outside to eat my lunch, weather permitting.

_____ ☐ **I will develop** a mind of peace by *(add your idea here)*

_____

_____

Action Steps: Developing a Heart of Joy

Instructions: Prayerfully choose one or two action steps to experiment with this week.

Start Date

_____ ☐ **I will make eye contact** with every person I meet this week, and I will be generous with my smiles.

_____ ☐ **I will watch my vocabulary** and eliminate negative words such as *struggle, hassle, exhausted, frustrated, draining,* and *impossible.* I will inject more positive words such as *adventure, explore, exciting, potential, hope,* and *celebrate.*

_____ ☐ **I will enjoy the journey** by singing songs when I'm driving alone, or using a book of conversation starters to get to know my children or carpool partners better. And, yes, I'll drive within the speed limit while singing or chatting.

_____ ☐ **I will celebrate something.** I will allow myself to rejoice and be glad in this day that the Lord has made. I will not keep waiting for everything to be perfect before I celebrate. *(Identify a mini-celebration you can have today.)*

_____

_____ ☐ **I will develop** a heart of joy by *(add your idea here)*

_____

_____

MASTER ACTION PLAN

Now, select only one major action step from this Day 5 exercise and record it on your Master Action Plan in appendix A on page 322. When you have finished reading this book, continue to refer to that one major action step on your Master Action Plan (as well as this Contentment Action Plan, of course, as your season of life permits!). Remember, in order to become more like Christ in your character, you need to collaborate with God in three ways: preparation, prayer, and practice. You have done the work of preparation by learning God's truth about contentment. Now, internalize it by praying for the Holy Spirit's help and practicing your action steps, one by one.

CONTENTMENT PRAYER

Precious Lord,

I'm so tired of not being content and of looking for greener pastures. Settle me down to enjoy today and see your magnificence. I want the peace, joy, and calm I see in others who understand that you didn't intend our lives to be lived as if we are waiting to exhale. Help me not only to breathe deep the beauty and adventure of today, but also to rest in your loving arms as you help me deal with the not-so-good side of living in a fallen world. Like you allowed Paul to pray, help me also to pray: I am content.

In the name of Jesus, amen.

Chapter 7

Generosity

Command them to do good, to be rich in good deeds,
and to be generous and willing to share.

1 Timothy 6:18

Being Like God

The world asks, "What does a man own?"
Christ asks, "How does he use it?"

Andrew Murray, 1828–1917,
South African evangelist

WELCOME BACK TO MY PLACE!

Ah, welcome to one of my favorite spots in the world, my front porch. The reason I like it so much is because I told God that I would not buy a porch bench or otherwise renovate my home in any way, until I was convinced that he wanted me to stay here. Finally, after four years of asking God whether I should sell my house or not, I was convinced that I was to stay—and proceeded, as my first order of upgrading business, to find the perfect bench for me. I know the slats are wood, which might get a bit uncomfortable, so we will plan to take a stretch break midway by standing up for a bit to get a better view of the mountain range. Let's read this prayer aloud together now:

All-knowing God,

Thank you for sitting with us today on the porch. In fact, thank you for loving us at all. We don't deserve your grace and mercy, but we are certainly grateful for how generously you give it to us. Inspire us with your heart of generosity. And thank you that there is so much joy involved in becoming more like you in this area. We are excited to discover what you have for us to learn about generosity.

Amen.

That shared praying was nice. Thank you! Shall we get started on today's topic? Generosity.

A Coach Who Had Impure Generosity Motives

I've always been generous, to a fault. I have a tendency to give away everything to everybody. Awhile back, I stopped to check my motives for being so generous with my time, money, and energy, and what I discovered about myself was not pretty. I must confess that I had a partially impure motive as a people-pleaser. I wanted people to like me, so I catered to their wishes—giving them things to ensure that they would like me better. Now, I think I have finally wrestled that monster to the ground, but if not, I usually have the common sense to check my motives at some point along the way!

Out of all the character qualities we are examining, I think that generosity is the one that most clearly shows us God's passionate, all-out, go-for-broke, get-their-attention, over-the-top love for us. If you want to pick a characteristic to work on that will make you most like God, generosity is your ticket. But you'll have better success with generosity if you have first worked on contentment. Contentment is that inner restfulness that says, "I've got enough." Generosity goes a step further and demonstrates outwardly what contentment believes inwardly. In other words, generosity sees a need and says, "I've got enough—let me share with you!"

God Gives ... Extravagantly

If you want to grasp the scope of God's generosity, just try looking at the world around us. All creation shouts that God is *extravagantly* generous. Think about it ... he didn't just give us a few flowers to smell nice and perk up our centerpieces. He gave us thousands of varieties of flowers—wildflowers, roses, exotic orchids, and ridiculously huge peonies. God didn't just give us three primary colors. He gave us more colors than we can come up with silly names for (like my personal favorite, Chocolate Licorice). And, he didn't just turn on the cosmic radio to the "white noise" setting. We get to hear bird serenades, rivers tumbling over boulders, the crackling of a campfire, and rainfall on the roof.

Not only does creation tell us about God's extravagance, but it also shows his generosity. He made the whole world in order to give it away! Genesis 1 tells us that after God spoke the earth into existence, he gave it all to Adam by putting him in charge of the animal world and the garden of Eden. If it were me, I don't think I would have handed the earth over to a guy who was only a few hours old. That would be like buying a new sports car and throwing the keys to your teenager who has had his license for a day and saying, "Here! Take it for a spin! And by the way, it's yours—be good to it." But that's precisely what God did. He entrusted it all to us.

WHOSE STUFF IS IT, ANYWAY?

Yet, in our mythical car story, there is one hitch. You may have bought the car for your teenager to use, but in reality, you are keeping the title. So it is in the case of God's world-class generosity. God created the world and gave it to Adam to feed him and give him an occupation, but God still owns the world; we humans are simply caretakers: "The land is mine and you reside in my land as foreigners and strangers" (Leviticus 25:23).

You may say, "God doesn't own my house. I do! I worked hard to buy this house."

To which God might reply, "Oh really? Where exactly do you think you got the ability to earn the living that bought you that house?" Check out Deuteronomy 8:10–20. It is a powerful Scripture passage in which God reminds us that we can't take credit for the food we eat, the land that grew it, the houses we build, or the money we have earned, because even our ability to acquire what we have was given to us by him. That's pretty humbling to think about, isn't it?

GIVE IT UP

Just like our other character traits, generosity is based on humility. It is humbling to credit God for everything we acquire, but when we do so, it helps us loosen our grip on our belongings and give them up to his control. Think about it this way: What is one of the ways toddlers first learn not to be so self-centered? When they are taught to share. Learning to share can take a lifetime for some of us, because of our unruly ego which insists on that toddler word, *mine!* Just read these thoughts from Albert Day, a nineteenth-century physician and leader in the treatment of alcoholism:

> Left to itself, the ego is persistent in acquiring and keeping. Sharing is not one of its passions. Giving is not a trait of the ego. Owning is! "Mine" is its dearest adjective. "Keep" is its most beloved verb.
>
> The ego is possessive. Its possessiveness in property manifests itself as stinginess, miserliness, greed. Its possessiveness of people makes jealous friends, wives, parents.

... Faithfully practiced, generosity weakens the ego's authority. (*Discipline and Discovery*, Nashville: The Upper Room, 1947)

If you think you can't afford to share what you have, read this next Scripture passage and look for the possessions Jesus asks us to share:

> *"For I was hungry and you gave me something to eat, I was thirsty and you gave me something to drink, I was a stranger and you invited me in, [36]I needed clothes and you clothed me, I was sick and you looked after me, I was in prison and you came to visit me.... [40]Truly I tell you, whatever you did for one of the least of these brothers and sisters of mine, you did for me."*
>
> Matthew 25:35–36, 40

Jesus tells us to share some very simple things: food, drink, shelter, clothing, and time. (Yes—time is a possession.) We don't have to be wealthy or talented to share simple things like that with people in need.

GOD GIVES ... ABUNDANTLY

God is an extravagant giver, which we have seen exhibited in his creation and provision. He is also an *abundant* giver, which is dramatically demonstrated in the gift of his Son. Anyone who receives Jesus is automatically entitled to a deluge of other gifts, such as spiritual blessings, a secure inheritance, a purpose for living, and a hope for the future.

God's *giving formula* is so different from the way many women operate. They give a very expensive gift to a girlfriend, present it with a drum roll, watch her open it, bask in her gratitude, wait for the gushing thank-you note, and then don't give her anything else until she gives a nice gift in return. But God's process is astonishing. First, he gives the sacrificial gift of his Son. Upon our acceptance of that gift, he immediately follows it with another unmerited gift, that of adoption into his family. Then without pause, he pours on more gifts, like an abundant, fulfilled life and spiritual gifts, such as serving, encouraging, forgiving, leading, teaching, helping, and giving. All the while, as we are enjoying our gifts, he is busy preparing a heaven full of unimaginably glorious gifts for our eternal enjoyment (see Ephesians 1:3–6). Now, that's an abundant giver!

WHOSE LIFE IS IT, ANYWAY?

This life, which is full of purpose and meaning, is one of the most precious gifts God gives. Jesus said, "I have come that they may have life, and have it to the full" (John 10:10b). Aren't you glad we get to live life to the fullest? I don't know about you, but I aim to get every ounce of energy, joy, adventure, and fulfillment out of life that any one lady can muster!

But this wonderful gift of life to the full comes with a caveat: "You are not your own property, then; you have been bought at a price. So use your body for the glory of God" (1 Corinthians 6:20 NJB). So, your possessions are not your own—God loaned them to you; and you are not your own—God paid a price for you.

LAY IT DOWN

Since God gave us the ultimate, best, non-repayable, unsurpassed gift, how are we expected to respond? The verse we just looked at says, "You have been bought with a price. So use your body for the glory of God." Since our body is the repository for the full life God gave us, we are to use our body respectfully and generously give away the gifts that came with the full life:

- Did he give you grace? Use your voice to speak words that believe the best in your friend when she disappoints you.
- Did he give you rest? Use your hands to straighten up, providing a restful atmosphere for your family when they come home.
- Did he give you hope? Use your arms to hug an elderly shut-in who needs encouragement.
- Did he give you forgiveness? Use your lips to kiss your child who messed up again.

And here's the cool thing about giving these gifts away: they don't diminish with the giving; they multiply! Look at the two-way street that starts when you give away what you have received:

"You must be compassionate, just as your Father is compassionate. 37Stop judging others, and you will not be judged.... If you forgive others, you will be forgiven. 38If you give, you will receive. Your gift will return to you in full measure, pressed down, shaken together to make room for more, and running over."

Luke 6:36–38 NLT

What amazing gifts God gives us that we can in turn give away: grace, hope, forgiveness, compassion, mercy, and acceptance. The list is endless. It is mind-boggling to have the added bonus of knowing that they are returned to us more abundantly than we gave!

Journal

What things can you share? Is this a new concept for you: that you are simply God's steward of what he is allowing you to own? How would it change (or has it changed) your attitude toward sharing to look at your possessions as God's?

_____

_____

_____

From the following list, check the top five gifts of a full life that you enjoy the most or make your life feel the richest:

☐ Acceptance   ☐ Heaven
☐ A ministry   ☐ Hope
☐ Answered prayer   ☐ Joy
☐ Belonging   ☐ Love
☐ Changed life   ☐ Mercy
☐ Compassion   ☐ Peace
☐ Energy   ☐ Power
☐ Faith   ☐ Purpose
☐ Forgiveness   ☐ Rest
☐ Freedom   ☐ Right with God
☐ God's Word   ☐ Singing
☐ Grace   ☐ Wisdom
☐ Guidance   ☐ Other: _____
☐ Healing

Now, how can you give those gifts away this week? Think of two or three people who may need to receive these gifts from you, and plan at least one "gift-giving" event for each person. You may give a word of encouragement, a cup of tea with a listening ear, some of your time to help somebody get organized, or a "Get Out of Jail Free" card for the next time a child blows it! By the way, the more humbly you can do it, the better.

_____

_____

_____

_____

PRAYER

Precious Lord,

Thank you for your bountiful, extravagant, abundant, lavish generosity. I long to get close to your heart by practicing the lifestyle of a generous person. Help me to hold my stuff loosely, as if it's not mine, because it's not. Help me to share some of my things I would normally hold back from sharing. Help me to live as if my life is not my own, because it's not. You paid for me, and you gave me a life full of gifts to give away. I surrender my body to you — use me to deliver hope, help, grace, joy, mercy, and forgiveness to people who need those gifts this week. You have given me so much. It's the least I can do.

In the name of Jesus, amen.

Greed: Exposing Your Inner Scrooge

One of the dangers of greed is that it often
doesn't set off the alarms that other sins do.
Gary Thomas, author, speaker

Then he said to them, "Watch out!
Be on your guard against all kinds of greed;
life does not consist in an abundance of possessions."
Luke 12:15

A VIRTUAL MESSAGE

 NOTE: It's Day 2, so you have the option of listening to today's message by downloading it from my website, www.LifePurposeCoachingCenters.com/ CM, or reading the message text below. Enjoy the virtual coaching and don't forget to open in prayer!

THE FLIP SIDE OF GENEROSITY

There are two classic Christmas movies you may happen to watch year after year, which portray two sides of this generosity theme: *It's a Wonderful Life* and *Scrooge*. In *It's a Wonderful Life*, an angel shows George Bailey how his lifetime of sacrifice and generosity has transformed his town for the better. In *Scrooge*, an angel shows Ebenezer Scrooge how his lifetime of being "a squeezing, wrenching, grasping, scraping, clutching, covetous old sinner" has made him lose everyone who meant anything to him. *It's a Wonderful Life* ends with the townspeople of Bedford Falls rallying around George's crisis and showering him with money. *Scrooge* ends with Ebenezer awakening to his folly and giving away his money. George Bailey reaped the rewards of being generous. Scrooge was reaping the consequences of being greedy until he faced himself and learned the joy of giving.

Consider these contrasts:

Generosity is grateful.	Greed is covetous.
Generosity sees God as the source.	Greed sees self as the source.
Generosity lets go.	Greed hoards.
Generosity gives.	Greed gets.
Generosity trusts God.	Greed distrusts God.

That last one—greed distrusts God—is a biggie. Many years ago I noticed that I was once again struggling with greed, and I wrote in my journal, "Greed slaps God in the face and says, 'You won't have enough for me, so I will hoard for myself.'" Slapping God in the face may sound harsh, but think about how you would feel if your child were to say something like this to you: "You might not give me enough food for dinner tonight, so I'm just saving this bread from lunch, and I'm sneaking some of Johnny's lunch too. I got some cans out of the cupboard, and I have them hidden away in my sock drawer—you know ... just in case you don't come through for me." That would be like a slap in the face, wouldn't it? Well, that's what I feel I am doing to God when I forget about his habitual generosity and start hoarding what he has given me or grasping for more than I need.

Let's look at greed a little deeper, starting with its many faces.

THE MANY FACES OF GREED

Greed can take numerous forms. It is seen in an inordinate *craving* for more than is needed (i.e., food, wealth, possessions, sex, power, love, entertainment, comfort, popularity, control). This form of greed was at the root of the original sin in Eden. When Adam and Eve indulged their craving for the forbidden fruit, they were greedily grasping for more than they needed, over and above what God had so amply provided.

Another form of greed is *hoarding*. This person protects what she has by holding on tightly and not letting go. Try this little self-test to see if you might possibly be a hoarder.

Hoarding Self-Test

Here are some interesting categories of hoarding you may not have considered. Rate yourself on a scale from 1 to 5 as to how much you experience each of these types of hoarding, with 1 meaning "rarely" and 5 meaning "frequently."

1 2 3 4 5 Do you have a hard time sharing your possessions?

1 2 3 4 5 Are you usually too busy to spare the time to serve others?

1 2 3 4 5 Are you so protective of your agenda that you resent interruptions?

1 2 3 4 5 Do you close out people by guarding your personal space?

Another insidious form of greed is a *sense of entitlement*. This is the type of person who says, "I deserve that," or "The world owes me," or "It's all about me." The entitlement mentality justifies putting oneself before others when:

- **I believe I have suffered greatly.** "My son just moved out and I'm depressed, so I can be rude to the woman who is going on and on about her precocious child."
- **I think someone is inept.** "I can be demanding with that waitress because she keeps bungling our order."
- **I think my needs trump everyone else's.** "I'm tired and I'm the queen and I need a break worse than you, so leave me alone."

GREED NEVER WALTZES ALONE

Greed not only has several faces — craving, hoarding, and entitlement — but it also has many companions. Greed often waltzes with another sin. After all, in the garden of Eden, greed was the sin that launched all sin! Greed is at the core of character flaws such as pride, bragging, addiction, and obsession. It can promote financial crises like compulsive spending, gambling, embezzlement, and shoplifting. Greed fosters gluttony and eating disorders; and it is at the heart of the sexual sins of pornography, adultery, and incest.

RESULTS OF GREED

So, have the insidious tentacles of greed invaded your life? Are you aware of evidences of craving, hoarding, entitlement, or any of greed's companions listed in the previous paragraph? Here are some signs to look for to know if greed has made itself at home in you. You may want to ask someone who knows you well if they have seen any of these results of greed in your life.

Greed squeezes out God. Instead of depending on God, greed depends on self-effort. Instead of waiting on the Lord, greed grabs what it can get now. Instead of obeying God's promptings to give, greed hoards what it has. The more you try to keep for yourself, the less room there is for God.

Greed shuts out others. Greed puts me, me, me first. The entitlement mentality shuts out everyone's needs but your own.

Greed brings out insecurity. Greed is ego-driven. If you think your self-worth is improved by what you can get, greed is faking you out. *More* doesn't make you *more secure*. The desire to acquire, which is a sign of insecurity, is actually self-deception that can lead to many other sins.

Greed snuffs out peace. Greedy people are characterized by anxiety. A greedy person is never fully at rest. She is in perpetual pursuit of something else, something more, something beyond.

So, if you are feeling distant from God or people, or lacking in self-worth or peace, greed may be the culprit.

Journal

What kind of greed do you suffer from (or have you experienced in the past)—craving, hoarding, or entitlement? Describe how it typically looks in your life. What companion sins has greed brought with it into your life?

_____

_____

_____

_____

_____

Next, note the top two or three reasons you experience greed:

- ☐ **Fear:** I had better get my fair share fast before we run out (Middle Child Syndrome!).
- ☐ **Selfishness:** I don't want to share.
- ☐ **Entitlement:** I deserve it more than you.
- ☐ **Control:** I want to be in charge.
- ☐ **Happiness:** The more I have, the happier I'll be.
- ☐ **Mask:** My things hide my pain.
- ☐ **Self-esteem:** I'll be worth something if I have this.
- ☐ **Pride:** Me, me, me first. I'm more important.
- ☐ **Vanity:** I'm the queen of the world.

Looking at the top reasons you experience greed, explain how they have squeezed out God, shut out others, brought out your insecurity, or snuffed out your peace.

_____

_____

God will be generous to forgive, and he will give you overflowing peace and acceptance in response. Just ask him to point out specifically where greed tends to show up in your everyday life and what the root cause is. Then tell him that you are ready, willing, and able to work on it with him.

PRAYER

Precious Lord,

I do not want to be like Ebenezer Scrooge, "a squeezing, wrenching, grasping, scraping, clutching, covetous old sinner." Help me to care less and less about more clothes, bigger closets; more furniture, a bigger house; more money, a bigger checking account. Help me to let go of hoarding my possessions, my time, my prestige, and even my pride in how much I am able to give. Help me to truly see others as your precious children and to get rid of my entitlement mentality. If I am blind to any form of greed in myself, set off alarms, so that I do not continue to tolerate this sin in my life.

In the name of Jesus, amen.

How to Be a Generous Giver

That's what I consider true generosity. You give your all and yet you always feel as if it costs you nothing.

Simone de Beauvoir, 1908–1986, French philosopher

YOU'VE GOT MAIL

To:	"The Best You" Woman	Sent: **Day 3**
From:	Katie Brazelton	
Subject:	Generosity	

It's Day 3, so here is your weekly Email Message. Feel free to blog me a response at my website, www.LifePurposeCoachingCenters.com/CM, if you'd like. Enjoy the email-coaching and don't forget to open in prayer!

THE GENEROSITY HALL OF FAME

You may have never thought about this, but the Bible describes several different types of givers. We read about the *persistent givers* of Israel who had to be restrained from giving too much toward the tabernacle fund (Exodus 36:6–7). There are the *poor givers* of Macedonia who gave sacrificially to the persecuted church in Jerusalem (2 Corinthians 8:2–3). Zaccheus, the *guilty giver*, was making up for a lifetime of graft (Luke 19:8). Or there are the Egyptians, the *terrified givers*, who practically threw their donations of silver, gold, and clothing at the escaping Israelites to keep any more plagues from happening (Exodus 12:35–36). But some of the finest Hall of Fame givers in Scripture are the *women*:

258

- **Most lavish giver:** The Queen of Sheba. Her gift to Solomon of gold alone amounted to three and a half million dollars in today's currency, and that doesn't count all the shiploads of spices and jewels and mahogany (see 1 Kings 10:1–13).
- **Most astute giver:** Abigail. Her gift to David of provisions for his army averted a murder (see 1 Samuel 25:14–35).
- **Most unsung givers:** The women who sponsored Jesus. We don't hear much about them, but they fed and supported Jesus and his followers throughout his ministry (see Luke 8:3).
- **Most broken giver:** The woman of ill repute who tearfully anointed Jesus' feet with costly perfume and wiped them with her hair (see Luke 7:36–50).
- **Most generous giver:** The widow who put two pennies in the offering (see Luke 21:1–4). Isn't it remarkable that in all of Scripture, Jesus singles out this woman as *the* example of the greatest generosity he had seen; and yet, out of all these givers, her gift was by far the smallest imaginable amount? That shows us bluntly that God doesn't care *how much* we give; he cares about *how heartfelt* our giving is. He looks for a generous, cheerful, sacrificial, gracious attitude when we give. That is what gets applauded in heaven.

TIFFANI AND CHRIS'S STORY OF GENEROUS GIVING

Several years ago when Tiffani and her husband, Chris, were both new Christians, their pastor challenged the congregation to give to a building fund. He said something that struck them as counterintuitive: "God does not need your money." Hold on! That's not the type of thing you expect to hear from someone asking for money! He went on to explain that what you give is between God and you, and the amount you give should not be driven by the recipient's need, as much as by how willing you are to depend on God's leading.

Tiffani and Chris prayed separately for an entire month about the amount of their gift. Tiffani was afraid to tell Chris what God had been impressing upon her to give, because the dollar figure was so surprising to her. Interestingly, Chris had a similar fear, because the number was so much higher than they had ever given before. When they finally told each other their numbers, it turned out to be the exact same number.

That experience started a giving pattern that they have tried to maintain ever since. At the beginning of every year, each spouse has a time of separate prayer about their giving level for the coming year, beyond their tithe to the church. Amazingly, nearly every time they do this diligently, God reveals the same number to both of them.

Not only do they use this process with their annual giving amount to their church, but they do it throughout the year as they give away portions of that amount to different causes and people. On a case-by-case basis, as the Lord brings needs to their attention, they first evaluate the ministry and its effectiveness. Then, they pray about how much to give, compare their amounts, and rejoice when God reveals the same thing to both of them. If their numbers are different, they continue praying and discussing until they sense God's peace on an amount—then they give joyfully.

Chris and Tiffani try to give to the causes that were closest to Christ's heart: evangelism first; discipleship next; then meeting the needs of those most needy and helpless. Tiffani marvels at how true it is that "where your treasure is, there your heart will be also" (Matthew 6:21). She has found that once they start giving to a cause that God has put on their hearts, they develop an intense interest in everything having to do with that ministry. Their prayers and their involvement follow their dollars. She says, "I'm so thankful for the privilege of being able to partner with God to meet needs. I didn't know that giving could feel this good."

EIGHT PRINCIPLES OF GIVING

Here are eight principles that can be drawn from my friends' story to help guide your own giving decisions.

1. The amount doesn't count. Remember, God doesn't need your money. He wants your heart to be right about giving. As we become more like Christ we learn to let go, realizing that the amount we give is about pleasing our Father, not anyone else.

2. Compare after prayer. Pray about every giving decision. If you have a husband or a prayer partner, try praying separately about what to give, then compare the number God laid on your hearts. If you do not have a partner, it is still important to take every giving decision to the Lord and ask him what the dollar amount should be.

3. The Lord rewards. When you give, God not only stores up treasures in heaven for you, but he also gives you tremendous joy right now—a taste of eternity here on earth. Because of that joyful feeling, you may find your-self saying: "How can we *not* give?"

4. Delay before you pay (by predetermining your giving for the year). Allocating a generous sum to giving sets up an automatic delay when-ever you make a spending decision. It counteracts the impulse shopping mentality of "I deserve it and I can afford it, so I'll buy it" by literally causing you to stop and ask the Lord where he wants *his* money to go.

5. Decide against pride. A temptation for a generous giver is to be prideful about the amount of giving she does. It is not necessarily God's will that money goes to missions instead of replacing your threadbare carpet. Having unsightly carpet can become a badge of honor and a matter of pride, especially when you can say, "Yes, we need to replace that carpet, but I gave my money to missions instead." *Give even your giving* to God, and he will help you develop a healthy balance when it comes to using your resources for the needs of your family.

6. Invest in the best. Think of giving as a kingdom investment and ap-proach your investment as you would an investment in a property. Research the ministry and determine whether or not it is using its funds effectively. If it is not, you may need to make the hard decision to stop supporting a ministry.

7. Be wise and prioritize. After giving to your local church, prioritize your giving, using some type of filter like Chris and Tiffani did (for example, emphasizing evangelism, discipleship, and meeting the needs of the most needy).

8. Take part from your heart. Your heart follows your treasure. When God lays a ministry on your heart, don't just give money. Volunteer to help, contributing in whatever way needed, whether that's letter writing or deco-rating or bookkeeping or cleaning or reading to children—or praying!

Giving is an adventure in faith. Obeying God in the area of giving will probably be a stretch of your trust in God. Your giving should be viewed as an act of obedience, especially if you can't see how you are going to be able to meet the challenge God has laid before you. The most important thing to remember is that generosity is meant to be joyful!

Journal

"Bring all the tithes into the storehouse so there will be enough food in my Temple. If you do," says the LORD Almighty, "I will open the windows of heaven for you. I will pour out a blessing so great you won't have enough room to take it in! Try it! Let me prove it to you!"

Malachi 3:10 NLT

Are there any blessings you feel you are lacking because you are not obeying God in generous giving? Did you know that this Malachi verse is the only place in Scripture where God invites us to test him? By faith, write out at least one way you would like to test God with generous giving.

_____

_____

_____

Generous Giving Self-Test

Review the eight principles of giving and see how you're doing.

1. The amount doesn't count.	Are you giving to please God more than people?	Yes	No
2. Compare after prayer.	Do you pray before giving?	Yes	No
3. The Lord rewards.	Are you regularly storing treasures in heaven?	Yes	No
4. Delay before you pay.	Do you evaluate purchases in light of your giving commitments?	Yes	No
5. Decide against pride.	Have you given even your giving to God?	Yes	No
6. Invest in the best.	Do you research before you donate?	Yes	No
7. Be wise and prioritize.	Do you give where Jesus would give?	Yes	No
8. Take part from your heart.	Do you donate more than your money?	Yes	No

Yes 7 – 8 times: You're a giving superstar! Thank God for the joy you're experiencing in giving.

Yes 3 – 6 times: You're well on your way to being a generous giver.
Choose one area to work on.

Yes 1 – 2 times: Review the chapter on greed and practice a hand-release
motion. Are you holding on too tight?

PRAYER

Precious Lord,

*I have a burning desire in my heart to take you at your word and go
on an adventure of faith with you. I want to seek your will before I use my
money, and I want to listen to your prompting and give what you tell me to
give, to the places you tell me to give it. I give even my giving to you, releasing
my pride in how much I give. Show me ways to be generous with my life as well
as my money. Thank you that when I obey you, I not only store up rewards in
heaven, but you give me overwhelming joy here on earth.*

In the name of Jesus, amen.

Your Generosity Coach

It is an anomaly of modern life that many find giving to be a burden.
Such persons have omitted a preliminary giving.
If one first gives himself to the Lord, all other giving is easy.
John S. Bonnell, 1893–1992, pastor and author

PERSPECTIVE-CHANGING OUTING

Today, we are in for a beach treat! We came down to the ocean to see one of God's most generous gifts, with the expanse of the horizon; the pounding waves; and the interplay of the water, the shoreline, sea birds, and sunshine. We take off our shoes and wiggle our toes in the warm sand. We talk about how God knows the number of grains of sand in the world, and we marvel at how he took the time to make each grain different from the next. We sit quietly for a while, just listening to the crashing surf, watching the shimmer of light on the water, feeling the refreshing breeze on our faces—then we open our time in prayer. Somehow, we feel closer to God here. Let's take a walk down by the water's edge and talk about how you're doing in three aspects of generosity: how generous you are; the motivation for your generosity, and the impact your generosity is having.

HOW GENEROUS ARE YOU?

Generosity is giving more than you can.
Kahlil Gibran, 1883–1931, Lebanese-American author

Think for a minute about how generous you are. Think about how loosely or tightly you hold onto your possessions. Think about how you feel when you are donating money. Think about your first impulse when you are interrupted or when you are asked for help or when someone disappoints you. There. Do you have a sense of whether or not you are a generous person? Let's sit down for a moment and read together about a group of poverty-stricken Macedonians who have a few things to teach us about generosity:

> *In the midst of a very severe trial, their [the Macedonians] overflowing joy and their extreme poverty welled up in rich generosity. ³For I testify that they gave as much as they were able, and even beyond their ability. Entirely on their own, ⁴they urgently pleaded with us for the privilege of sharing in this service to the Lord's people. ⁵And they went beyond our expectations; having given themselves first of all to the Lord, they gave themselves by the will of God also to us.*
>
> 2 Corinthians 8:2–5

Let's take some cues from the story of the Macedonians to ask you a few questions about how generous you are.

1. The Macedonians were tested by troubles and were very poor. How have your troubles, or any fears you may have had about not having enough to spare, kept you from being generous?

---

2. The Macedonians were not held back by their troubles — they gave much because of their great joy. What type of joy, excitement, or results cause you to be the most generous?

---

3. The Macedonians begged and pleaded for the privilege of sharing with the Christians in Jerusalem, then gave more than they could afford. What cause or ministry or need makes you feel the most passionate about giving?

---

4. The Macedonians surprised Paul by giving of themselves first. Beyond your money, what do you give to the Lord and to others?

What Motivates Your Generosity?

> You can give without loving.
> But you cannot love without giving.
>
> **Amy Carmichael, 1867–1951, missionary to India**

Let's think about what is motivating you to be generous. Is it because you really like it when people thank you? Do you give more readily when you know you'll receive something in return? Or is your giving a financial transaction that feels like an obligation?

What if the primary reasons you give were (1) because God loves you and you love him, and (2) because God and you love people, and you see their needs as God sees them? When the needs of others reach down inside you and break your heart, you have probably noticed that you are not able to stop yourself from responding with generosity. Notice the inherent connection in this next passage between Jesus giving to us first and our compassion toward others, which results in our generosity.

> *This is how we know what love is: Jesus Christ laid down his life for us. And we ought to lay down our lives for one another.* [17]*If any one of you has material possessions and sees a brother or sister in need but has no pity on them, how can the love of God be in you?* [18]*Dear children, let us not love with words or tongue but with actions and in truth.*
>
> 1 John 3:16–18

1. What is your real motivation in giving? How would it change your giving if you were truly motivated to give in response to Jesus' sacrifice for you?

_____

_____

(To find out more about Jesus' sacrifice for you and how that can change your life, go to www.LifePurposeCoachingCenters.com/CM or see Appendix C.)

2. Who are the people in need in your world? What is your response to them internally, and what are your outward actions toward them? How would it change your giving if you were more motivated by compassion for others?

_____

_____

YOUR GENEROSITY FROM HEAVEN'S PERSPECTIVE

One of the most profound songs on the subject of the eternal impact of generosity is "Thank You" by Ray Boltz. The lyrics invite you to imagine that you are walking down heaven's streets of gold, and people are coming up to you to thank you for your sacrificial giving that changed their lives. One person, for example, a former Sunday school student of yours, tells you that he is in heaven because of your dedication. Another man, a missionary, thanks you for your small, heartfelt financial gift that God multiplied. One of the stanzas sums up the song so well:

> *One by one they came, far as the eye could see*
> *Each life somehow touched by your generosity*
> *Little things that you had done, sacrifices made*
> *Unnoticed on the earth, in heaven now proclaimed*
>
> 1988 Gaither MusicASCAP. All rights reserved.

Following this long line of grateful souls, the song says that Jesus approaches you, takes your hand, and tells you of your rich reward in heaven!

1. My friend, when Jesus takes your hand in heaven, who will be lining up to tell you how your generosity touched their lives and why?

_____

_____

2. When you think about your generosity from the perspective of heaven, what sacrifices have you been unwilling to make that you could reconsider?

_____

_____

For more assessment questions on generosity, go to www.LifePurpose CoachingCenters.com/CM.

PRAYER

Precious Lord,

Would you examine my heart right now? Am I as generous as I think I am? Do I have true compassion for people? Do I stop and really look at the people around me and see their needs? Do I respond to them like you would? Lord, I want to be more like you. I want to overflow with generosity. I want to find a cause that I feel so strongly about that I'm begging for the chance to support it. I want to be so aware of others and so unconscious of my own limitations, that I give more than I'm able, for you are my supply. Help me to exude generosity in the way I behave at work and on the road and in a restaurant and with my family. I would love for you, Jesus, to see a stream of people in heaven who were touched by some smile or act of kindness or gift or service of love that I did for them on earth.

In the name of Jesus, amen.

Steps to Generosity

Dearest Lord, teach me to be generous.
Teach me to serve you as you deserve;
to give and not to count the cost;
to fight and not to heed the wounds;
to toil and not to seek for rest;
to labor and not to seek reward,
save that of knowing that I do your will.

**Ignatius Loyola, 1491–1556,
founder of the Jesuits**

SITTING QUIETLY WITH YOUR MAKER

Today is a time of reflection and solitude for you in the privacy of your own quiet-time space. You will be putting together a Generosity Action Plan. The action steps are divided into four areas: developing a heart of compassion, releasing your grip on your stuff, generous giving, and generous living. Go through the following options and note where you are doing well and what action steps you would like to take to build more generosity into your life.

Ask yourself how deeply you are able to focus on increasing your generosity during this season of your life. Then select the appropriate action steps on pages 270–273, whatever you feel you can realistically experiment with this week. It's your plan, your life, and your prayerful decision—nobody else's. If you feel God impressing on you to concentrate on your generosity right now, go for these exercises with gusto—without further ado or delay! I am confident that whatever effort you are able to devote to improving your generosity will be richly rewarded by him on earth and in heaven.

Generosity Action Plan

PRAYER FOCUS: Pray that God will open your eyes to needs of people around you, and that he will show you what he wants you to do about those needs. Assess what you have and ask God what he wants you to do with it. Give God your day, being open to interruptions as divine appointments. And pray about where to donate your money, asking God what amount to give.

DEVOTIONAL FOCUS: Choose one of the following Scripture passages on the topic of generosity: To focus on *developing a heart of compassion*, read Luke 10:29–37 and evaluate your compassion in light of the story of the Good Samaritan. To focus on *releasing your grip on your stuff*, read Matthew 6:19–34, which addresses attitudes toward possessions. To focus on *generous living*, read Romans 12 to discover how to offer your body as a living sacrifice. To focus on *generous giving*, read 1 Corinthians 9 to learn principles of cheerful giving.

EXTRA PERSPECTIVE: Read *Treasure Principle*, by Randy Alcorn, which teaches that the only way to hang onto treasure is to send it on ahead to heaven by giving it away on earth. Or get creative and explore the Generous Giving website (GenerousGiving.com) to learn about other generous givers now and in history, and how they did it.

Action Steps: Developing a Heart of Compassion

Instructions: Prayerfully choose one or two action steps to experiment with this week.

Start Date

_____ ☐ **I will volunteer** to serve at an event or a facility that helps the elderly. *(Identify the volunteer activity.)*

_____ ☐ **I will donate** first to my church; then toward ministries that conduct evangelism, discipleship, and helping those who are most in need. (Or, I will design my own filter for giving.)

_____ ☐ **I will help the homeless** by giving something appropriate to individuals when God prompts me to do so.

> IDEA: *Prepare sacks containing healthy snack foods, small toiletries, a gift certificate for a fast food meal, and a gospel tract, and have a supply in your car ready to give away when you see someone in need.*

_____ ☐ **I will give gifts from my "full life"** (see exercise in Generosity Day 1, pages 251–252) to people in my circles of influence who need them.

_____ ☐ **I will travel with a purpose**, choosing to visit a place where I will face people in need. I will not stay in a pampering hotel, but in a place where I become acquainted with the local people. I will use my time to do something to make their lives a little better. I will find ways to stay involved with their needs after I return home.

_____ ☐ **I will develop** a heart of compassion by *(add your idea here)*

_____

_____

Action Steps: Releasing My Grip on My Stuff

Instructions: Prayerfully choose one or two action steps to experiment with this week.

Start Date

_____ ☐ **I will affirm that my possessions are not my own**, and I will stop hoarding them. I will share them freely, and donate them when I have stopped using them.

_____ ☐ **I will affirm that I am not my own.** I will stop hoarding my time, my energy, my privacy, and my rights.

_____ ☐ **I will stay accountable.** I will give someone permission to ask, "How is your battle with materialism?" and to hold me accountable to set and reach giving goals.

_____ ☐ **I will simplify my lifestyle** so I have more time, energy, and money to give away. (Choose one of the following ideas or create one of your own.)

SCHEDULE-SIMPLIFYING IDEAS: *Quit activities. Stop thinking that I'm indispensable. Train someone to take my place. Spread the blessing of serving.*

CONSUMPTION-SIMPLIFYING IDEAS: *Downsize. Sell possessions that have payments. Implement money-saving measures. Budget. Reduce needs.*

(Add your own simplifying idea here)

_____

_____ ☐ **I will release** my grip on my stuff by *(add your idea here)*

Action Steps: Developing Generous Giving

Instructions: Prayerfully choose one or two action steps to experiment with this week.

Start Date

_____ ☐ **I will tithe** to the Lord the first portion of my income and gifts.

_____ ☐ **I will research** the fiscal policies of ministries before I donate.

_____ ☐ **I will give additional gifts** to the Lord's work out of my excess. I will set a limit on what I need to live on (and wisely investigate what I need to save for my retirement years) and give away whatever God provides beyond that.

_____ ☐ **I will evaluate** my major purchases in light of my giving goals.

_____ ☐ **I will become** more generous in my giving by *(add your idea here)*

Action Steps: Developing Generous Living

Instructions: Prayerfully choose one or two action steps to experiment with this week.

Start Date

_____ ☐ **I will encourage someone** with a phone call, handwritten note, or flowers.

_____ ☐ **I will invite people** into my home and share my food and shelter with them, even if I haven't cleaned my house or prepared a gourmet meal.

_____ ☐ **I will give away myself** by giving generous, loving attention to my family and by giving the time and energy it takes to be a caring, generous listener to my friends.

_____ ☐ **I will volunteer** and give my talents to support a ministry.

> IDEAS: *Ministries and churches can use volunteers in areas such as bookkeeping, correspondence, data entry, filing, envelope stuffing, phone calling, writing, event planning, babysitting, sewing, cooking, cake decorating, etc.*

_____ ☐ **I will transform my hobby** from a self-centered pursuit into an opportunity for sharing.

> IDEAS: *Gardeners can bring flowers to a resident in an assisted-living home; bikers can take a single-parent child on a ride to the park; scrappers (you know who you are!) can create a scrapbook memory page to commemorate a friend's accomplishment; knitters can make a baby afghan for an orphanage.*

_____ ☐ **I will pray for someone who needs grace from me.** If there is someone in my life right now who is troublesome to me, I will pray for him or her by name right now. Then I will give the gift of my mercy, forgiveness, and grace to that person, even though he or she doesn't deserve it — remembering that I don't deserve to receive the many gifts of God's generosity to me. *(Identify the person for whom you will pray.)*

_____

_____ ☐ **I will become** more generous in my living by *(add your idea here)*

_____

_____

MASTER ACTION PLAN

Now, select only one major action step from this Day 5 exercise and record it on your Master Action Plan in appendix A on page 322. When you have finished reading this book, continue to refer to that one major action step on your Master Action Plan (as well as this Generosity Action Plan, of course, as your season of life permits!). Remember, in order to become more like Christ in your character, you need to collaborate with God in three ways: preparation, prayer, and practice. You have done the work of preparation by learning God's truth about generosity. Now, internalize it by praying for the Holy Spirit's help and practicing your action steps, one by one.

GENEROSITY PRAYER

Precious Lord,

If I am not generous, what am I? As I learn more and more about your thoughts on this subject, I am convinced that, without generosity, I am nothing but a hollow shell of a woman. Teach me to be outrageously generous, just like you are to me. How can it be that the more I give, the more I receive? That is an amazing biblical truth—one that signifies the enormous emphasis you have placed on this principle. Create in me a generous heart and a quiet, humble method of giving myself, my possessions, and my resources away.

In the name of Jesus, amen.

PART 5

The Making of a Right Relationship to My Future

Chapter 8

Perseverance

Let perseverance finish its work
so that you may be mature and complete,
not lacking anything.

James 1:4

Inspired by God

Let me tell you the secret that has led me
to my goal: my strength lies solely in my tenacity.

Louis Pasteur, 1822–1895, inventor of pasteurization

WELCOME BACK TO MY PLACE!

I can't believe we are heading into our last week together, can you? I'd love to give you your choice of where we meet today for this character makeover grand finale. You may choose my living room, dining room, office, or even the front or back porch. But, before you lead the way to your favorite spot, let's say a special prayer that will tell God how serious we are about this final topic:

Lord of Lords,

Teach us to persevere against all odds. Train us to keep on keeping on. Send us role models who have this character strength, and let us model it for those who are watching how we live out our faith. You are our refuge, our rock, our shelter when things get tough. Help us to rest in you as we keep moving forward in spite of difficulties. Our strength lies solely in you and the perseverance you give us.

Amen.

What a great focus for our final coaching session: perseverance. In the Bible, you'll find the concept of perseverance addressed using words like persistence, patience, endurance, diligence, and pressing on. Let's both take a deep breath and see what God has in store for us today!

WHEN I NEARLY GAVE UP

For fifteen years I was rejected—and I actually have forty-seven rejection letters to prove it! Back in 1989, I started with an idea and a dream. My idea was to write a book about how to be a good person. My dream was that the book would succeed in the secular market as a unique answer to helping people reach their potential. After forty-two "no, thank you" letters, I surrendered my book to God, giving up my dream, my future, and my vision, and trusting him with it all. But there was no miraculous success story right after that. In fact, I received five more rejection letters! Then, when I finally got a book contract, it was cancelled four months before publication because of the September 11 terrorist attacks which caused budget cuts in the entire industry. It wasn't until eight long years after I had surrendered the book to the Lord, and had rewritten every sentence to reflect a Christian perspective, that my new agent secured a contract that turned into the four *Pathway to Purpose* books.

My story of perseverance is not unique. Nothing worthwhile is accomplished in this world without stick-to-itiveness. Think of the daily types of things people achieve because they persevered: organizing the garage (that takes extreme perseverance!), refinishing a piece of furniture, writing a song, graduating from school, remodeling a home, adopting a child, getting a promotion, painting a picture, teaching a class, losing weight, starting a ministry. When you have an idea, the process of pursuing your dream and making it a reality requires that you stay strong in your resolve.

As an example of that, let's consider the Old Testament story of Nehemiah, who was inspired by God to rebuild the walls of Jerusalem, a daunting task that required tenacity to complete.

DREAM GIVER

Nehemiah's story opens in the Persian palace, where he was in service to the king who held the Jewish people in captivity. Nehemiah asked a visitor how things were going back in Jerusalem, and he got some very disturbing news:

> *Those who survived the exile and are back in the province are in great trouble and disgrace. The wall of Jerusalem is broken down, and its gates have been burned with fire.*
>
> Nehemiah 1:3

God gives us our dreams in a variety of ways. For Nehemiah, God opened his eyes to a disaster. Nehemiah's heart broke over the plight of his people, and he had to do something about it. Likewise, God shows us a need, such as with homeless people, AIDS babies, or single mothers, and he gives us a burden for them that inspires us to find a way to help them. In other cases, God creates a desire within us that is borne out of what we do well, such as photographing nature or fixing computers, and we seek ways to create a business or a life's work out of the activities we enjoy. In addition, many of us have dreams related to our pain. We have suffered in some way—lost a child, been abused, gone through a divorce, endured chronic pain—and out of our suffering, we realize we are uniquely equipped to help others who are going through a similar life circumstance.

Has God given you an idea, a dream, an inspiration, a heart's desire, a sweet spot, a divine urge, a burden on your soul? When your dream lines up with your gifts, experiences, and background, oh boy—watch out! That's when you start getting that tingly, excited sense of certainty that God has crafted a dream just for you, and that he has specifically chosen and empowered you to carry it out. But . . . sometimes the road to dream fulfillment has its nightmarish potholes.

DREAM KILLERS

What types of things come along and threaten our dreams? Two of the most common dream killers are a project that seems too big and people who are unsupportive. As you read through the explanations on these topics, insert yourself into the Nehemiah story to make it more real!

The Project Seems Too Big

For Nehemiah, the first threat to his dream of rebuilding Jerusalem came when the wall was half done (see Nehemiah 4:6–9). Isn't that about the time discouragement sets in? You've come too far to change your mind, but there's so much more to do, you don't think you can keep going. It feels like it's taking too long; the job is too big; and there is too much about it that is just plain difficult. In Nehemiah's story, this is right about the time that the people complained to him:

> *The strength of the laborers is giving out, and there is so much rubble that we cannot rebuild the wall.*

> Nehemiah 4:10

Translation: "We've worked hard, but it seems like things are worse than when we first started. It feels like we'll never finish." Big projects generate messes, and things usually get worse before they get better. At times like that, your behemoth task can drain your energy. You start to lose heart, and you question whether or not your dream is really from God. It seems like the size of the project is bigger than the size of your dream.

Anne Sullivan, a Persistent Dream Builder

Seven-year-old Helen Keller was glad Anne Sullivan didn't give up. Anne thought she might draw upon her own experience with being visually impaired to try to help the deaf and blind Helen. But she soon found herself completely out of her element with this raging, uncontrollable child. Yet, even after Anne was bitten and had food thrown on her, she was doggedly determined to stay and teach Helen how to behave. The breakthrough finally happened when Helen connected the water at the pump with the letters w-a-t-e-r that Anne relentlessly spelled in her hand. That moment never would have happened if Anne had quit when the assignment got too messy.

People Are Unsupportive

One of the other big dream killers comes from people who are affected by your dream. It's no big surprise that not everyone will agree with you or support your vision. Big dreams have big detractors. The more daring your inspiration, the more naysayers will come around and tell you why it will never work. At the beginning of Nehemiah's project, he was ridiculed and his motives were questioned:

> *They mocked and ridiculed us. "What is this you are doing?" they asked. "Are you rebelling against the king?"*
>
> Nehemiah 2:19

From then on, until the completion of the project, his enemies didn't let up. They threatened, they spread rumors, and they tried dirty tricks, all to keep the wall from being built. When you're attempting big things, some people (out of jealousy or pettiness or just because they're negative people) will find all sorts of reasons why you should quit. It can seem like the force of the opposition is stronger than your dream.

Door-to-Door Salesman, Bill Porter

Bill Porter's story is a well documented, public record that has even been turned into a Turner Network Television (TNT) film staring Oscar®-nominated actor William H. Macy. It's all about proving naysayers wrong. Crippled with cerebral palsy, Bill was told that, because of his condition, he would never be able to hold a job. Nevertheless, he secured a territory in Portland, Oregon, selling Watkins products door-to-door. He was told he would never be able to do all the walking that the job would require, yet he walked seven to ten miles a day for more than thirty years. He was told it would be too difficult to deliver the products with no car, but he devised a method to get them delivered. He was told people wouldn't buy from him, because they would be afraid of him or wouldn't be able to understand his speech, but he has collected several awards from Watkins for being top salesman of the year. He persisted in spite of ridicule, thievery, injury, pain, the Oregon weather, and his own physical limitations. He was determined to succeed, no matter what people told him, and today, at age seventy-three, he runs a successful website business, still selling Watkins. In 1997 Bill was given "America's Award," which honors unsung heroes who personify the American character and spirit.

DREAM LAUNCHERS

So, how do you overcome the dream killers of discouragement and criticism? With perseverance. In the case of Nehemiah, he demonstrates how to persevere over dream killers in three ways: by praying effectively, by recalling God's past blessings, and by being prepared to fight for his dream.

Cover Your Dream with Prayer

Nehemiah covered his entire project with prayer. Right from the moment he heard about the broken-down walls, Nehemiah launched into a period of fasting and praying about the problem (Nehemiah 1:4–11). Midway through the project when the efforts were threatened, he prayed for protection (4:9). And at the end of the project, he and Ezra reinstituted public confession and worship (8:1–9:3). There is even a recorded instance where

Nehemiah prayed an emergency prayer—when the king put him on the spot for a reply:

> *The king said to me, "What is it you want?" Then I prayed to the God of heaven, ⁵and I answered the king …*
>
> Nehemiah 2:4–5

You've got to bathe the entire project—from beginning to end—in deep prayer, a habit of prayer, and emergency prayers.

Recall How God Has Worked

Nehemiah didn't stop with prayer. When you are launching your dream, it can be a nerve-racking time of self-doubt and fear. Nehemiah's strategy was to draw strength from how God had already led him. In his rallying speech, he inspired people to attack the problem by telling them how God prepared the heart of the king and provided their building materials to get them started.

> *"Come, let us rebuild the wall of Jerusalem, and we will no longer be in disgrace." ¹⁸I also told them about the gracious hand of my God on me and what the king had said to me. They replied, "Let us start rebuilding."*
>
> Nehemiah 2:17–18

> *[Nehemiah] stood up and said to the nobles, the officials and the rest of the people, "Don't be afraid of them. Remember the Lord, who is great and awesome …"*
>
> Nehemiah 4:14

So, to keep going when it's hard, remember how God has already come through for you.

Have Courage to Fight for Your Dream

Not only do prayer and remembrance help when your dreams are threatened, but some good old-fashioned "standing your ground" comes in handy. When Nehemiah came under attack, he did not cave in and question whether God really gave him his dream. He devised a plan for the people to protect themselves and fight back, in God's strength.

> *" … fight for your people, your sons and your daughters, your wives and your homes."… ¹⁷Those who carried materials did their work with one hand and held a weapon in the other.… ²⁰"Wherever you hear the sound of the trumpet, join us there. Our God will fight for us!"*
>
> Nehemiah 4:14, 17, 20

God inspires you for a reason, yet he does not put you in a bubble and keep you perfectly protected while you're working toward your goal. Be prepared to defend the dream and call upon God when you come under attack.

In order to persevere, many of the character qualities we have discussed in this book come into play. Think about that as you take the following self-test.

Perseverance Factors

The following factors play a key role in your ability to persevere. On a scale of 1 to 10, with 1 being not at all and 10 being perfect, rate your level on each of these factors.

_____ 1. **Clarity** (Do you know your purpose in life and have clear goals?)

_____ 2. **Humility** (Are you honest with yourself about your dependence on God?)

_____ 3. **Confidence** (Do you have faith in God — God-confidence?)

_____ 4. **Courage** (Can you keep going in the face of opposition?)

_____ 5. **Self-control** (Do you have healthy habits?)

_____ 6. **Patience** (Can you wait on God's timing?)

_____ 7. **Finisher** (Do you finish projects you start?)

_____ 8. **Resilience** (Can you bounce back quickly from setbacks?)

_____ 9. **Health** (Do you have good stamina and an adequate energy level?)

_____ 10. **Support** (Do you have effective support from the people around you?)

_____ Total Score

What Does Your Score Reveal?

0–50: Take a fresh look at everything you do well, and focus on developing those factors further. The desire to persevere will follow.

51–60: You need to pick somewhere to start, so work on raising your lowest scores.

61–80: You're in great shape to go. Maybe do a little fine-tuning along the way.

81–90: Excellent — just don't get too comfortable.

91–100: You are a Perseverance Machine. Keep up the incredible work!

Journal

What inspiration has God given you? (You can describe a short-term dream, such as going on an overseas missions trip, or a long-term dream, such as starting a business.)

_____

_____

What type of dream killers have you encountered (i.e., getting halfway and wanting to give up; things getting worse before getting better; strength giving out; detractors and naysayers)?

_____

_____

Describe your experiences with the following dream launchers. Which one do you think would be most helpful to you right now to overcome any discouragement about your dream? (Put a star by it.)

- *Use of deep prayer, habit of prayer, and emergency prayers.*

_____

_____

- *Recalling how God prepared the way or has helped you in the past.*

_____

_____

- *Fighting for your dream, defending your dream, and not caving in when your dream was attacked.*

_____

_____

PRAYER

Precious Lord,

You are the giver of dreams, and I thank you for the one you are revealing to me. Thank you for equipping me specifically and perfectly to see this dream through to the end. When my strength gives out because I feel overwhelmed by the size of this dream, or because of the mess it's making, please renew me by reminding me why you gave me this dream in the first place. When people discourage me and tell me all the reasons this won't work, give me the passion to fight for my dream. And from now to the end, help me to pray as my first impulse, my last resort, and my habit throughout.

In the name of Jesus, amen.

The Quitter: Exposing Your Inner Mowgli

I've got a woman's ability to stick to a job and
get on with it when everyone else walks off and leaves it.

Margaret Thatcher, former British prime minister

A VIRTUAL MESSAGE

 NOTE: It's Day 2, so you have the option of listening to today's message by downloading it from my website, www.LifePurposeCoachingCenters.com/ CM, or reading the message text below. Enjoy the virtual coaching and don't forget to open your time in prayer!

THE FLIP SIDE OF PERSEVERANCE

Mowgli is a quitter. In *The Jungle Book*, the classic tale by Rudyard Kipling later made into a Disney film, a young boy, Mowgli, is determined to stay in the jungle despite the fact that he is a target of a man-eating tiger, Shere Khan. A panther named Bagheera tries to escort Mowgli to safety in the man-village, but Mowgli quits the journey because he's having too much fun. He teams up with Baloo the bear, whose carefree nature is right up his alley, but he quits that friendship too when he thinks Baloo has betrayed him. It's not until Mowgli sees a pretty village girl that he is lured out of the jungle.

There is a lot of Mowgli-thinking in society these days. If you're committed to one course of action, but you come across something that looks like more fun, quit. If you're in a friendship, and you have a misunderstanding, quit. If you're feeling incompatible with your husband, quit. If a difficult class might ruin your grade point average, quit. If a job is underutilizing your talents, quit. If your team is going through a losing season, quit. If you're on day three of your diet and you are offered an éclair, quit. (No duh on that last one!)

HOW TO BE A QUITTER

Since quitting is such a popular modern pastime, let's get some great pointers on quitting from a famous quitter in the Bible, the prophet Elijah.

When the going gets tough, quitters run away.

In 1 Kings 19, Elijah had just scored a major triumph over four hundred fifty prophets of Baal, the fertility god. This, in turn, majorly ticked off Queen Jezebel, who worshiped Baal. So she sent Elijah a nasty-gram via her personal messenger, threatening to kill him by that exact hour the next day. And so, Elijah beat a hasty retreat, abdicating his role as God's prophet.

You might be facing a nasty-gram right now, perhaps an eviction notice, a pink slip at work, divorce papers, a note from your child's school principal, an overdue bill, or a cancelled contract. These types of situations pierce our confidence and make us feel like failures. Our first impulse is to run, leaving the promises unfulfilled and the commitments unfinished. That's what quitters do. They don't stay around when the problems pile up. They leave them for someone else to deal with.

After a failure, quitters put themselves down.

When we catch up with Elijah after his day-long marathon fleeing from Jezebel, he has collapsed under a broom tree, moaning and claiming that he wants to die.

> *He came to a broom bush, sat down under it and prayed that he might die.*
> *"I have had enough, LORD," he said. "Take my life; I am no better than my*
> *ancestors."*

1 Kings 19:4

Elijah compared himself to his failure-prone ancestors, admitting to himself that, like them, he came up short. But let's take a time-out from that story for a moment and remember that even the most competent people in the world are susceptible to self-recrimination. When Raphael, arguably the greatest painter who ever lived, was in the middle of painting the *Trans-*

figuration, he suddenly sat down and burst into tears and said: "I am not a painter; I cannot complete it."

Sometimes we persevere in one arena, but we quit in another. For instance, if you're a singer, do you quit singing if you don't do well on one audition? Probably not. But, if you are trying to have a daily quiet time, and you miss three days in a row, you might think, "I can't be consistent. I'm going to give up." If you're a lawyer, do you give up your profession when you lose your first case? Unlikely. But if there was a period of time when you were far away from God, you may say, "It's too late. I've wasted so much time in my life that I've blown my chance to be of any use to God now." Well, that's quitter thinking.

Just because you failed once, or even several times, doesn't mean you should throw in the towel. God specializes in redeeming failures and transforming them into masterpieces: "For we are God's masterpiece. He has created us anew in Christ Jesus" (Ephesians 2:10 NLT). If you don't ask God to pick you up and and help you keep going, you might deprive the world of the next Raphael!

By exaggerating their problems, quitters get paranoid.

One way that quitters justify quitting is by feeling sorry for themselves and making their problems seem insurmountable. Elijah did this:

> *He replied, "I have been very zealous for the LORD God Almighty. The Israelites have rejected your covenant, torn down your altars, and put your prophets to death with the sword. I am the only one left, and now they are trying to kill me too."*
>
> 1 Kings 19:10

Get out the violins. Elijah is singing his self-pitying whiner blues: "I've worked so hard to clean up this town. Now I'm all God's got, and they're hunting me down." Do you ever feel overworked, underappreciated, and alone? If so, that's right where Satan wants you. He loves to use discouragement to disarm and defeat Christians. The famous evangelist D. L. Moody said, "I have never known God to use a discouraged person." I'm not sure if I agree with that statement completely, but I do know that if Satan can get a perfectly capable, successful, fruitful Christian to succumb to discouragement, he has gained himself one more quitter and removed one more threat to his agenda for the world.

GOD'S PERSEVERANCE PROGRAM

The great thing about Elijah's story is that he doesn't stay a quitter. God doesn't let him. God intercepts Elijah mid-plunge, and he gives him a four-step program to get back in the game.

Step 1: When you're exhausted, God gives you rest and nourishment.

> *Then he lay down under the tree and fell asleep. All at once an angel touched him and said, "Get up and eat." ⁶He looked around, and there by his head was some bread baked over hot coals, and a jar of water. He ate and drank and then lay down again. ⁷The angel of the LORD came back a second time and touched him and said, "Get up and eat, for the journey is too much for you." ⁸So he got up and ate and drank.*
>
> 1 Kings 19:5–8

I love the tenderness that the angel of the Lord expressed to Elijah—"for the journey is too much for you." When you have been running too far, too long, working on your dream night and day without rest and nourishment, you'll wear out and feel like quitting. (Allow me to make a plug for the mandatory Sabbath rest each week that helps alleviate this problem.) God will sometimes force you to stop and rest, using an illness or an injury or a layoff or some other method to slow you down long enough to replenish you physically, emotionally, and spiritually. He cares for us in practical ways. Notice how God takes Elijah to Step 2 of the perseverance program.

Step 2: When you're discouraged, God lets you vent.

Elijah got rest and nourishment, yet he still had all his emotions of panic, desperation, loneliness, self-pity, and discouragement to deal with. So God met him and gave him a way to vent:

> *And the word of the LORD came to him: "What are you doing here, Elijah?"*
>
> 1 Kings 19:9

Elijah answered God by pouring out all his feelings and telling him what was on his mind. Do you trust God with your feelings? God knows them already, but there is something therapeutic about verbalizing to him your worries, fears, and discouragement. Even though Elijah was overdramatizing his problems, God didn't get frustrated with him. He wasn't horrified. He didn't turn away from Elijah. Instead, he introduced him to the third step in his perseverance program.

Step 3: When you want to give up, God reminds you who he is.

God listened to Elijah's feelings about wanting to give up, and then he gave him an experience that let Elijah see who he really is.

> *The LORD said, "Go out and stand on the mountain in the presence of the LORD, for the LORD is about to pass by."*
>
> 1 Kings 19:11

God showed Elijah his power in the wind, earthquake, and fire. When you think you've got big problems, God will let you know in some unmistakable way that he's bigger than your problems. If you think you're the only one who can solve everything, God will remind you that solving everything is his job. God wanted Elijah to stop trying to be God.

Step 4: When you're full of self-pity, God gives you a task and friends.

God's last therapy for this quitter was to get him to stop being self-absorbed.

> *The LORD said to him, "Go back the way you came.... When you get there, anoint Hazael.... 16Also, anoint Jehu ... and anoint Elisha ... to succeed you as prophet....18Yet I reserve seven thousand in Israel—all whose knees have not bowed down to Baal and whose mouths have not kissed him."*
>
> 1 Kings 19:15–16, 18

God gave Elijah a task and some friends. He gave Elijah a new primary companion, Elisha, someone to whom his mantle of leadership would someday fall. But God went one step further: he gave Elijah (who felt all alone) a crowd to belong to—seven thousand strong! When you're full of self-pity, God's solution is to get your eyes off yourself by giving you a job to do and people with whom to do it. He might restore to you your original dream, or he might give you a new thing to do.

Journal

Second Corinthians 4:7–10 is a passage about persevering under intense pressure. The entire text has been inserted in the chart below, in pairs of contrasting phrases. For each part of the passage, think about an area in which you feel like quitting and write your own paraphrase of the text starting in verse 8.

7But we have this treasure ... **Example:** *I have the treasure of the Holy Spirit ...*	in jars of clay ... **Example:** *in the jar of clay that is my broken body. I am not worthy to hold God's spirit, yet he chooses to live in me ...*
to show that this all-surpassing power is from God ... **Example:** *to know that God's power is sufficient with my credit card debt ...*	and not from us ... **Example:** *and that reducing my debt will not be by my power or might ...*
8We are hard pressed on every side...	but not crushed ...
perplexed ...	but not in despair ...
9persecuted ...	but not abandoned ...
struck down ...	but not destroyed ...

¹⁰We always carry around in our body the death of Jesus ...	so that the life of Jesus may also be revealed in our body.

What has this exercise revealed to you about how to persevere in your situation?

_____

_____

_____

_____

_____

PRAYER

Precious Lord,

    Thank you so much that when I feel like quitting, you pursue me. Thank you that you make sure I get the rest and nourishment I need to revive me. Thank you for being gracious enough to let me vent my feelings of discouragement and self-pity on you. Thank you that no matter how big my problems may feel, you are bigger than that which is dragging me down and making me want to quit. And, thank you so much that at the right time, you will give me even more kingdom-building things to do and someone with whom I can do them.

                               In the name of Jesus, amen.

How to Keep On to the End

Eternity … think of it
when you are hard pushed.

**Elizabeth Ann Seton, 1774–1821,
formed relief society for widows**

You've Got Mail

To:	"The Best You" Woman	Sent:	Day 3
From:	Katie Brazelton		
Subject:	Perseverance		

It's Day 3, so here is your weekly Email Message. Feel free to blog me a response at my website, www.LifePurposeCoachingCenters.com/CM, if you'd like. Enjoy the email-coaching and don't forget to open in prayer!

Gladys Aylward Perseveres

One of the most remarkable stories of perseverance I have ever heard is about Gladys Aylward (1902–1970). In 1930, as a twenty-eight-year-old English parlor maid, she had just been rejected by the China Inland Mission to serve as a missionary in China. She had failed their probationary courses in theology and linguistic aptitude, and she was considered too old for the remedial training to prepare for overseas service. Dejected though she was, Gladys did not give up her dream. Look at this dramatic litany of determination shown by this young, single woman:

- She found an elderly missionary in China who needed an assistant, and she went on her own. (Don't gloss over the fact that this was the 1930s!)
- Travel by ship was too costly, so she booked a train ticket, even though the travel agent warned her that overland travel through Russia and Siberia would be quite impossible due to a Russian-Chinese war.
- She left on her perilous, six-week, solo journey to China, during which she endured the dangers of war, arrest, interrogation, a stolen passport and money, sleeping on the train tracks in the Siberian snow, wolves, kidnapping with the intent to send her to a work camp, and rescue by a Japanese ship captain.
- She finally arrived, only to be pelted with mud because she was a "foreign devil." It was weeks before she could venture out of her house without dodging mud, spit, and curses.
- She overcame these difficulties and gained the trust of the people, eventually becoming fluent in the five dialects of her province!
- When war with Japan threatened her village, she took one hundred orphans, ages three to sixteen, on a month-long trek through a war zone over mountain passes to safety, with no food supplies, blankets, or shoes for many of them, and carrying at least one child the entire way.

Gladys had perseverance that was possible because she kept sight of a long-term reward: to save the lives of children, so they would have the opportunity to know Jesus and live forever with him in heaven. When you're motivated by such a phenomenal, long-term reward (in this case an eternal reward), you'll have perseverance too.

Linda's Story of Perseverance

My colleague, Linda, spent many years of her life working with teenagers, so she knows all about perseverance. After fifteen years of youth ministry (as if that wasn't challenging enough), she went to work at the public middle school and was assigned to teach the at-risk students in the in-school suspension class. None of her predecessors in that job had lasted for more than a year; they treated it like glorified babysitting by having the "bad kids" copy dictionary pages for their hour of detention. But Linda looked at her role as a ministry to an entire culture of students about whom she had never given much thought before.

Her principal gave her free rein in the classroom, even knowing she was a minister's wife and former church youth director. She put up Christian posters and kept a student Bible out on her desk. She developed enrichment activities for the students to help them discover the root causes of their problems, and then she taught them how to correct their behaviors.

Throughout her time in this assignment, Linda had to persevere on many levels. She had to learn to love teenagers who were stubborn, hardheaded, and downright rude. She had to battle with other teachers who questioned her teaching techniques. She had to find enough qualified volunteers to work with students one-on-one, so she recruited Christian moms. She invited her students to church, and then had to contend with her own church ushers who turned away her students at the door, because they rode up on skateboards or smelled of cigarette smoke. One Sunday she had to pursue a student who ran out of church when he recognized the man singing a solo. (A few days earlier, the soloist had rudely run the student off his property.) The Lord taught Linda to show love, mercy, compassion, grace, and patience toward these difficult teens, and many of them received Christ and got connected to churches because of her methods. Her five years in that job is still an all-time record—no one else has stayed as long in that public school's most notorious classroom!

PERSISTING IN FAITH FOR ETERNAL REWARDS

Sometimes, when Linda was having a rough day at school, she got through it by thinking of the hot bubble bath that would be her reward in the evening. But on other days, a luxurious bath just wasn't enough to keep her there. Sometimes, the only reward big enough to get you and Linda to stick with a tough assignment is God's promise of heavenly rewards. So, when you feel like giving up, here are two principles about rewards to help you persevere.

Life is a race and there's a prize at the end.

The apostle Paul pictures life as a race, and at the end of the race, prizes are awarded. When you know there are going to be prizes, and when you know the prizes are things you really want, you are more effectively motivated to run your best in a race.

Do you not know that in a race all the runners run, but only one gets the prize? Run in such a way as to get the prize.

1 Corinthians 9:24

The quality of the prize helps determine how long we persevere. Paul says that our crown will last forever. Aiming for an eternal crown—having eternal perspective—motivates us to go into strict training.

Everyone who competes in the games goes into strict training. They do it to get a crown that will not last; but we do it to get a crown that will last forever.

1 Corinthians 9:25

It's that eternal perspective, the knowledge that the real adventure is going to be eternity in heaven, which enables us to persevere through the strict training here on earth.

Winners *always* focus on the prize.

To maintain the highest level of devotion to the training and the race itself, winners always focus on the prize—whether that's the weight loss, a gold medal, prestige, a world record, or the residual sponsorships and endorsements! When there is a big prize at stake, a true champion will not weaken her concentration by thinking about past failures, which is paralyzing, or past victories, which causes carelessness.

Forgetting what is behind and straining toward what is ahead, [14]I press on toward the goal to win the prize for which God has called me heavenward in Christ Jesus.

Philippians 3:13–14

TRAINING WELL AND PUSHING THROUGH TO THE END

If you've read one of my other books, *Pathway to Purpose for Women,* you may have gotten a chuckle over the story about my pitiful struggle to train for a marathon. But I must say that those days taught me two important lessons that pertain here: (1) real racers follow a regimen, and (2) real racers finish the race.

Real racers follow a regimen.

A serious runner knows that the less weight she carries, the greater her stamina. She is willing to be disciplined in this area and follow any diet/exercise regimen her coach prescribes. The training regimen we go through in the Christian life involves, in part, getting rid of any entanglements that slow us down.

> *Let us throw off everything that hinders and the sin that so easily entangles. And let us run with perseverance the race marked out for us.*
>
> Hebrews 12:1

Notice that there are two types of things to throw off—hindrances and sin. Sin, we know, keeps us from competing in the spiritual race of life—it's like being a smoker and trying to run in the Olympics. But what are the hindrances to which this verse is referring? What's tying you down? Your possessions? A relationship? A habit? Worry? Guilt? This race of life is not a sprint; it's a marathon. This means we need to divest ourselves of everything that is holding us back and depleting our stamina.

Real racers finish the race.

Stay diligent until the end of the race. If you let up when you think you're getting close to the end, you could lose all for which you have so diligently strived. If you think your hard work has given you the right to slack off a little and coast, think again.

> *We want each of you to show this same diligence to the very end, in order to make your hope sure. [12] We do not want you to become lazy, but to imitate those who through faith and patience inherit what has been promised.*
>
> Hebrews 6:11–12

Diligence, commitment, persistence, right to the very end; whether you feel like it or not. That's a mark of character. That's perseverance.

Robertson McQuilkin, a Persevering Hero

In 1990, *Christianity Today*'s memorable story about Robertson McQuilkin, "Living by Vows," caught my eye. Robertson stunned the academic world when he left the presidency of Columbia Bible College and Seminary to care full-time for his wife, Muriel, who was dying of Alzheimer's. He had been advised to put her in a home or hire a nurse, but that did not set right with Robertson. He declared in his farewell speech that the decision about her care had been made forty-two years earlier, when he promised to "care for Muriel in sickness and in health ... till death do us part." Although Robertson did try the in-home nurse route for several months, Muriel grew more and more distressed and terror-stricken whenever he was not with her. As soon as he would leave for work, she would follow him, sometimes walking the mile to school as many as ten times a day. Their family doctor surmised that the love she had developed over the years for Robertson was the predominant thought she retained as her mind failed her. "When the time came, the decision was firm," said Robertson. "It took no great calculation. It was a matter of integrity, of keeping my commitment. This was no grim duty to which I was stoically resigned, however. It was only fair. She had, after all, cared for me for almost four decades with marvelous devotion; now it was my turn. If I took care of her for forty years, I would never be out of her debt. I don't *have* to care for her. I *get* to."

Journal

Gladys, Linda, and Robertson demonstrated perseverance despite their stamina being regularly depleted. Which of the following issues are depleting your stamina?

☐ Conflicting priorities	☐ Lack of resources
☐ Criticism	(money or other)
☐ Danger	☐ Loneliness
☐ Difficult learning curve	☐ Loving with no return
☐ Difficult people	☐ Overload
☐ Extreme exertion	☐ Persecution
☐ Failure	☐ Prejudice
☐ Hopeless task	☐ Self-sacrifice
☐ Keeping a commitment	

Referring specifically to any issue(s) that may be depleting your stamina, write out the text of Philippians 3:13b–14 in your own words.

But one thing I do: Forgetting what is behind and straining toward what is ahead, I press on toward the goal to win the prize for which God has called me heavenward in Christ Jesus.

_____

_____

_____

_____

_____

PRAYER

Precious Lord,

I praise you for the heavenly rewards that make my earthly trials worth enduring. Thank you that even the most extreme sacrifices and difficult commitments can be endured because of the promises you have made to take care of me and reward me. I need your strength to keep my focus in the right place. A focus on my past troubles is demotivating; a focus on my failures is debilitating; but if I focus on the eternal prize, that's invigorating. Help me to live the disciplined life of a real racer. Help me to disentangle myself from the encumbrances that are dragging me down. Help me to finish well, keep my commitments, and not lose heart at the end, even when I have spent my last ounce of energy. My character is seen not in how I get off the starting blocks, but in how I run the race and cross the finish line. Give me your power to persevere to the end with honor, integrity, and love.

In the name of Jesus, amen.

Your Perseverance Coach

Nothing in this world can take the place of persistence. Talent will not; nothing is more common than unsuccessful individuals with talent. Genius will not; unrewarded genius is almost a proverb. Education will not; the world is full of educated derelicts. The slogan "Press on" has solved and always will solve the problems of the human race.

Calvin Coolidge, 30th president of the United States

PERSPECTIVE-CHANGING OUTING

For our last coaching conversation together, you have a surprise for me. You invite me to a nearby open field, where you have been building something ever since we started this character-coaching journey. You proudly show me a three-foot-long, knee-tall retaining wall, hidden off the beaten path, that you have built out of river rocks. You chose beautiful stones that you carefully lodged into place with mud. You show me a few meaningful stones that you have placed in the wall, your "stones of remembrance": a small, insignificant brown stone for humility; a rock glittering with quartzite for self-confidence; one that juts out and anchors the corner of the wall for courage; the entire retaining wall itself really signifies self-control; the rock with a crack that reminds you to be patient; a rock with a smile-shaped indentation for contentment; the rock glistening with fool's gold speaks to you about true generosity; and the capstone, which you placed only when you had completed the wall, signifies perseverance. We'll sit under a shade tree close by, say an opening prayer, and talk about how well you're persevering in the areas of challenges, prayer, and your focus on long-term rewards.

PERSEVERING IN CHALLENGES

Ninety-nine percent of the failures come from people
who have the habit of making excuses.

George Washington, first U.S. President

In our culture, *determination* is so passé — it's much more preferable to be flexible. We can't express our *convictions* anymore — we'd be labeled intolerant. Those who exercise *discipline* are considered control freaks. The problem is, without determination, conviction, and discipline, we shrivel up in boredom and despair. When you remove every challenge, reduce every standard, and soften every obstacle, there are no meaningful rewards to gain.

When Shelley Saw How People Need a Challenge

One of the most riveting altar calls I, Shelley, have ever observed took place in a youth group meeting I attended as a teenager. The speaker did not paint the usual picture of a rosy Christian life with every problem solved as we await the bliss of heaven. Instead, he spent the time telling the kids that the Christian life is the most difficult life we can choose. He said things like, "You are guaranteed to have trials. If you live right, you'll be persecuted. Character development hurts." He told the students that there is no more challenging, more frustrating, more demanding, yet more deeply rewarding life in all the world; and even if there were no promise of heaven, the Christian life would still be the most fulfilling way to live. Well, I have never seen a non-stadium altar call with a higher percentage of the audience going forward to receive Christ. The front of the room was jammed with students responding to this tough, almost "I dare you" type of call. That message of truth resonated with those students. Why? Because people need to have something in their lives that is bigger than they are.

James talks about Christian challenges and perseverance like this.

Consider it pure joy, my brothers and sisters, whenever you face trials of many kinds, ³because you know that the testing of your faith produces perseverance. ⁴Let perseverance finish its work so that you may be mature and complete, not lacking anything.

James 1:2–4

Think about the trials, tests, and challenges you face in your life right now. In light of that, list at least three skills you are developing as a result of what you are enduring.

Example:

1. *My mother's cancer treatments are causing me to become a deeper student of my mother by trying to really understand her and not just project my own feelings onto her.*
2. *I'm getting good at finding new ways to make her smile.*
3. *I'm learning to release my own expectations of how life should be for me right now.*

1. _____

2. _____

3. _____

PERSEVERING IN PRAYER

We must be in earnest when we kneel at God's footstool. Too often we get faint-hearted and quit praying at the point when we ought to begin. We let go at the very point where we should hold on strongest. Our prayers are weak because they are not impassioned by an unfailing and resistless will.

E. M. Bounds, 1835–1913,
Methodist minister and author on prayer

Now, I want you to recall something about which you have prayed for a long time. Maybe you have prayed off and on about this situation for years, or perhaps you have given up praying about it because God just never seemed to answer you. Jesus told a parable of a widow who prevailed over an unjust judge and got him to meet her request (see Luke 18:1–8). The widow represents each one of us, as a powerless, helpless, hopeless person, unfairly treated, with no other weapon than our persistence. And Jesus' point? If an unjust judge will grant the request of a persistent person, how much more will your loving, heavenly Father respond to your prayers of trust in him?

So, if God loves answering our prayers, why do we sometimes have to persist in prayer about a matter? There are four principles of persistent prayer that we need to understand and evaluate in our lives.

1. Unanswered prayer is how God gets your attention.

Do you look to everyone else to solve your problem before you turn to God? Psalm 105:4 (NCV) says, "Depend on the LORD and his strength; always go to him for help." If you pray perfunctory lip-service about something and then move on to your support group or your mother or the Internet for the "real help," God may delay his answer to your prayer until he has your full attention.

It is important to be aware of the resources you draw upon when you have problems. List the people or places you typically turn to for solutions, and place "Persistent Prayer" on the list in the order in which you usually get to it.

1. _____

2. _____

3. _____

4. _____

5. _____

2. Persevering in prayer adjusts your desires.

Sometimes God uses a time of prolonged prayer in a given area in order to test the depth of our desire or to help us adjust our request.

"I will test them as gold is tested. Then they will pray to me, and I will answer them."

Zechariah 13:9 GNT

What have you prayed for over a period of time, and then realized you didn't really want what you were asking for?

_____

_____

What have you prayed for over a period of time, and as time went by, you modified your request, made it more specific, or altered your direction?

_____

_____

3. Persevering in prayer changes you.

Effective prayer is having meaningful communication with the living God. It connects you to him in conversation and moves you into an intimate union with him. Prayer over time reveals your innermost self to God. It is a crying out, a pouring out, to him from the depth of your soul. It can even be a wrestling with him in dark times. Persistent prayer isn't blackmail, where we threaten God with an "or else" statement. Prayer doesn't change God; it changes us.

What have you prayed for in such a way that you were trying to bargain with God, convince God, or blackmail God?

_____

_____

How has God turned the tables on you and changed you in some way over the course of praying for something?

_____

_____

4. Persevering in prayer is an exercise of faith.

When you persevere in prayer, God grows your character, faith, and hope. Persevering in prayer prepares you for God's answer, which may be bigger than what you are praying for.

> *Now glory be to God who by his mighty power at work within us is able to do far more than we would ever dare to ask or even dream of—infinitely beyond our highest prayers, desires, thoughts, or hopes.*
>
> Ephesians 3:20 LB

The size of your God determines the size of your prayer. What are you praying for that is bigger than you can accomplish through your own power?

_____

_____

Persistent Trust

God expects us to ask continually for the same thing until we get our prayer answered. James 5:16 tells us that the "earnest prayer of a righteous person has great power and produces wonderful results" (NLT). But God wants our sincere and earnest trust, not our insistence. He may answer our prayer after one sincere request, or he may impress upon us to talk with him about it over a long period of time.

PERSEVERING FOR LONG-TERM REWARDS

Everyone who receives Christ is given a place in heaven by the grace of God, and we also receive rewards that make heaven "heavenlier." That means everything I do on earth *by faith* is rewarded: every prayer I pray in faith, every act I perform in faith, every word I speak by faith. Sometimes, the only thing helping us to persevere is the motivation of receiving a reward for what we're doing. In order for those rewards to be a powerful motivation for us to persevere today, we need to understand them and how they work.

Turn to pages 308–309 and let's look at the five types of crowns or rewards mentioned in Scripture. Assess how you are doing at living your life in such a way as to receive these rewards in heaven.

Heavenly Reward	To whom is it awarded?	In what ways are you earning it?
Crown of Joy 1 Thessalonians 2:19 *For what is our hope, our joy, or the crown in which we will glory in the presence of our Lord Jesus when he comes? Is it not you?*	*To people who lead others to Christ*	How are you influencing others to know Christ? **Example:** *I invited my neighbor to my support group for young mothers.* **Your answer:**
Crown of Righteousness 2 Timothy 4:7–8 *I have finished the race, I have kept the faith. ⁸Now there is in store for me the crown of righteousness, which the Lord, the righteous Judge, will award to me on that day—and not only to me, but also to all who have longed for his appearing.*		In what ways (large or small) are you keeping the faith?
Crown of Life James 1:12 *Blessed are those who persevere under trial, because when they have stood the test, they will receive the crown of life that God has promised to those who love him.*		In what are you persevering?
Crown of Glory 1 Peter 5:2–4 *Be shepherds of God's flock that is under your care … ³not lording it over those entrusted to you, but being examples to the flock. ⁴And when the Chief Shepherd appears, you will receive the crown of glory that will never fade away.*		How are you being an example to others?

Heavenly Reward	To whom is it awarded?	In what ways are you earning it?
Imperishable Crown *1 Corinthians 9:24-25* *Do you not know that in a race all the runners run, but only one gets the prize? Run in such a way as to get the prize. ²⁵Everyone who competes in the games goes into strict training. They do it to get a crown that will not last; but we do it to get a crown that will last forever.*		How are you exercising self-control?

As you consider the crowns you have been promised in heaven, how does this encourage you to persevere today?

PRAYER

Precious Lord,

Thank you that there truly is joy in the trial, joy in the testing, and joy in completing the journey of perseverance. These are not just empty concepts, but the true reality for me as your child. Thank you that there are things bigger than me in my life, things I cannot handle. Those are the very motivators you use to teach me joy in trials and perseverance in testing. Continue to teach me that you are completing me and will reward me. Thank you that you set up situations in my life for which I have had to pray with persistence. I thank you that you are a righteous judge who will bring about justice in your incredible timing. Your delays have forced me to pray when my standard circle of support did not have answers. I come again before you to ask specifically and boldly for the request I have had on my heart for some time now. I want you to change me, so I am prepared for your answer. Give me perseverance to keep praying until you answer, the discernment to know when you have answered, and the faith to accept your answer, no matter what it is. Adjust my desires and help me to see my prayer request the way you do.

Thank you for the rewards you promise me just for living life by faith. Help me to shine for you in such a way that others will come to know you. Help me to stay faithful, persevere, be a good example, and live in a self-disciplined manner, so as to earn the ultimate reward, your greeting, "Well done, good and faithful servant. Come and share my joy with me."

In the name of Jesus, amen.

Steps to Perseverance

I will persist until I succeed. I will consider each day's effort as but one blow of my blade against a mighty oak. The first blow may cause not a tremor in the wood, nor the second, nor the third. Each blow, of itself, may be a trifling, and seem of no consequence. Yet, from childish swipes the oak will eventually tumble. I will be like the rain drop which washes away the mountain; the ant who devours a tiger. I will build my castle one brick at a time, for I know that small attempts, repeated, will complete any undertaking.

Og Mandino, 1923–1996, *The Greatest Salesman Who Ever Lived*

SITTING QUIETLY WITH YOUR MAKER

Today is a time of reflection and solitude for you in the privacy of your own quiet-time space. As you put together a Perseverance Action Plan, you can actually say that you persevered to the end because you have nearly finished this book! This week's action steps center on developing diligence, finishing well, and goal-setting. Way to persevere—you just need this one last hurrah and you're done!

Ask yourself how deeply you are able to focus on increasing your perseverance during this season of your life. Then select the appropriate action steps on pages 311–314, whatever you feel you can realistically experiment with this week. It's your plan, your life, and your prayerful decision—nobody else's. If you feel God impressing on you to concentrate on your perseverance right now, go for these exercises with gusto—without further ado or delay! I am confident that whatever effort you are able to devote to improving your perseverance will be richly rewarded by him on earth and in heaven.

Perseverance Action Plan

PRAYER FOCUS: Pray for God's perspective on your work, and ask him to show you ways you can be more diligent. Ask God to help you persevere to the finish line and to live so you please him as an audience of one. Persevere in prayer, asking God to show you his vision for your life and for diligence to continue doing what he has given you to do today.

DEVOTIONAL FOCUS: Choose one of the following Scripture passages on the topic of perseverance: To focus on *developing more diligence*, read 2 Timothy 4:1–5 regarding the benefits of spiritual diligence. To focus on *finishing well*, read 2 Timothy 4:6–8 regarding the motivation to finish well. To focus on *goal-setting*, read 1 Corinthians 9:24–27 and apply the principles of preparing for a race to goal-setting.

EXTRA PERSPECTIVE: Read about reaching goals in *Nine Things You Simply Must Do: To Succeed in Love and Life* by Henry Cloud. Or get creative and grab a Purpose Partner (a girlfriend!) or a Life Purpose Coach® (from www. LifePurposeCoachingCenters.com/CM) to help you understand your life calling more clearly as you go through *Conversations on Purpose* by Katie Brazelton.

Action Steps: Developing Diligence

Instructions: Prayerfully choose one or two action steps to experiment with this week.

Start Date

_____ ☐ **I will improve my quality.** I will choose one task that I have grown lazy doing, and I will improve the quality with which I complete it (i.e., making dinner and setting a table worthy of guests or working in the church nursery). *(Identify the task and the manner in which you want to improve the quality.)*

_____

_____ ☐ **I will be prompt.** I will choose one area in which I tend to miss deadlines (i.e., paying bills, turning in forms, replying to correspondence, completing projects), and I will make the changes necessary to be prompt. *(Identify the area in which to be prompt.)*

_____

_____ ☐ **I will get good advice.** Whether I'm starting a business, running a marathon, or growing a garden, I will seek advice from someone who has succeeded at it. *(Identify your area of interest and the person you will ask to help you.)*

_____ ☐ **I will take responsibility.** I will take ownership and be account-able for my actions. I will stop acting like someone else will take care of things (i.e., disciplining the children, repairing the car, doing the taxes, finding a job). *(Identify the area for which you will take responsibility.)*

_____ ☐ **I will handle success carefully.** When I succeed at something, I will undertake as much self-evaluation as if I had failed. *(Failure naturally causes me to look at where I went wrong and course-correct; whereas, unexamined success can fool me into com-placency, allowing me to ignore potential problems.)* *(Identify a success you need to examine more closely.)*

_____ ☐ **I will develop** diligence by *(add your idea here)*

Action Steps: Finishing Well

Instructions: Prayerfully choose one or two action steps to experiment with this week.

Start Date

_____ ☐ **I will finish a project.** I will choose one unfinished project around my house and complete it. *(Name a project to complete.)*

_____ ☐ **I will evaluate and let go.** I will clear my plate of any unfinished projects that are not worth completing, because they no longer hold interest for me or have ceased to be beneficial or are using my energy unwisely. I will pray for wisdom to discern whether

I am being a quitter or getting smarter! *(Name a project to eliminate.)*

_____

☐ **I will keep a promise.** If there is a vow, promise, commitment, or pledge I made that I have not been honoring, I will restate my intention to keep my word and, with God's help and my dogged determination, I will start honoring my vow again. *(Write a vow you will start honoring.)*

_____

☐ **I will memorize a promise.** I will memorize a biblical promise to help me persevere here on earth. God's promises help me look forward to his rewards in heaven. (Biblical promises to consider: Romans 8:37–39; Hebrews 7:25–26; 1 Peter 1:6–8.) *(Choose a verse to memorize.)*

_____

☐ **I will finish** well by *(add your idea here)*

Action Steps: Goal-Setting

Instructions: Prayerfully choose one or two action steps to experiment with this week.

Start Date

_____

☐ **I will assess responsibilities.** I will evaluate and define my responsibilities for people, organizations, and things. I will own those duties that are mine, while not taking on responsibilities that belong to others.

_____

☐ **I will set responsibility goals.** Some of my purpose in life pertains to my influence on others. I will set goals for those responsibilities that I have to teach, influence, or help other people (i.e., teaching life skills to my children; coaching my team on sportsmanship; helping my aging parent downsize to a smaller home). *(Identify an area of responsibility for which you will set goals.)*

_____ ☐ **I will understand my competencies.** I will develop a clear picture of both my capabilities and the things I cannot do. I will find ways to do what I'm good at more of the time. And I will get help and stop frustrating myself in areas where I am not skilled.

_____ ☐ **I will set competency goals.** I will determine what skills or areas of expertise I would like to develop, and I will establish goals and a plan for developing myself in that area. I will stretch myself to learn something new. *(Choose a competency on which you would like to work.)*

_____

_____ ☐ **I will find my passion.** I will take steps to discover what I am passionate about — what important cause or activity I return to again and again out of enjoyment, interest, concern, or fulfillment.

_____ ☐ **I will write a life mission statement.** I will prayerfully craft a mission statement that will succinctly summarize what kind of person I want to be (my characteristics), what I believe God wants me to do (my purpose), the kind of impact I want to have (my influence), and the source of my power to accomplish this (God). (To see some sample life mission statements, go to www.LifePurpose CoachingCenters.com/CM.)

_____ ☐ **I will set goals** in the areas of *(add your ideas here)*

_____

_____

_____

_____

MASTER ACTION PLAN

Now, select only one major action step from this Day 5 exercise and record it on your Master Action Plan in appendix A on page 322. When you have finished reading this book, continue to refer to that one major action step on your Master Action Plan (as well as this Perseverance Action Plan, of course, as your season of life permits!). Remember, in order to become more like Christ in your character, you need to collaborate with God in three ways: preparation, prayer, and practice. You have done the work of preparation by learning God's truth about perseverance. Now, internalize it by praying for the Holy Spirit's help and practicing your action steps, one by one.

PERSEVERANCE PRAYER

Precious Lord,

We made it to the end of this topic and the end of this book—together! Thank you so much for sticking by me and encouraging me along the way. I could not have made it to the finish line without you. You are magnificent. You are holy. You are worthy of all praise, especially mine. You finish what you start—even as you continue to pour your grace and love into this good work you have begun in me. Thank you that you yourself persevered, even to death on the cross for me. Thank you that you have never given up on me. Thank you that my character makeover was, is, and will continue to be a top priority to you!

In the name of Jesus, amen.

Afterword

Good character is more to be praised than outstanding talent. Most talents are, to some extent, a gift. Good character, by contrast, is not given to us. We have to build it piece by piece, by thought, choice, courage and determination.

John Luther

PBPGINFWMY

You may be heading to the finish line of this book, but you already realize that your journey of remodeling your character has only just begun. I know I'm *dating* myself here, but do you remember many years ago when there was a proliferation of buttons and bumper stickers that read, "PBPGINFWMY"? Well, if you don't recall, don't be alarmed—the keys on my keyboard did not get stuck. The acronym stands for "Please Be Patient; God Is Not Finished With Me Yet." We used to wear this slogan back in the Stone Age as a way to tell others to give us time to let God do his work in us. But I want to alter the direction of this slogan. Instead of saying it to someone else, turn it inward, and say to *yourself* about *yourself*, "Be patient with me." Don't expect of yourself that you will have all these character qualities wired at this point. Give yourself grace. God is at work in you, and he's not done with you yet. We have assurance in Scripture that what God starts, he finishes:

> *Being confident of this, that he who began a good work in you will carry it on to completion until the day of Christ Jesus.*
>
> Philippians 1:6

God's character makeover is a lifelong process. He started it with the good work of salvation, and he won't put the finishing touches on our Christlike character until we are united with Jesus in heaven. In the meantime, the task of transforming our character is still a collaborative effort that takes both God's strength and our choices.

What to Do After the Last Page

When you have finished reading this book, here are some suggestions for sticking with your plan:

1. Review your journals. Go back and read through your written responses throughout the book. Where do you see growth already? Where have you made changes? What relationships have improved as a result of actions steps you have taken? How has your prayer life changed since you started reading this book?

2. Start on your top three priorities. Go to your completed Master Plan and put an asterisk next to your three most urgent action steps. Begin working on those, if you haven't already. Accomplishing a few of these priorities will get the pump primed for doing the rest of your Master Plan, which in turn, will motivate you to work through your Action Plans in Day 5 for each character trait.

3. Keep praying. As you practice the disciplines of each character trait and hone them into habits, be sure to pray through the daily character prayers, asking for the Holy Spirit's power to make each character quality real in your life.

What to Do When You Need a Real-Life Coach

If you have steadily followed along through *Character Makeover*, you have already experienced milestones, turning points, and victories in your quest to deepen your character and be the best woman God created you to be. You may have also gotten stuck, made mistakes, or experienced some frustration with yourself as you have gone through this book. That is to be expected when you're serious about becoming more like Christ.

Now, I encourage you to take this journey to the next level. You have gotten this far with me as your coach on paper, and perhaps with a prayer partner with whom you have shared your progress. From here on out, there are a few ways you can fortify your character development process for added community and accountability.

1. Find a real-life coach. At www.LifePurposeCoachingCenters.com/ CM, my ministry website for Life Purpose Coaching Centers, International®, you will find a wonderful group of certified Life Purpose Telephone and Face-to-Face Coaches and 2-Day Intensive Facilitators, some of whom were featured in this book. If you want to go further with a personal coach who can help you with your specific issues of character development, contact one of our coaches for further information.

2. Use the other terrific web resources at www.LifePurposeCoaching Centers.com/CM. Join our Character Builders Open Forum where many of our Life Purpose Coaches, Shelley, and I dialogue with you about our experiences with character building. There is an Idea Exchange where readers share with each other their character prayers and the action steps that are working for them. You'll also get to read character-building articles, and try out additional self-testing tools. And, here is where you will find contact information for the Coaches whose stories are included in this book.

3. Download a small group curriculum for *Character Makeover*. Life change takes place best in community. Go to the website to order study guides for your small group members to deepen your experience with the book.

Thank you for the privilege of being your character coach throughout this book. Congratulations on your stick-to-itiveness! I close with something that the apostle Paul often did in the openings of his letters—he prayed for the character of his readers. This is the prayer I am praying for your character, adapted from Paul's prayer for the Colossians:

Precious Lord,

I ask you to fill my sister in Christ with a special knowledge of your will for her life. Lord, she'll need deep, Christlike character in order to fully realize her godly dreams. Plus, she'll need spiritual wisdom and insight for all the character-building circumstances in which she finds herself. Deepen her character to equip her to live the kind of life that shines your light in her world. Grow her into a Christlikeness that pleases you in every way, as her capacity for every kind of good work grows and expands because of the depth of her knowledge about you. I ask you to strengthen this precious daughter of yours by your unparalleled love, with all the joy and conviction she needs to follow her/your Master Action Plan. Bless her abundantly for having found the courage, humility, and perseverance to do a character makeover that glorifies you!

In the holy name of Jesus, amen.

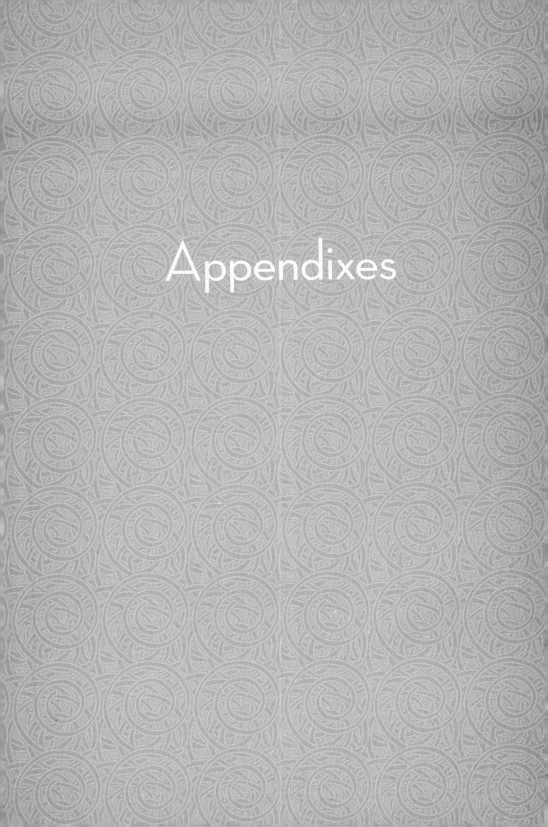

Appendixes

Master Action Plan

This is your Master Plan for building godly character qualities into your life. With so much to process every week and numerous action steps possible for building up each character trait, it can be overwhelming. This Master Action Plan is designed to help you condense your action steps from each week's work down to your eight most important goals: one for each character quality. Select the most important action step from each of your Day 5 exercises, and write each one in the space provided below, indicating a date you would like to begin to take the step.

By When

Humility _____

Confidence _____

Courage _____

Patience _____

Self-Control _____

Contentment _____

Generosity _____

Perseverance _____

Top Three Priorities: Now, place an asterisk by those three characteristics you listed that you feel need your earliest attention. Plan to focus on those first! Review and update your Master Action Plan regularly with your Accountability Partner (or new Character Coach), using any of your Day 5 answers or, perhaps, fresh ideas God brings to mind.

Scripture-Rich Prayer for Each Character Trait

Enjoy these in-depth, Scripture-rich prayers about all the character traits you have studied in this book, or choose one prayer in particular that your Master Plan suggests would be most beneficial to you. Each prayer represents a summary of the biblical teaching within its character-related chapter of the book. Let the Lord be your guide as you pray about which Bible passages he would like you to look up and meditate on more deeply. Don't feel compelled to look up all the references! We've simply included them to save you time, if you are interested in going deeper on a given subject. God will convict you of which ones you are to stop and ponder. The idea is to simply enjoy praying in a "concept summary" fashion, while being refreshed (spontaneously) by God's Word.

HUMILITY PRAYER

Lord, I want to humble myself under your mighty hand. When I focus on you, how can I help but be humble? When I look at creation and see the work of your hands, I become deeply aware, not of my worthlessness, but of my unworthiness *(Psalm 8:3–4)*. You are powerful to heal, kind to redeem me from destruction, merciful to bless me, bountiful to provide for me, patient to withhold the judgment I deserve, gracious to forgive me, and fatherlike to make allowances for my immaturity *(Psalm 103:1–18)*. Help me focus more and more on you so I reflect your glory *(2 Corinthians 3:18)*. Help me want, wholeheartedly, to discover things about you I didn't know before *(Deuteronomy 4:29)*.

Forgive me for the pride of self-sufficiency, when I live by my abilities instead of by your Word *(Luke 4:3–4)*. Forgive me for the pride of being spectacular, when I choose to show off instead of giving you glory *(Luke 4:9–12)*. Forgive me for the pride of being powerful, where I haughtily take charge instead of waiting on you for your place to use my gifts *(Luke 4:5–8)*. Forgive me for the pride of disobedience, when it seems too demeaning to do things your way *(2 Kings 5:11–13)*. Forgive me for the pride of self-pity, when I need to feel like a hero but instead I feel unrecognized, unapplauded, and ignored *(Esther 6:6–12)*. Forgive me for the pride of conspicuousness, serving where I'll be noticed and trying to appear holy *(Matthew 6:16)*. Forgive me for the pride of a judgmental attitude, ignoring my own shortcomings even as I criticize others *(Matthew 7:1–5)*. When disaster strikes or something I care about is destroyed, show me if, perhaps, it was my own pride that brought it about *(Proverb 16:18)*.

Straining to become humble only leads to self-consciousness and pride; but training my attention on you decreases my self-consciousness and has a side effect of making me humble *(John 3:30)*. Lord, help me focus on your will and surrender my own will in obedience to you *(Luke 22:42)*. Help me focus on your goals, plans, agendas, and choices, and die to myself *(Galatians 2:20)*. Help me focus on your power and sufficiency, and release my need to be ever-capable *(2 Corinthians 12:9–10)*. Help me focus on your example of leaving heaven to submit to death, and help me give up my rights, as needed *(Philippians 2:5–10)*.

Focusing on you also allows me to see others as you see them. Help me to regard the needs of others as more important than my own *(Philippians 2:3)*. May I be more interested in others than I am in talking about myself *(Philippians 2:4)*. Help me see the needs of others; then make me humble enough to meet those needs, even if it is not in my gift area *(John 13:3–5)*. May I treat others with gentleness and have the genuine, winsome spirit that a truthful, humble person exudes *(Matthew 11:29)*. Amen.

CONFIDENCE PRAYER

Lord, it boosts my confidence to know that you have loved me with an everlasting love *(Jeremiah 31:3)*; that you chose me before the creation of the world and made me perfect *(Ephesians 1:4)*; that you made me acceptable *(Ephesians 1:6)*; that I am valuable to you *(Luke 12:24)*; that your thoughts about me outnumber the grains of sand *(Psalm 139:17–18)*; that I can always approach you and receive grace *(Hebrews 4:16)*; and that I can always pray to you and be heard *(1 John 5:14)*.

Forgive me for those times when I place my confidence in the wrong things *(Job 15:31)*: my own strength *(Psalm 33:16)*, my appearance *(1 Peter 3:3–4)*, my achievements *(Jeremiah 48:7 NASB)*, my possessions *(Psalm 49:6–7)*, my goodness *(Ezekiel 33:13)*, my wisdom *(Jeremiah 9:23–24)*, what other people can do for me *(Jeremiah 17:5)*, or the opinions of others *(Job 19:1–3)*. You want me to place my confidence in you *(Psalm 38:15)*. Forgive me for letting my self-esteem be harmed by the talk of godless people *(Proverbs 11:9)*, and for all the time I've wasted being wounded by their thoughtless words *(Proverbs 12:18)*. You want to establish my self-esteem on the firm foundation of you *(1 Corinthians 3:9, 11)*. Forgive me for unwisely comparing myself with others *(2 Corinthians 10:12)*; you want me to look to you for approval *(2 Corinthians 10:17–18)*. Forgive me for mistaking my feelings for facts; you want me to tell the truth to myself, because the truth will set me free *(John 8:32)*. Forgive me for my negative self-talk; you want me to focus on what is true, noble, right, pure, lovely, admirable, and praiseworthy—even if it's about me *(Philippians 4:8)*.

Thank you for preserving my confidence when it could be shaken by my circumstances *(Isaiah 54:10)*, by being abandoned *(Psalm 27:10)*, by sudden trouble *(Proverbs 3:25)*, by what people can do to me *(Hebrews 13:6)*, or by being thrust into a situation I'm untrained to handle *(Acts 4:13)*. Thank you that when I keep my eyes on you, my face will not be covered with shame *(Psalm 34:5)*.

You have given my life meaning by appointing me to bear fruit *(John 15:16)*, perform my unique function in the body of Christ *(Romans 12:4–6)*, and be your temple *(1 Corinthians 3:16)* and your ambassador *(2 Corinthians 5:20)*. You give me confidence and security when I honor you *(Proverbs 14:26)*, respect you *(Job 4:6)*, and live in fellowship with you *(1 John 2:28)*. I have strength for all things in you, Christ, who empowers me—I am ready for anything and equal to anything through you who infuse inner strength into me; that is, I am sufficient in your sufficiency *(Philippians 4:13 AB)*! Amen.

COURAGE PRAYER

Lord, thank you that you want my life to be a fulfilling, joyous adventure *(John 10:10)*. It gives me courage to know that you will be with me wherever I go *(Joshua 1:9)*, that you hear me when I'm in trouble and call for help *(Psalm 34:6)*, and that you have set your angels to encamp around me and defend me from harm *(Psalm 34:7)*. Whenever I feel afraid, I just say to myself, "If God is for me, who can be against me?" *(Romans 8:31b)*.

I confess that I feel worried when I focus on the past *(Philippians 3:13b)* and when I imagine what could happen in the future *(Matthew 6:34)*. My fearful spirit saps my energy and plays tricks with my mind *(2 Timothy 1:7)*. My anxiety destroys my peace and makes me feel vulnerable *(Philippians 4:6–7)*. But your perfect love for me drives out all my fears *(1 John 4:18)*. When I'm afraid that I won't have enough, you provide for me *(Matthew 6:33)*; when I feel depleted and cowardly, you restore my energy *(Isaiah 40:31)*; and when I turn my anxieties into prayers and thanksgiving, you replace my unrest with a surprising peace *(John 14:27)*.

Help me to have the courage to put off falsehood and speak the truth to my neighbor *(Ephesians 4:25)*. Give me the courage to take on a daunting task, knowing that you are with me and that you will see it through to its completion *(1 Chronicles 28:20)*. When I feel threatened by people, help me to trust in you and not be afraid, because what can mortal man do to me *(Psalm 56:3–4)*? When my world is falling down around me and I feel all my security crashing, help me to find courage by taking refuge in you *(Psalm 46:1–2)*.

You have not given me a spirit of fear, but of power and of love and of a sound mind *(2 Timothy 1:7)*. And, Lord, thank you for the gift of courage that you give me when I embrace the power of your presence in me that is greater than anything that can threaten me in the world *(1 John 4:4b)*. Amen.

SELF-CONTROL PRAYER

Lord, thank you so much for the power that I can tap into, through you, to exercise self-control *(Philippians 4:13)*. Even though I have your power in me, I still need your help to unplug from my old power source ("reckon myself dead to sin"), and plug into the right power source ("reckon myself alive to God") *(Romans 6:11)*. Help me put to death the sinful, earthly things lurking within me *(Colossians 3:5)* and to take hold of your power that is already at work within me and that is able to do exceedingly abundantly more than I can imagine *(Ephesians 3:20)*.

Control my words, Lord, for they have power to wound or power to heal *(Proverbs 12:18)*. They can bring death *(Matthew 5:22)* or life *(Proverbs 15:4)*. They can stir up gossip or keep a confidence *(Proverbs 11:13)*. They can be rash and hasty *(Ecclesiastes 5:2)* or well-considered and wise *(Proverbs 3:21)*. They can exasperate *(Ephesians 6:4)* or encourage *(Proverbs 12:25)*. They can be unwholesome or beneficial to the hearer *(Ephesians 4:29)*. They can explode with anger *(Ecclesiastes 7:9)* or show remarkable patience *(Proverbs 14:29; 15:18)*. They can be full of poison or rich with kindness *(Ephesians 4:31–32)*. They can be judgmental *(Romans 14:13)* or forgiving *(Mark 11:25)*. Help me remember that self-control means controlling my tongue! *(Proverbs 13:3 LB)*.

Control my impulses, Lord, and make me a woman of self-discipline *(1 Corinthians 9:24–27)*. Help me to practice those positive actions that will lead to good habits *(Galatians 6:7–10)* and avoid things that will tempt me *(Proverbs 4:14–15)*. Help me to habitually study your Word *(Psalm 1:2)*. Help me to make good choices about those with whom I spend time *(Psalm 1:1)*. Always provide an effective accountability partner for me *(Ecclesiastes 4:9–10)*. And, Lord, I know you want me to stop each week and devote myself to the joy and peace that comes from worshiping you, just as you instructed your people in the Old Testament *(Exodus 20:8–11)*. Tired, worn-out people have a very hard time exercising self-control, which is why you invite me to enter into your rest *(Matthew 11:28–29)*, so that I can be rejuvenated and restored for your work *(Isaiah 40:31)*. Thank you. Amen.

PATIENCE PRAYER

I'd like to adopt this prayer for patience: Lord, give me patience, and give it to me ... whenever it pleases you. I'll wait.

I confess my self-centeredness, which makes me forget how much mercy and unlimited patience you have shown me *(1 Timothy 1:16)*. Help me to show more love by being more patient *(1 Corinthians 13:4)*. Give me a deeper understanding of people, so I may overcome my impatience with them *(Proverbs 14:29)*. Help me to listen first and answer later *(Proverbs 18:13)*. I want to be known for showing grace by making wise allowances for the faults of others *(Ephesians 4:2)* and for ignoring insults *(Proverbs 12:16)*. I ask for the strength to follow your example, Jesus, and not force people to change *(Mark 10:21–22)*. Give me the wisdom to not smother people—to know when to embrace, and when to refrain from embracing *(Ecclesiastes 3:5b)*.

As I go through my day, help me to slow down, be still, wait patiently for you, and stop fretting *(Psalm 37:7–8)*. Forgive me for being haughty, rude, demanding, irritable, touchy, and for keeping a record of wrongs when one of my pet peeves surfaces *(1 Corinthians 13:5)*. Help me to replace those reactions with the unfading inner beauty of a gentle and quiet spirit *(1 Peter 3:4)*. When it feels like things are taking too long, remind me that you're never late *(Ecclesiastes 3:11)*, and that if I trust you, you will act on my behalf *(Psalm 37:5)*. Help me not to jump the gun, but to count the cost *(Luke 14:28)*, and wait to move ahead until you give me peace *(1 Corinthians 14:33)*.

When I find myself in a wilderness time, use it to help me know you better *(Philippians 3:10)*. Refresh me through the waiting *(Isaiah 40:31)*. Remind me that you're not being slow; you're gracefully being patient with me, waiting for me to change enough to be prepared for the next thing *(2 Peter 3:9)*. Give me patience to trust in your timing, even when it doesn't agree with mine *(Isaiah 55:8–9)*. Amen.

CONTENTMENT PRAYER

Lord, thank you, thank you, thank you. I thank you for everything I have, and everything I don't have *(Ephesians 5:20)*. I thank you for what I do during the day that I enjoy and for the activities that I don't enjoy *(Colossians 3:17)*. Thank you for my circumstances that are pleasant and for some things I am going through right now that I don't understand *(1 Thessalonians 5:18)*. I thank you in faith *(Psalm 37:5)*.

I am sorry, Lord, for the way envy has crept into my life. When I start acting like Saul, and burn with envy over someone's accomplishments or accolades *(1 Samuel 18)*, help me instead to rejoice for her and give her a sincere compliment *(Romans 12:16)*. When I feel as insecure as Joseph's brothers and wish I had someone else's family relationship or specialness *(Genesis 37)*, help me to reach out in love to the one who is unsettling me *(1 Corinthians 13:4)*. When I get as anxious as Eve about what I don't have, and start grasping for that which will hurt me *(Genesis 3)*, remind me of everything I already possess, and fill me with thankfulness *(Ephesians 5:20)*. Help me to think and act without covetousness, to be content with what I have *(Hebrews 13:5)*. I can live without envy because you have promised to be there for me, to not let me down, to be my helper, to battle my fears, and to keep me from being vulnerable to the slights of others *(Hebrews 13:6)*.

Thank you for the gift of finding satisfaction in my work *(Ecclesiastes 2:24)*. I can handle even the most difficult challenges and mundane tasks with enthusiasm, because my work gains more meaning when I picture myself serving you instead of my boss or my pastor or my husband or even my children *(Ephesians 6:7)*.

Thank you for the gift of finding joy in difficult circumstances *(James 1:2)*. By faith, I obey your commands to always be full of joy in the Lord *(Philippians 4:4)*, and to give thanks no matter what happens *(1 Thessalonians 5:18)*. I can obey this when I pray continually *(1 Thessalonians 5:17)*, which helps me remember that you are always right beside me, keeping me from being shaken by what is happening, and keeping me at peace inside with an overwhelming sense of safety. No wonder my heart can be filled with joy no matter what *(Psalm 16:8–9)*.

Thank you for the gift of finding peace in my mind by trusting in you *(Isaiah 26:3)*. I know if I'm feeling unrest, dissatisfaction, anxiety, envy, or worry, that it's a signal that I'm not trusting in you right then *(Philippians 4:6–7; 1 Peter 5:7)*. You will meet all my needs, and I can rely on that when I'm trying to be content *(Psalm 34:9–10)*. Teach me, Lord, to be satisfied with the things I have *(Philippians 4:11)*. Teach me to truly live even when I feel poor, and to truly enjoy my plenty when you give it *(Philippians 4:12)*. I can only live this absurdly contented life through you, because you give me the supernatural strength to do so *(Philippians 4:13)*. Amen.

GENEROSITY PRAYER

Lord, thank you for being an extravagantly generous God. I love discovering the delights of creation, and I am so thankful for your bounteous provision *(Genesis 1)*. Lord, please keep me from thinking I own what I possess. The earth is yours and everything in it *(Psalm 24:1)*. I can't claim credit for even the intelligence it took to acquire my food and my home and my clothes and my possessions *(Deuteronomy 8:17–18a)*. I also can't claim to own my own self, because you paid the ultimate price to buy me *(1 Corinthians 6:20)*. I am yours. My stuff is yours. I release it all back to you, because it was never mine in the first place.

Forgive me for hanging onto my possessions too tightly. Forgive me for times I have hoarded, because I have been afraid you would not provide *(Exodus 16:19–20)*. Forgive me for my entitlement mentality that makes me say, "It's all about me" *(1 Kings 21:1–16)*. Forgive me for times I have been obsessed with getting more things than I need, because in the end they cannot make me happy *(Ecclesiastes 2:26b)*. Forgive me for loving the idea of being wealthy, because money never satisfies *(Ecclesiastes 5:10)*. Forgive me for measuring my life by how much I own *(Luke 12:15)*.

Instead, Lord, I want to measure my life by how much I give. I pray along with Jabez, "Bless me and enlarge my territory!" *(1 Chronicles 4:10)*, but today I specifically pray that you would enlarge the territory of my giving. You have made me rich in every way, so instead of being arrogant or self-sufficient because of my plenty *(1 Timothy 6:17)*, help me instead to find every excuse to be generous with what you have given me *(2 Corinthians 9:11)*. And, Lord, at times I really don't feel all that rich; sometimes I feel depleted, inadequate, and used up. But, when I'm in that place, help me remember that you specialize in taking my little and turning it into much. That little boy (in the story of you feeding the five thousand) must have felt like his lunch was so small when he looked out at that sea of people, yet when he generously gave you all he had, you stretched his lunch and used it, and only it, to feed multitudes *(John 6:1–14)*.

So I give up my need to give a certain amount. Like the poor widow who gave two pennies *(Mark 12:42)*, my everything may be small, but if I give it to you out of love and sacrifice and devotion, you will bless it, multiply it, and use it beyond what I can imagine. Thank you that the more I give, the more thanksgiving takes place. First of all, there is the thanks offered to you from those to whom I give *(2 Corinthians 9:12)*; and, secondly, there is my thanks to you for the joy you allow me in the giving!

Finally, Lord, I want to be rich in good deeds, generous, and willing to share *(1 Timothy 6:18)*. I want to generously share with others the spiritual gifts you have given me, such as serving, encouraging, forgiving, leading, teaching, helping, and giving *(Romans 12:7–8)*. Help me even to be generous with people who are hard to love. Help me to bless those who persecute me *(Romans 12:14)*; to feed my enemies if they are hungry *(Romans 12:20)*; to befriend people of low position *(Romans 12:16)*; and to invite strangers into my home, because you may just be sending me angels in disguise *(Hebrews*

13:2)! You have said that if I have resources and I see someone in need, but don't show compassion, I don't have your love in me! Help me, Lord, to not just talk like I love people, but to put my money and my possessions and my self where my mouth is *(1 John 3:17–18)*. Amen.

PERSEVERANCE PRAYER

Lord, thank you for giving me the perseverance to finish this book! Forgive me for the times I have been a quitter, because I have forgotten that I am not alone *(Hebrews 12:1)*; I have grown tired *(2 Thessalonians 3:13)*; I have lost heart *(Galatians 6:9)*; or I have lost sight of the purpose of my work *(1 Corinthians 15:58)*. Because of your power in me *(2 Corinthians 4:7)*, I am no longer a quitter, but I'm an overcomer of pressure, confusion, persecution, and pain *(2 Corinthians 4:8–9)*. I can even be joyful when these trials come, knowing you are using them to mature and complete me *(James 1:2–4)*.

Help me to do the things perseverers do: keep standing firm *(Galatians 5:1)*; continue in what I have learned *(2 Timothy 3:14)*; diligently practice the Christian virtues *(2 Peter 1:10)*; let go of encumbrances *(Hebrews 12:1)*; let go of what lies behind *(Philippians 3:13b)*; hold fast to my confidence *(Hebrews 3:6)*; hold fast to that which is good *(1 Thessalonians 5:21)*; and run with endurance *(Hebrews 12:1)*.

Then, help me to finish well *(Matthew 24:13)*. Help me to make plans and set goals *(Proverbs 21:5)*; to stay diligent to the very end *(Hebrews 6:11)*; to keep my hope fixed on Christ *(1 Peter 1:13)*; and to press on to win the prize *(Philippians 3:14)*. Help me, also, to run in such a way as to win the crowns that you promise for living the Christian life *(1 Corinthians 9:24–25)*, such as the Crown of Joy for bringing people with me to heaven *(1 Thessalonians 2:19)*; the Crown of Righteousness for living obediently *(2 Timothy 4:8)*; the Crown of Life for enduring temptation *(James 1:12)*; and the Crown of Glory for leading by example *(1 Peter 5:2–4)*. By your grace, I will persevere until you say, "Well done, good and faithful servant! Come and share my joy with me" *(Matthew 25:21)*. Amen.

Appendix C

Fresh Start with Jesus

Therefore God exalted him [Jesus] to the highest place and gave him
the name that is above every name, that at the name of Jesus every knee
should bow, in heaven and on earth and under the earth, and every tongue
acknowledge that Jesus Christ is Lord, to the glory of God the Father.

Philippians 2:9–11

Over the course of reading this book, have you agreed to let Jesus be your Savior? If you are ready to take the first step today on the character makeover journey, here's a simple prayer you can say:

Jesus,
I believe that you died for me and that God raised you from the dead.
Please forgive my sins. You are my Savior. You are my only hope. I want to
follow your will for my life. I bow and confess that you, Jesus Christ, are Lord.
Amen.

If you decided just now to accept Jesus as your Savior and Lord, you are assured forever of salvation. Nothing can snatch you now from the hand of God. Please let someone know about your decision, so he or she can encourage you and thank God for his grace-filled, purposeful plan for your life.

If you decided not to say the prayer, I urge you to mark this page and to keep seeking truth with an open heart and mind. If you need help, ask a pastor or a Christian friend. Some Scripture verses that I highly recommend are the ones I have summarized here:

Romans 3:23	All have sinned.
Romans 6:23	Heaven is a free gift.
Romans 5:8	Jesus has already, out of love for you, paid the penalty for your sins by dying on the cross.
Romans 10:9–10	If you confess that Jesus is Lord, and if you tell God that you believe he raised Jesus from the dead, you will be saved.
Romans 10:13	Ask God to save you by his grace. He will!

Acknowledgments

Without a faithful team surrounding us, this book would not have been written. Thank you to those who believed in our message—that God cares deeply about our character and that being holy is even more important than accomplishing countless goals for him:

- Our dear families, who have always been our most constant cheerleaders— who continued to love us during the writing process, even when our character waned under the stress and we ourselves began to exhibit just about every negative quality in the book!
- Our friends who shared their stories with such authenticity and vulnerability, especially our insightful Life Purpose Coach® contributors: Chris Crowley, Linda Graber, Bette Hamby, Lisa Kindermann, Kathryn McColskey, Jan Stanish, and Geri Swingle. (You will find their contact information on my website.)
- Our dedicated review team: Bill and Jackie Ogdon, our most incisive and discerning reviewers who made sure we stayed true to Scripture; Andria Panchal, who thought up challenging new angles for every character quality; Ginny Caldwell, whose journey of courage was an inspiration; Miriam Mohler, who always provided a thoughtful, balanced perspective; Robin Breakey, from whom a compliment meant a LOT; Tiffani, who started out as a featured story, and ended up as an encouraging tester of all the exercises; Alf and Marilyn Paul, who read the pages like a devotional and responded with conviction; Shannon and Heather Leith, who injected their youthful perspective and irreplaceable encouragement; special friends Fern, Marti, Merle, Allie, Vonette, Tina, and Lisa, who were wonderful cheerleaders throughout the whole process; and Bob Kelly, who contributed so many great quotes. Special mention must be made of Greg Leith, who exhibited the character quality of *patience* as he endured the vagaries of living with an author-wife, of *generosity* as he gave of himself endlessly to make this book a reality, and of *perseverance* as he stayed cheerful and supportive to the end.
- Our incomparable literary agent, Nancy Jernigan, who made all this possible, through her godly vision and wisdom.
- Our enthusiastic, grace-filled team of Zondervan experts: Greg Clouse, developmental editor; Cindy Davis, cover designer; Beth Shagene, interior designer; Scott Heagle, marketing manager; and the incredible Sandy Vander Zicht, Zondervan's associate publisher and executive editor who prayerfully guided the process.

Thank you to each one of you for your "way above the call of duty" contribution to this manuscript! May God replenish all the time and energy you spent helping us bring it to fruition.

Katie Brazelton

To learn more about bestselling author and life coach, Katie Brazelton, PhD, MDiv, MA, founder of Life Purpose Coaching Centers, International®, regarding an upcoming online or on-site Coach/Facilitator training; a personal, 2-Day Life Purpose Intensive Facilitation called "Your Life on a Movie Screen"; or to read about her dream of opening 200 Life Purpose Coaching Centers, please visit her website:

www.LifePurposeCoachingCenters.com

Or email her at *one* of these addresses:

WomensInfo@LifePurposeCoachingCenters.com
MensInfo@LifePurposeCoachingCenters.com
CouplesInfo@LifePurposeCoachingCenters.com.

Or write to:

Life Purpose Coaching Centers, Intl
Katie Brazelton
P.O. Box 80550-0550
Rancho Santa Margarita, CA 92688

To invite Katie to speak to your organization, contact:

Ambassador Speakers Bureau in Tennessee
(615) 370-4700 x. 237
Naomi@AmbassadorSpeakers.com

———

An adjunct professor at Rockbridge Seminary, Katie is also author of the *Pathway to Purpose for Women* books and has been thrilled to see each of her books translated into four to ten languages. She has been a featured guest for such radio shows as Jim Burns's *HomeWord* and Moody's *Midday Connection*, and has been interviewed for publications such as *Today's Christian Woman* and *www.pastors.com* and television broadcasts including Canada's *100 Huntley Street*. She writes a regular column in *Extraordinary Women* for the American Association of Christian Counselors (AACC), and she has been honored to speak at AACC's World Conference, as well as Focus on the Family. For years, she was Director of Women's Bible Studies at Saddleback Church in Lake Forest, California. Katie has two adult children, a daughter-in-law, and her first grandson—who all live nearby.

Shelley Leith

To learn more about Shelley Leith, who is on staff as a writer at Saddleback Church, and her ministry of speaking on character makeover, self-esteem, life mission statements, parenting, or marriage; or regarding a personal, 2-day Life Purpose Intensive Facilitation called "Your Life on a Movie Screen," please visit her website: *www.ShelleyLeith.com*.

Shelley has been married to her husband, Greg, for twenty-eight years. Throughout those years they have shared God's timeless blueprint for marriage and family through leading Bible studies, appearing on the television show called *Marriage UnCensored*, and speaking to national audiences at *FamilyLife*™ marriage conferences.

They are both Life Purpose Facilitators with *Life Purpose Coaching Centers International*®. Greg and Shelley love to communicate together or individually about how God's truths can change lives, businesses, marriages, and families—as they help people come to know and fulfill their life purpose. They live in Southern California with their five children, ages fifteen to twenty-one.

To reach either of them, write or email:

Shelley or Greg Leith
P.O. Box 80903
Rancho Santa Margarita, CA 92688-0903
Shelley@shelleyleith.com
GregoryLeith@msn.com

To do the additional self-assessments mentioned in this book,
or to connect with other women working on their character,
or to get a Life Purpose Coach® list of book contributors,
or to download small group curriculum,
please visit the website:
www.LifePurposeCoachingCenters.com/CM

Products from Katie Brazelton for Women Searching to Learn More about Their Purpose

All Pathway to Purpose books work together to enhance a woman's journey as she searches for her God-given purpose. Each book provides its own unique benefit that enriches her walk down the pathway.

Pathway to Purpose for Women is a stand-alone book that takes the five universal purposes from *The Purpose Driven® Life* and helps women drill down to their own unique life purposes. This book is also available as an Abridged Audio CD.

Conversations on Purpose for Women is a companion book to *Pathway to Purpose for Women*, specifically designed for those women who want to find another woman who can serve as their Purpose Partner to help them down the path toward purpose.

Praying for Purpose for Women is a 60-day prayer experience that can change a woman's life forever. Sixty influential Christian women share how *their* lives have changed.

Pathway to Purpose for Women Personal Journal allows women to reflect during their quiet time on how the principles they discover can and will affect their lives.

Pathway to Purpose for Women	ISBN: 0-310-25649-6
(In Spanish) *Camino hacia el propósito para mujeres*	ISBN: 08297-4506-8
Pathway to Purpose for Women Abridged Audio CD	ISBN: 0-310-26505-3
Conversations on Purpose for Women	ISBN: 0-310-25650-X
(In Spanish) *Conversaciones con propósito para mujeres*	ISBN: 08297-4508-4
Praying for Purpose for Women	ISBN: 0-310-25652-6
(In Spanish) *Oración con propósito para mujeres*	ISBN: 08297-4507-6
Pathway to Purpose for Women Personal Journal	ISBN: 0-310-81174-0

Spanish products also available.

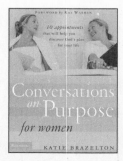
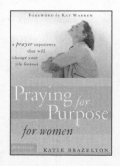
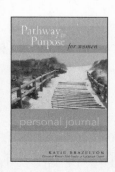